## SURVIVE. DRIVE. WIN.

'The story of Brawn GP is legendary. Imagine sitting at home at Christmas thinking you were out of a job, then by next Christmas you were a World Champion. This is F1's Leicester City story – it's every bit as exciting and magical.' **Damon Hill**

'It is refreshing for a book to be written about a sport as exciting as Formula One which covers the enormous amount of work that happens behind the scenes to bring two cars to the grid. Until now I had not seen this in a book about our sport.' **Sir Jackie Stewart**

'Nick Fry and Ed Gorman take us behind the mysterious and tightly closed doors of F1 to tell the remarkable story of the 2009 season, through the eyes of someone at the centre of the action.' **Martin Brundle**

'Fascinating detail covering efforts behind the scenes to keep Brawn GP alive and on course for their extraordinary World Championship. Nick Fry gives a refreshingly honest and, at times, self-deprecating account. Reporting from the sidelines, it's clear we only knew half the story...' **Maurice Hamilton, award-winning motor-sport writer and broadcaster**

'This book portrays all that is good about Britain. The very best talent in motor sport, excellent designers, engineers and sound business leaders who kept their heads in a crisis... and then went on to win a World Championship against all the odds in the most ruthlessly competitive sport there is. A truly inspiring story.' **Lord Digby Jones, Former Director-General of the CBI and Former Minister of State for Trade and Investment**

# NICK FRY with Ed Gorman
# *SURVIVE.*
# *DRIVE.*
# *WIN.*

### The Inside Story of Brawn GP and Jenson Button's Incredible F1 Championship Win

Atlantic Books
London

First published in hardback in Great Britain in 2019 by Atlantic Books, an imprint of Atlantic Books Ltd.

This paperback edition first published in Great Britain in 2020 by Atlantic Books.

1 2 3 4 5 6 7 8 9

A CIP catalogue record for this book is available from the British Library.

E-book ISBN: 978-1-78649-891-5
Paperback ISBN: 978-1-78649-892-2

Printed in Denmark
Atlantic Books
An Imprint of Atlantic Books Ltd
Ormond House
26–27 Boswell Street
London
WC1N 3JZ

www.atlantic-books.co.uk

*In memory of Richard Fry 1929–2019*

# CONTENTS

*Foreword: Bernie Ecclestone*                                          1

Prologue: Our dream start                                             5

**1** Bombshell from Honda                                           13

**2** Pulling the team from the fire                                 25

**3** Now it's our turn to become team owners                       45

**4** One hell of a tunnel and getting Ross on board                57

**5** Bringing the RA109 to life as BGP001                          71

**6** Testing the rocket ship                                        81

**7** Now Bernie wants to buy us                                     89

**8** Branson steals the show at Melbourne                           99

**9** Winning with no money                                         109

**10** A night to remember in Monaco                                127

**11** Keeping our heads as Ron calls for the aero number           139

**12** The buying game: Mercedes, the Glazers and Air Asia          149

**13** The dip                                                      161

**14** Rubens on a charge as Jenson struggles                       171

**15** Brawn GP scales the heights in Brazil                        185

**16** Splitting with Jenson                                        199

**17** Michael                                                      211

**18** The long road to hiring Lewis Hamilton                       225

Epilogue: Looking back on a sporting fairy tale                     237

*Cast of characters*                                                245

*2009 FIA Formula One World Championship Results*                   250

*Illustration credits*                                              269

*Acknowledgements*                                                  271

*A note about the authors*                                          272

*Index*                                                             276

# FOREWORD

The story of Brawn GP and how the old Honda team was taken on by Ross Brawn and Nick Fry is one of the most remarkable in the long history of Formula One. Few of us imagined that the team could carry on, let alone win the world championship. It was something different in an era when the sport was dominated by big-spending teams like Ferrari, Red Bull and McLaren – and, really, I was delighted to see it.

At the time I was probably a bit exasperated by Jenson's runaway start to the season, but actually – looking back – 2009 was one of our most exciting battles as Jenson made his mark early and then the others tried to catch him.

Of course, it was all a bit tragic for Honda, who saw the chassis they developed romp home to both the constructors' and drivers' titles without their name on it. I guess in sport and in business you have to hold your nerve and they didn't do that. But I can't blame them.

This is not to forget that the Brawn car was powered not by Honda but by Mercedes, and this story would not have happened without the offer by Martin Whitmarsh at McLaren to help a fellow British team in need. Modern Formula One is not known for that sort of generosity of spirit, as it was in the good old days.

I have seen some great champions over the years and some super British ones going right back to the likes of Mike Hawthorn and Graham Hill in the late 1950s and early 1960s, Jackie Stewart in the early 1970s, then James Hunt, Nigel Mansell and Damon Hill.

I was thrilled to see Jenson win at the end of the three-year period, 2007–09. Those years stand out in retrospect in a modern era that has been far too one-sided, with Ferrari, Red Bull and then Mercedes dominating more than is good for the sport.

Admittedly those guys are spending big bucks. What both Max Mosley and I liked about Brawn was the way they slimmed down their operation at Brackley – they had to, of course – and yet were still able to win. This has to be the future for Formula One.

*Bernie Ecclestone*

*SURVIVE. DRIVE. WIN.*

# OUR DREAM START

There were seconds to go. Thousands of people were on the edge of their seats around the street circuit at Albert Park in Melbourne and millions more were watching on television.

Our mechanics sat in front of me in the team garage, kitted up in their black race suits and protective helmets, transfixed by Jenson Button on the monitors. It was a warm and sunny early autumn afternoon and the shadows were just starting to lengthen on the grandstands.

The man on pole was sitting apparently impassively in the cockpit of his Brawn GP Formula One car, his white-gloved hands gripping the wheel, his head encased in a white and yellow crash helmet, his eyes focused on the road ahead.

Ross Brawn, our eponymous team principal, was in his usual place for races, running the show on the pitwall, headphones on and outwardly calm. In front of him on the monitor desk sat a banana – sustenance for later in the race but a good-luck charm too. I knew what he was thinking. This was what we lived for as racers and this was a moment of truth for us.

Two lights on the gantry above the start–finish straight went red, then three, then four. The roar of twenty V8 engines rose to a crescendo that shook my heart in my chest. The fifth red light came on and then, a fraction of a second later, one of the most hotly awaited Formula One world championships of the modern era was underway.

At the opening race of his tenth season in motorsport's most illustrious category, Jenson showed all his experience as he launched his car from stationary almost instantaneously. Within the blink of an eye the car was accelerating like a jet fighter taking off on an aircraft carrier, as the Englishman moved up through the gears at the beginning of a race in which he would never be overtaken.

Alongside him, in identical machinery but just slightly staggered on the grid, his Brawn GP teammate Rubens Barrichello was less fortunate. When the lights went out, his car sat motionless as the Brazilian former Ferrari driver stalled and then, after what seemed an age, grabbed first gear.

In the stampede to Turn 1 Rubens was already down to seventh place, running behind Sebastian Vettel in the Red Bull, Robert Kubica in the BMW Sauber, Nico Rosberg in the Williams and the two Ferraris of Felipe Massa and Kimi Raikkonen.

When they got to the sharp righthander, all hell broke loose. Rubens arrived with Mark Webber in the Red Bull ahead and to his left and Nick Heidfeld's BMW to the left again, each trying to get through the corner first. Behind the Brazilian, Heikki Kovalainen in the McLaren locked up under braking and hit the rear of Rubens' car, his front tyres hissing burning rubber. This sent Rubens sideways into Webber who, in turn, took out Heidfeld. How on earth did Rubens get away with that, I was thinking, as he roared on down to Turn 2, apparently unscathed?

This was the first wheel-to-wheel combat of the Formula One season in 2009 – a season that few thought Brawn GP would even take part in. That was because only four months earlier Honda had abruptly pulled the plug on their Formula One team, as the Japanese car giant retreated to lick its wounds after the 2008 global financial crisis wrecked its order books and stung its shareholders.

Refusing to acquiesce to Honda's plan to simply shut the team down, we had made it to Melbourne after weeks of crisis management, including the painful business of letting more than a third of our 700-strong workforce go. At the same time, after having failed to find a suitable new owner, we had convinced Honda to allow Ross and me, the chief executive, to lead a management buyout of the team for the princely sum of one pound in return for taking on all its liabilities.

Just about everything about our presence that day in Melbourne was unprecedented. So certain was everyone Down Under that we would not be competing in 2009 that Brawn GP was not even listed in the official programme for the race. There were no driver profiles, no predictions for the team's likely performance and the team was not shown in the full-season points table that you were invited to keep and fill in after each of the seventeen races. In summary, no one thought we would exist as a Formula One team by the time the race at Albert Park took place.

Minutes before the start our two cars, which we had such high hopes for after working on them under Ross's expert guidance throughout 2008, had stood out like beacons on the front row of the grid, gleaming in the sunlight. With no title sponsor, they appeared almost pure in their plain white livery with fluorescent yellow flashes, reminding the thousands of people trackside and millions more watching around the world that we had virtually no sponsors at all (apart from a small deal with Richard Branson's Virgin empire).

And we had arrived in Australia with hardly any mileage on the clock, having missed the first two pre-season test sessions when all the teams try out their cars together at European circuits over three days. When we did make it to the third and final session at Barcelona three weeks before the trip to Australia, our car had shown devastating pace, suggesting we could run at or near the front of the pack. But we had no real idea about whether the Brawn machines would make it to the end of the race without suffering mechanical failure. Would the gearboxes last the fifty-eight laps and 191 miles of the rough ride round the street circuit at Albert Park? And how would the much-modified suspension cope on a car that had been brutally altered to fit the Mercedes engine that we were using to replace the Honda one for which it had been originally designed?

It wasn't just the fascination with how Brawn GP might fare that had ignited interest in the 2009 season. There were new tyre rules in play, new design rules to savour, including the use of energy recovery systems on Formula One cars for the first time, and the championship was taking place against a sharply deteriorating world economic outlook, with the prospect of a spending cap being introduced for the first time in Formula One the following year.

Among ardent race fans, the focus was on Britain's Lewis Hamilton, who had won a thrilling first drivers' championship the year before. The question in many minds was how would the sport's youngest-ever world champion fare in the new cars and in a McLaren Mercedes that had the same engine we were using, but that had looked off the pace during pre-season testing? And what of Massa, who had so narrowly lost out to Lewis at the last race of the 2008 season in Brazil – could he lead the charge for Ferrari? This all left Jenson and Rubens rather nicely on the sidelines, regarded by most as also-rans in a season that would be dominated by others.

Our cars certainly stood out that day and not just because they were almost entirely free of sponsor logos. From an aerodynamic point of view they were simple and clean-looking, but with a finely detailed front wing and a lethally competitive design at the rear where the exhaust gases are channelled out of the engine. This area, known as the diffuser, was where we had made a huge step ahead of our competitors.

We had spotted a loophole that we could exploit in the design rules, and our so-called 'double-diffuser' gave our car more grip on the road and thus more speed through corners. Our opponents didn't like it one bit and throughout the build-up to the start the paddock at Albert Park was full of talk about protests, which were duly made and then dismissed by the stewards at the track. These were then followed by an appeal against the stewards' decision to the sport's governing body – the Fédération Internationale de l'Automobile (FIA) – which would be heard after the second race of the season took place in Malaysia. There was a possibility that we could be retroactively disqualified from the first two races of the campaign but we had no difficulty putting that to the back of our minds. Now was the time to focus on the here and now...

Jenson drove a smooth and controlled race, expertly piloting his car through the twists and turns of a track that rewarded a machine that, as he put it, could 'dance on its tyres'. In the engineering briefing before the start we had agreed that our plan would be for him and Rubens to go as fast as necessary to try to win, but no faster. Operating on a shoestring budget, we needed to preserve the cars as much as possible. We had few spare parts available if there was any damage in crashes – and we did not want to show our full pace, given the furore over our diffuser design.

On an eventful afternoon during which there were two safety-car periods, Jenson produced a virtually faultless drive save for a tiny blemish when he slightly overran his pit box as he came in for his second stop. At all times he kept his lead at 4–5 seconds while maintaining a close eye on Vettel, who was chasing him until the young German crashed after tangling with Kubica three laps from the finish.

Rubens survived a bump with Raikkonen's Ferrari while taking fourth place. That became third when Kubica made a pitstop, only for the Polish BMW driver to take the place back before going on to collide with Vettel. By the time the second safety car came out in the dying laps, the two Brawn cars were running one and two and they cruised across the line, taking the chequered flag just metres apart.

Then the celebrations began. We had done it. We had won our first race of the season. We had brought the cars home first and second. We were in the almost preposterous position of leading the drivers' and the constructors' championships. Our mechanics were beside themselves, and Jenson and Rubens were ecstatic as they climbed out of their cars in parc fermé, with Jenson immediately running over to his teammate to shake his hand in the cockpit. A tearful Ross and I followed suit, giving each other the biggest of bear hugs.

This was elation and relief all mixed together in an intoxicating cocktail. In an interview on the pitwall immediately after the finish, Ross spoke movingly about what this victory meant for a team that was struggling merely to survive. He dedicated the win to the hundreds of employees we had been forced to make redundant only days earlier in the wake of the Honda pull-out. 'This was for them,' he said.

Jenson captured the emotions perfectly. 'I think people understand what we've been through the last few weeks and I think we've got a lot of support out there,' he said as the crowds cheered him to the rooftops. 'This is not just for me, but for the whole team,' he added. 'This is the fairy-tale ending to the first race of our career together. We are going to fight to keep the car competitive and, with the limited resources we have, to keep it at the front.'

This was Button's second victory in 154 starts in Formula One. His first had come at the Hungaroring in the rain back in 2006 when we were still under the Honda banner. This was the 200th victory in Formula One by a British driver, and it was the first one-two finish by a new team on debut since Juan Manuel Fangio of Argentina and Karl Kling of Germany finished first and second at the French Grand Prix in 1954. As a beaming Button stood grinning from ear-to-ear on the podium and the British national anthem struck up on the Albert Park PA system, Jonathan Legard of the BBC summed it all up in a sentence: 'The sun is going down but Brawn has arisen from the ashes of Honda.'

My girlfriend Kate – soon to be my wife – had watched the action from the team base in the paddock. A superstitious character, she had been completely spooked by the fact that the official race programme had been printed without the

Brawn cars included in it. Could that in some way presage something terrible that day, she wondered? She resolved not to touch the offending document before the race, let alone open it. But afterwards she went running round, buying up as many copies as she could. What better souvenir could there be for our friends and family back home than the guide to a race that never mentioned us and that we had won hands down?

That night we all piled into a Melbourne nightclub called Boutique, where we celebrated until four in the morning. In the run-up to the race the idea that we might have a shot at a drivers' title seemed unthinkable. After the race it still seemed beyond our reach, but all of us had a feeling that – FIA Court of Appeal rulings notwithstanding – we had a tremendous chance to build a lead on our rivals before they started catching us up.

We knew we had the first four so-called 'flyaway races' – Australia, Malaysia, China and Bahrain – in which to establish an early lead in the points table, but that we would inevitably be pegged back as the likes of Red Bull and Ferrari started to upgrade their cars. While we were operating on a tiny budget and had next to no money available to improve our cars, Red Bull, with their design wizard Adrian Newey calling the shots, were rumoured to be spending £2 million a race on new parts – more money than we had available for the whole of the season. Everyone would be making a big step up in performance at the first European race of the campaign, at Barcelona, so we had to push as hard as we could until then.

We were the foxes running before the hounds and they were out to get us, whether in the FIA's court of law, in the design race or on the track...

# CHAPTER ONE

## *BOMBSHELL FROM HONDA*

It was a cold and grey November morning, almost exactly four months before the Australian Grand Prix that would open the 2009 season so spectacularly for us. Mr Hiroshi Oshima, the Honda Motor Company's bespectacled chief operating officer, with his trademark shock of greying hair, looked nervy as we greeted him in the black and grey marble reception of Heathrow's Renaissance Hotel.

'Good morning,' I said, shaking his hand and then standing to one side to make way for our team principal, Ross Brawn, to follow suit. Greetings were always formal with our Japanese counterparts. Without further delay Oshima-san, as we generally referred to him, ushered us into a tiny conference room where the three of us sat huddled around a small table, uncomfortably close.

It was immediately clear that this was going to be no ordinary meeting. Mr Oshima was extremely tense and finding it difficult to compose himself. Eventually he took his glasses off and began speaking very quietly. The top man at Honda was close to tears. The news he said was 'not good, not good at all'.

Motorsport is at the core of Honda's DNA. One of Japan's greatest post-war companies, founded in 1946 by the legendary engineer Soichiro Honda, it enjoyed a proud history in both motorbike and car racing. After working with the company in Formula One for seven years – four when it was the engine supplier and three more when it owned the team – I knew just how passionate Honda's people were about racing. They loved it, they viewed it as a display cabinet for the excellence of their engineering and regarded the racetracks of the world as battlegrounds where they would take on their road-car rivals – especially Toyota.

This came home to me most vividly on one of my first visits to Honda's HQ in Tokyo not long after I took over as managing director of the BAR Honda Formula One Team in 2002. We were taken to a nondescript warehouse not far from the great Formula One racing track at Suzuka. From the outside it looked run-down and altogether unremarkable and when we got inside it was dark. It felt like the set of Bond movie. Then someone flicked a switch and panels of dusty fluorescent lights burst into life – and there, stretching into the distance before us, were the serried ranks of Honda's motor racing thoroughbreds and all their road cars too.

There was one example of every model. In the racing section there were scores of Formula One cars going back to the mid-1960s, including the unrepaired wrecks of cars that had been written off in big crashes. There were motorbikes too and there was not just one copy of each model but three or four, including those driven by legends like Freddie Spencer and Mick Doohan. In the Formula One collection the stars were the immaculately preserved examples of the iconic red and white McLaren Hondas driven by the great

Ayrton Senna to world championship glory in 1988, 1990 and 1991.

So for Mr Oshima on that day at Heathrow in the autumn of 2008, ten weeks after the collapse of Lehman Brothers investment bank in New York, to have to be the person to deliver the news that Honda was pulling out of Formula One was an especially onerous – not to say humiliating – undertaking. I felt for him as he sat before us; he was a good man, a serious man and he was speaking to us from the heart.

Ross and I had known something was up. In the weeks before the meeting, with increasing concern we had watched the dramatic onset of what would turn out to be the worst global recession since the Great Depression. Big multinationals were being hit all around the world, people were losing their jobs and order books were dwindling.

Nigel Kerr, our financial director at Brackley, had been picking up signals that Honda was not going to be able to escape this without serious retrenchment and we had noticed a few straws in the wind, like the sudden repatriation of key Japanese members of staff back to Tokyo. But we assumed – as a worst-case scenario – that we were looking at a hefty funding cut.

In the days leading up to the meeting, we had been working on an emergency plan to cut 30 per cent from our £200 million annual budget, but we had been careful to try to protect the promising work we had been doing on RA109. This was our new car for the 2009 season and the first car that Ross had overseen since his much-heralded arrival at the team a year earlier. It incorporated what we believed was a highly competitive chassis with innovative aerodynamic solutions, including a design for the whole rear end of the car that would eventually become highly controversial. Our goal for that machine was to try and break into Formula One's top three for the first time in Honda's history as a team owner, and we were quietly confident we might be able to make a big step up in performance as the 2009 season drew ever closer. We had no idea that Honda was about to stun the motor racing world by announcing that it was abruptly ending its involvement in Formula One, a move that would eventually be followed by Toyota and then BMW.

Our recent results were not in our favour. Nor, indeed, was our long history of under-achievement stretching back to 2000 when Honda had first re-entered Formula One as an engine supplier after an eight-year absence. Although we finished second in 2004 in both the constructors' and drivers' championships, we never properly understood why our car was so fast that year and thus we were not able to build on that success in 2005. In short we had never managed to escape the also-ran category and our recent results in 2008 had been woeful. At the final race that year at Interlagos in Brazil, Jenson managed thirteenth place while Rubens could only finish fifteenth at his home Grand Prix. That season Honda finished ninth out of eleven in the constructors' championship, with Rubens fourteenth and Jenson eighteenth in the drivers' standings.

Even so we were not quite ready for what Mr Oshima had come to tell us. He was brief and to the point.

'The financial crisis has had immediate and severe consequences for Honda Motor Company, which is anticipating "red ink" for 2009, with losses of the order of three thousand million dollars,' he said. 'US dealers are refusing to take more new cars into stock because they don't see how they are going to sell them. Our sales in America have fallen by 32 per cent already and it is likely that our plant at Swindon is going to have to shut down for a few weeks to try to weather the storm. In the light of all this,' he told us, 'Honda Motor Company must cut its spending and protect its core business. Our shareholders simply would not understand it if we continued to pursue something as expensive and esoteric as Formula One, especially given our long run of poor results.'

And that was it. In less than ten minutes our world had caved in. Mr Oshima was clear that it was over. There was no debate. The decision had been taken by the top management tier in Tokyo a week earlier. Honda was departing Formula One, lock, stock and barrel. There was going to be no process or a gradual wind-down; it was going to stop with immediate effect.

Mr Oshima stood and we took our cue. There were other people, he said, in the conference room next door who we would now have to see.

We had turned up for an execution. Our own.

I had sat, winded for a second or two, listening to this genial man telling us politely that our business life had collapsed. But even before we had got up from the table we were thinking about how we were going to save this situation. We knew we were sitting on what our early assessments suggested was a pretty decent car for 2009 and I also knew that we could not let down the more than 700 people who worked with us at Brackley. There were designers, engineers, aerodynamicists, electricians, race teams – even drivers – secretaries and catering staff who all had livelihoods and families and we had to fight to protect them.

The phrase that was pinging around my mind as I listened to Mr Oshima was: 'You can't do that!' I didn't mean Honda had no right to close its Formula One business. Of course it could do what it wanted with its team. But they couldn't just shut down the company as if it had never existed – something I suspect would have been politically impossible had we been talking about a company solely based in Japan.

As we were ushered into the much bigger conference room where twenty Honda executives were sitting around a large glass table, some from Tokyo, others from Honda UK, I was ready to mount a rearguard action. We needed time – as much of it as possible – to find an alternative to simply going back to Brackley and closing the door and turning the lights off.

Ross looked stunned. I guessed his initial thought was: 'What on earth have I got myself into here?' Having only joined us a year earlier and reportedly turned down lucrative offers to work either for Toyota or McLaren, or perhaps to rekindle his glory days at Ferrari, he must have been thinking he had made a dreadful mistake. But who could have guessed that Honda would have reached the point where it wanted out without any warning whatsoever?

The discussion with the lawyers and accountants began and I started to push back.

'Look, you cannot simply sack 700 people and sell the plant,' I told them. 'There are procedures to go through; government has to be informed – this is a significant business within the UK – the sport's governing body has to be notified and we have obligations not only to our staff but to our suppliers. We have to have time to work this through and find a solution and you have to give us that time.'

I could see from the puzzled looks on some of the Japanese faces staring at me from across the table that this was not what they had come to hear. The contingent from Tokyo had come to London to oversee an immediate shutdown and sell-off.

After an hour or two of discussion, Mr Oshima suggested we bring other senior managers from the team to assist us. I called Caroline McGrory our company lawyer, John Marsden our head of HR, and Nigel Kerr. They all jumped in their cars and headed to Heathrow to help us deal with the massed ranks of Honda's finest. In Caroline's case this was a heroic undertaking as she was heavily pregnant with her third child.

Eventually we managed to get agreement to one month's grace. We would be given thirty days – until Christmas – to pull this thing from the fire, even if we had no idea how we were going to do it. There had been no time for detail. There was talk of limited funding to tide us over for thirty days, but the Tokyo contingent was adamant that there would be no more engines for the car, for example. And there was nothing on how we were going to continue to pay Jenson's considerable salary.

I pressed them on the decision – was it final? Was there any leeway at all? The shaking heads opposite couldn't have been clearer.

Racing ahead, in a room where you could have heard a pin drop, I asked about a disposal: 'Would Honda Motor Company be prepared to sell the team? I recognize that even that would be a tough goal in the current climate,' I added, filling a rather awkward silence.

Mr Omura, a Honda F1 board member, said the company had not had time to consider selling the team but that there would be a further full board meeting the following week to discuss the decision. It felt like the first glimmer of light on a bleak day for us.

Ross, meanwhile, was also thinking ahead and told the visiting executives that he would go back to Brackley and start discussions with senior technical staff on drawing up plans for the team to compete in the 2009 Formula One world championship as an independent entity. It seemed both of us were looking for the opportunity in this crisis.

On the way home that evening my head was spinning. Who could we get to buy the team and who might the buyers be? How would we find them? What would be the price and the process? What would we tell the staff and when would we tell them? What about Jenson and Rubens? And what about Fernando Alonso, the former world champion who was back with Renault after his unhappy spell at McLaren, whom Ross and I had been wooing for months to join us for 2009? I knew immediately that that project was doomed. We were going to be firefighting all the way to the first race of the season – if we even managed to get that far – and changing our drivers was a luxury we could no longer afford.

During a break in the meeting I had popped out to make a quick call to Kate back home in Oxford.

'They are out,' I told her breathlessly. 'You can't tell anyone. I'll speak to you later.'

An American from Detroit with a typically enthusiastic – even gung-ho – approach to life, Kate was stunned and cried when I rang off. In the days leading up to the meeting she had listened to me speculating about what might happen but she hadn't been expecting this. When I got home though, she was already on the front foot as I stood in the kitchen, glass of wine in hand, running through some of my more outlandish schemes to save the company.

'You can fix this,' she said and she meant it. Over the coming months she and Ross's wife, Jean, would form a vital part of our team, encouraging us and convincing us that we would succeed when the doubts threatened to overwhelm us, as we did our best to fight back from the brink.

On the following Monday morning – 1 December 2008 – Ross and I informed the team's directors of Honda's decision at our weekly strategy meeting. Caroline, Nigel and John were there alongside Ron Meadows, sporting director, Joerg Xander, head of chassis engineering, and Graham Miller who was operations manager for the plant. Of course they were stunned and surprised but Ross and I did our best to convince them that we were going to find a way out of this and that the team was going to survive. At that stage the grim news was to remain under wraps.

A few days after that there was a pre-planned meeting of the Formula One team principals group – the so-called Formula One Teams Association (FOTA), a sort of trade body of F1 team owners and bosses. The meeting took place at Brown's Hotel on Albemarle Street in London's Mayfair, a favourite haunt of the then-chairman of FOTA, Luca di Montezemolo, the charming and statesmanlike chairman of Ferrari.

Ross knew Luca extremely well from his Ferrari days at Maranello. As technical director there, Ross had played a key role in helping the team win five drivers' titles with Michael Schumacher. When we arrived, we asked Luca if we could brief him first, before we spoke to the full group. He was just as shocked as we had been when we told him what Honda was doing and that we no longer had an engine for our 2009 car, if it ever made it onto the track. We had no expectation that Luca might offer to assist us in any material way but, as we sat with him in Suite 201, he stunned us by making a generous offer that (even if ultimately we would not take it up) was hugely encouraging.

'Ross, I know you very well,' Luca said in his heavily accented English, 'and Nick, I don't know you so well, but you seem a good guy, so this is what I will do. We want Honda on the grid – we cannot afford to lose you. If you go, who will be next?'

He paused for a second.

'You can have our engines for 2009,' he continued. 'I will organize that for you if you wish.' Then with a smile, he muttered: 'But don't beat us with them.' We all laughed heartily at the impertinence of such a suggestion.

It was a rare example of F1 rivals coming together to protect their sport. Luca could see we were in imminent danger of crashing out of Formula One and neither he nor his fellow team bosses wanted to see fewer cars on the grid.

The mood was grim when Luca informed the full meeting a few minutes later about Honda's decision. John Howlett was there as head of Toyota's very expensive Formula One operation (which was just as unsuccessful as Honda's), alongside his Japanese boss Tadashi Yamanashi, and the anxiety on their faces was plain for all to see. Ron Dennis and Martin Whitmarsh from McLaren were, like Luca, immediately positive and indicated that they would help if they could.

Later that day we told our drivers. I called Richard Goddard, Jenson Button's manager, at his home in Guernsey and broke the news. There was a long silence followed by expressions of support. I had a good relationship with Richard and I spent some time setting out my determination to find a solution. But I knew he had a job to do and the fear of losing Jenson was immediately on my mind. There was a clear risk that he would go elsewhere, although at that late stage in the year and in this commercial environment, where would he go?

That evening Ross and I returned to Brackley to inform our staff. Undoubtedly the rumour mill had been turning but it was important that they hear what was happening from us. The mood was solemn as almost all the 719 employees gathered around the bays where the new cars were being put together. That night two chassis of the RA109 were sitting in a state of advanced assembly along with their gearboxes and new Honda V8 engines on trolleys next to them. These were the engines that we had hoped would be a big improvement on the previous season's power unit. But we already knew that those cars in that configuration would never turn a wheel on a racetrack.

I started off with the bad news: Honda was going and there was nothing we could do to change it. We had secured a month's breathing space to find a buyer and, consequently, we would have to place everyone on three months' notice from the start of January, unless that buyer was found.

Then Ross took over to talk about the opportunity. This was the start of our new double act forged in crisis – me as chief executive and Ross gradually morphing from a team principal with a strong bias towards the technical aspects of the job to more of an all-round leadership role. Ross was inspired that night and spoke in Churchillian tones, asking rhetorically whether we – as a company and a group of friends and colleagues – were up for the fight to survive.

'Can we recover from this? Do we want to see all our work go to waste? Are we prepared to pull together to keep this great team alive?' he asked in his mellow and sonorous voice. 'Nick and I are committed to doing all in our power to find a solution to this crisis and we will do our best not to let you down, but please be patient and give us a little time to work out the best way forward.'

Ross exuded calm in the face of what otherwise seemed like impossible odds, and I could see the emotion swirling through the crowd of faces watching him. Ross gave them hope and the determination to get our cars to the start line of the first race of the 2009 season, in Melbourne. It was less than four months away.

As I mingled with the staff after the announcement, I did my best to try to reassure everyone that we *would* survive intact as a team. I was especially concerned about losing our star performers – our incredible engineers, mechanics, designers and aerodynamicists. I knew other teams would be hovering in the wings, looking for opportunities to snap people up. Losing our buildings and other physical assets was one thing; far worse was the much more likely prospect of losing the talent we had painstakingly assembled at Brackley over the previous eighteen months. The only thing in our favour was that we were not the only ones in the pitlane feeling the full effects of the world financial crisis, so cheque books were not going to open as readily to tempt staff to rival teams as they might have done a few months earlier.

That evening we issued a press release announcing Honda's withdrawal from Formula One. The headlines were lurid the following day as the media digested what was described by *The Times* as a 'seismic shock' to motorsport's most prestigious championship, amid much speculation that Williams, Renault or Toyota could be next.

My phone was hot all day. The main message I hammered home was that we were looking for a buyer. Already it was becoming clear that a lot of people had identified this as an opportunity to get into Formula One, and I knew that some media exposure would help those conversations happen. In the meantime I was ready for what I knew was going to be the biggest challenge of my professional life.

# CHAPTER TWO

## *PULLING THE TEAM FROM THE FIRE*

Normally the run-up to Christmas in a Formula One team is a relatively quiet time when senior management starts to plan the racing campaign for the following year, but things were very different in the run-up to Christmas 2008. Ross and I threw ourselves into a rescue mission and we left the planning for 2009 to department heads, while we devoted ourselves to trying to save the business inside the deadline set by Honda.

After that first meeting with the staff at Brackley, the job of sorting out our future began the following day, with Ross and I devoting most of it to doing interviews with the media. Obviously what we were saying was for external consumption and we had a team to sell. But we were both acutely aware that those inside the company would also be reading and listening, and wanting to know what was going on and what our plans were.

The important thing at that point was to put forward a boldly positive position. We needed to give the impression from the start that we were being looked at, and that good people were genuinely interested in the opportunity Honda had created for someone to get into Formula One with a big team and first-class facilities that were all ready to go.

In those press interviews I did my best to dispel the widespread assumption in the paddock that a buyer for our team was extremely unlikely to be found, especially in the short time left before the start of the 2009 season. I said that we had already received a 'stream' of enquiries from potential purchasers, and that Ross and I believed there were already at least three potential buyers who had what I described as the 'resources and background' to take the business on.

I have to admit that this positive spin was initially little more than a fabrication and we were talking our prospects up with a big dose of hope. But that was the only way forward; it was the only way to dispel the gloom that inevitably began to seep into the fabric at Brackley. We needed to fill everyone in the team with enthusiasm that there *was* a future and that we were going to find investors.

In our position Ross and I had no other option. What were we going to say? You can't go out there and say 'it's all a disaster' and 'there is no hope'. What you've got to say is 'we are going to fix this'. And this comes back to leadership in a crisis – you have to be prepared to be a little bit exposed and take risks because if you are not out there shouting from the rooftops and imploring people to greater heights and telling them that it is all going to be all right, then it is never going to work.

We knew immediately that we were going to have to decide which people we could afford to lose and which we could not afford to let go under any circumstances. At that stage the Honda F1 team had grown to be one of the biggest – if not *the* biggest – in the pitlane and this made the inevitable contraction all the more painful.

In the good times it is all very well having a benevolent owner who is prepared to spend a lot of money, but the other side of that coin is that as soon as the economy or the fortunes of that company turns, the more you've taken off them and the more exposed you are. I had been aware for some time that we could be very exposed if something went wrong at Honda. So it was evident right from the start that there would have to be major cutbacks because the team was completely unsustainable with more than 700 people on its books and with a wage bill running at a couple of million pounds per month.

The individuals we needed to keep were the bellwethers for the rest of the group. These were people like Ron Meadows, the sporting director who had been there from the start, and Andrew Shovlin, one of the most senior engineers and Jenson's race engineer. They were important because they were skilled and they were stalwarts of the team, and because other people would look to them. If Ron had gone, I suspect a lot of others would have concluded that if he saw no hope then neither could they.

To make a Formula One car go fast the three most vital aspects are the aerodynamics, the engine and the tyres and how you use them, otherwise known as race strategy. In terms of priority as to where you spend your money, those three areas were – and still are – the key elements. If you had to pick one above the others, it would be the dark art of aerodynamics. The head of that department was a French guy called Loïc Bigois. I brought him in from Williams and he was there pre-Ross. He was experienced in the F1 world, was at the top of his game and had played a key role in developing our car for the new season. We did not want to lose him.

On race strategy we had James Vowles, who had been there since starting in a lowly position as a teenager. He turned out to be the most brilliant strategist. Simon Cole, who was the chief race engineer, had come to Honda with me from Prodrive where he had been chief engineer for Richard Burns in the World Rally team. Simon is one of those low-key, underrated characters who is worth his weight in gold – he was behind Richard when we won the championship and he was about to play a key role during our remarkable 2009 season.

Then there was Jock Clear, who was Rubens Barrichello's race engineer. He is not the most modern of engineers but a rugby man through and through who gives motivational speeches and works on the emotional side of drivers; he's a player you want on your side. All of these people stayed with the team after I left in 2013, though Jock would later move to Ferrari.

That's the interesting element: all those guys are still in the sport, their longevity underlining their class. For example, 'Shov', as we all knew him, and Jock were the perfect pairing. Jock is an old-school engineer but with vast experience and is excellent on the man-management side of things. The younger Shovlin is massively intelligent and analytical and comes at it from a very detailed engineering point of view. Having the two of them together was a great strength because they had subtly different ways of doing things that were complementary. Jock was the guy you needed going over the top in the trenches; Shov was the man you would want designing the weapons you were carrying.

Slimming the team down started the following week after the meeting at Heathrow as Ross and I, alongside Caroline, Nigel and John, divvied up responsibilities. We asked department heads to look at their staffing and to suggest where we could afford to make cuts. If we had four people doing something then we would look to cut two of them, and we did this right through the team, eventually coming up with around 300 redundancies. We needed to protect the race team – the group that goes to Grand Prix weekends – and knew we could afford to reduce our research and development staffing levels and put the 2010 season on hold. It was a painful process, but we had no choice; if we were going to survive we would have to be leaner and meaner and take some shortcuts and risks.

As any manager in any business will attest, calling people in to break the news to them that they are being let go is not pleasant, and we were doing it on an industrial scale. There were some gloomy days at Brackley but I am glad to report that many of our staff quickly found good jobs in other teams or in other areas of motorsport, and within a year some of them would be back on our payroll.

This is the sort of period when you earn your money as a manager. When things are going along in a fairly regular fashion and change is incremental, there are others who are much better than me. In those circumstances I can get bored and lose focus. But in a full-on crisis there are people – and I am one of them – who rise to the challenge because it is exciting and it's risky; there is huge opportunity but it is unknown territory. You are hard-pushed to rationally plot your way out of this sort of problem; there is planning and detail that needs to be done, but it has to be carried out underneath an overriding umbrella of optimism and charging from the front.

The principle I have always lived by is trying to avoid fighting battles unless I have to. We all fall into the trap of getting into scraps because it is a bit of fun, but generally you shouldn't get stuck into something unless you absolutely have to. The second thing, which is probably more important, is looking at something and saying: 'Can I live with the consequences of failure?' Ross and I discussed this over the next few weeks and we decided that, if it all went belly-up, then our plan was for that to happen at the end of the 2009 season. We both felt that by then we should be able to look ourselves in the mirror and say: 'We gave it our best shot; it wasn't good enough but we did everything that we could have done to rescue the situation.' The worst thing that could have happened is that some of the team would have had a year's more work than they would have done if the team had shut down immediately. In my mind it was clear; apart from the personal reputational risk, there wasn't much other downside. With regards to the reputational risk, if we could show that we had tried our hardest to rescue the situation then yes, we'd have failed but at least we would have tried, as opposed to just rolling over and letting the whole thing collapse.

Within a few days my positive spin in the press about buyers queuing up to take over the team started to become a reality as people began contacting us with interest in investing. It was the start of a roller-coaster ride through Christmas and into the New Year.

The first person to get in touch was Vijay Mallya, the flamboyant Indian beer-and-airlines tycoon who already owned his own Formula One team, Force India. Vijay knew from the team principals' meeting at Brown's what was going on, and in fact he expressed interest in the team briefly at that stage.

A thick-set, bejewelled character from Kolkata, with a fleet of luxurious homes and cars and a massive superyacht, Vijay was one of the most extravagant spenders in Formula One, which put him in fairly extreme company. Every time there was a charity do in the paddock, for example, Vijay was always the one who led the way. At Monaco, where the drivers used to parade as fashion models to help raise money for good causes, Vijay always sat at the right hand of Bernie Ecclestone, the commercial rights holder of Formula One, and was encouraged to spend enormous amounts of money on flashy watches and other self-indulgent baubles.

He may have been a larger-than-life character in the paddock but what Vijay really wanted was to be a contender. However, his team – based at Silverstone, which had previously been owned by Eddie Jordan among others – wasn't blessed with great facilities. So the modern-day Indian mogul was very interested in picking up where Honda had left off and he was the first on the phone to me. We arranged for him to come and have a look around the factory at Brackley on the next Saturday afternoon.

We did a 'royal tour' for him on 6 December. Although clearly no engineering expert, Vijay knew what lots of expensive stuff looked like. The years of investment by Honda had produced a dazzling array of state-of-the-art kit designed to help a car go fast. This included the best wind tunnel in the sport and one of the best machine shops, which was filled with new tools from Japanese manufacturers.

It was a bit like showing a rich, wide-eyed customer some expensive and exotic diamond-encrusted watches through the shop window of a Bond Street dealer. We were tempting someone with lots of stuff that they clearly desired. The shininess and the scale of it was a massive leap forward from what Vijay had with the old Jordan team, and it was pretty clear that he wanted to move to Brackley and just take it all over and start again. At least from a location point of view, Force India would have been closed down and a new team would have been created at Brackley, presumably with some of the talent from his old team and some of our people.

Even at that point there was a sense that it wouldn't be a normal deal in terms of someone buying the team for lots of money. We all knew that if Honda closed us down, there would be a hefty bill that came with it because making more than 700 people redundant in the UK required them to be paid off in a legally compliant way. So the headline price was not going to be high in an environment where the world had just gone into a deep recession and Mr Mallya was itching to write a cheque.

Following his visit, Ross, Nigel and I were invited to dinner two days later at a place that sums up Vijay to a tee – Stowe Castle near Silverstone. This is an eighteenth-century 'eye-catcher' that looks like a castle from one side but, when you walk around to the other side, you find that the battlements and corner towers are missing. In their place are what were originally – and slightly disappointingly – a series of farmworker's cottages that are now a restaurant.

That dinner – when it was finally served – was the start of the fall as far as Vijay's ambitions of buying the Honda team were concerned. Ross had already turned down this opportunity to break bread with Mallya. Accustomed to operating at the highest levels with the likes of Ferrari, Ross did not see a team run by this rather flamboyant character with no motor racing background as someone he wished to work with. Vijay is about as far from a Ross Brawn-type of person as you could imagine. But we were committed to explore every opportunity that might be available, so Nigel and I duly turned up.

We arrived at Stowe at about 8 p.m. and sat around, awaiting the arrival of Vijay. There was a coterie of attractive ladies in attendance who kept coming and going.

'Don't worry, Mr Fry,' they confidently told me every twenty minutes, 'Mr Mallya is now on his way and will be here very soon.' Then they went off fluttering around, going over arrangements and generally fretting about where their boss would sit, what he would eat and so on. It was as if God himself was about to descend from heaven.

By 11.30 p.m. my patience was wearing thin.

'Any news from Vijay?' I wearily asked a flunky.

'I assure you, not much longer now,' came the reply.

'This is getting ridiculous,' I confided in Nigel as we sat twiddling our thumbs.

Mallya eventually walked through the door at 1 a.m., a mere five hours late. The big upside of this was that we then tucked in to the best curry I've ever had. But in reality, even at the poppadom stage, with my background in blue-chip car companies, I was struggling to see myself working with Vijay Mallya. I am not used to an environment where people are so poorly disciplined and think nothing of turning up three, four or even five hours late for meetings with no good reason – and we were never given one. By 2 a.m. I was struggling to stay awake and to stay interested.

Vijay didn't want to talk to Nigel, who he considered to be too lowly, so Vijay and I adjourned to a small lounge adjacent to the dining room and sat on a sofa with our curries on our laps. It was all slightly bizarre. Vijay waffled on about how he would take the team on, and take it to the top of the grid and find new sponsors, but there wasn't much substance to anything he was saying, and by this time I was too tired to care.

Over the following weeks the Indian multi-millionaire would ring every so often to see what was going on, but there was never any substantial evidence that he was putting a lot of effort into buying us. It almost started and finished on that Saturday night.

The following Thursday, suitor number two who contacted us was Achilleas Kallakis. Four years later, Kallakis would be jailed for seven years for Britain's biggest-ever mortgage fraud and for duping banks out of more than £750 million. This would make him, as the media put it, 'Britain's most successful serial confidence trickster'. At his trial it would emerge that Kallakis – real name Stephan Kollakis with an 'o' at the beginning of his surname rather than an 'a' – was not the high-flying Greek businessman we encountered but the son of an unsuccessful nightclub owner, who had been brought up in Ealing, west London, and had started out in life working in a travel agency. We would have done well to remember the age-old saying: 'Beware of Greeks bearing gifts.' But back in December 2009 Kallakis, an expensively wined and dined balding individual in a classy-looking suit and tie, was in his pomp, playing his part to perfection and hoodwinking everyone left, right and centre. What's more, he quite fancied the idea of entering the rarefied world of Formula One so that he could add 'motor racing tycoon' to his apparently mega-successful career as a Mayfair property baron.

After Kallakis had made contact with our sponsorship team, Ross and I went to see him in a grand office just off Berkeley Square in London's West End. Achilleas was styling himself as a billionaire Greek shipping owner (weirdly, he was in fact the nephew of a bona fide Greek shipping magnate) and he also referred to himself as the 'Ambassador of the Republic of San Marino'. Ross and I found ourselves perched on a sofa in a sumptuously appointed reception room. In front of us was a coffee table littered with official-looking letters from the

English National Ballet, the National Portrait Gallery and other charities and esteemed bodies. These congratulated him on his appointment to senior positions in their organizations and for his significant donations. Whether any of them were true we had no idea (in fact Kallakis's accomplice, Alex Williams, was an accomplished forger), but at that point we were grasping for anything we could get, and we were very taken in.

Then in swept Achilleas, making a theatrical entry, rather as a minor royal might do at an official audience.

'Good morning gentleman,' he uttered. 'No, do sit down. Very good of you to come at short notice.'

I have to say he was very convincing – he wasn't Britain's most successful confidence trickster because he was an amateur – and he got down to business immediately. He wanted to buy the team and he wanted to come to the factory to see our wares. He was direct and to the point and we found ourselves giving him our sales pitch.

We explained how Honda had invested a huge amount of money in the physical assets that you need to be successful in Formula One, that we had the equipment to do the job and we had the people to do the job, including Ross, one of the most successful motor racing engineers of all time. It was a relatively simple pitch and Kallakis lapped it up.

We arranged for him to come to Brackley the following Saturday at 10 a.m. for another 'royal tour'. This one was even more 'royal' than the Mallya's tour because of the – in retrospect – hilarious matter of trying to find a parking space for Kallakis's massive helicopter. We had a purpose-built helipad at the factory, but Kallakis's people let it be known that he would be arriving in a machine that was so big it wouldn't fit on a standard pad. So we had to clear a car park for this aircraft, which appeared to be some kind of military machine.

There was an interesting unintended consequence of the visit of this giant chopper. Someone who saw it coming in to land that day concluded that its markings identified it as the private helicopter of the Mexican telecommunications billionaire and the world's second-richest man, Carlos Slim. This was duly leaked to the motor racing media and from that point on all sorts of journalists confidently – and wrongly – reported that Slim was one of our suitors. He never was but I did speak to his son, Carlos Slim Jnr, who confirmed that they had no interest. We had a bit of a laugh together about it and he was happy for us to play the story along; it certainly did us no harm.

Once the 'copter was on the ground, the Kallakis visit was virtually a repeat of the Vijay tour and done in a similar fashion. A few days later Ross and I were invited to dinner in a private room at the Ritz in London where the staff greeted Achilleas as if he were a Greek God.

'Good evening, Mr Ambassador,' they would offer as he entered. 'Yes, Mr Ambassador… no, Mr Ambassador…' and so on.

We had a rather stilted evening, which got a little awkward at one point when Achilleas startlingly revealed that he couldn't really understand why either Ross or I were stupid enough to pay taxes in the UK.

'What? You actually pay income tax here? You must be out of your minds,' he sniffed.

Ross and I laughed nervously to fill the ensuing silence. This gave us our first hint that Mr Kallakis was perhaps not all that he was pretending to be. Nothing more was said but it was a comment that neither of us overlooked and it was an indication of what was to come.

Not happy making small talk, Ross made his excuses and left straight after dinner, so I was left with Kallakis and a couple of his colleagues at the Ritz. After it was over, I walked from the hotel to Victoria to get the bus – the so-called Oxford Tube – back to my home near Oxford. We were so money-conscious at the time that I didn't dare take a taxi or stay overnight in a hotel in London. I got back home at 4 a.m., wondering if Mr Kallakis really was the man to save us.

The following night Ross and I were invited to his house in Brompton Square in Knightsbridge. The aspect of this meeting that struck both of us as rather strange was that there was a maid who served us dinner, but she kept leaving the dining-room door open and Kallakis kept getting up to shut it. His behaviour seemed odd and it was obvious he didn't want other people in the house to hear what was going on.

After dinner Kallakis ostentatiously took us round the house, showing us his art collection that, he claimed, was worth tens of millions of pounds. Some paintings were familiar and well-known pieces of artwork, but neither Ross nor I was in any position to tell a fraud from the real thing. So we stood around, making suitably enthusiastic comments about how wonderful they were and he was. All in all, it had been the most bizarre couple of days with a person who we had some suspicions about, but about whom we had no evidence that he was anything other than who he said he was.

The doubts lingered. We asked Nigel Kerr to try and get in touch with a Swiss banker who had written a reference that we had been given by Achilleas. And we decided to spend £10,000 of our hard-earned money on employing Kroll, a corporate detective agency, to try to find out a bit more about Kallakis. Caroline McGrory was given the task of working with them to try and get to the bottom of who the hell this guy was. I decided to make my own enquiries. I rang the font of all knowledge, Jackie Stewart, because I knew from my previous dealings with him that Jackie was friendly with the former King of Greece. I asked him if he would ask the King if he had ever heard of Achilleas, which Jackie agreed to do.

In the meantime, during the following week, we received two letters in support of Kallakis's candidacy as future owner of the team. One was from a junior member of the British Royal Family, another from an MP, and each was saying what a wonderful person Kallakis was. They appeared to be genuine and were on official-looking letterheads. I remember sitting at my desk with the three letters in front of me, just staring at them. One thing that seemed odd was that these were three letters from important people that had been produced in short order in the run-up to Christmas. This struck me as slightly improbable. But the more I stared at them, the more I became concerned about something else: the sentence construction in each letter was uncannily similar.

Although it would be fair to say we were somewhat worried about Kallakis's bona fides, he was at the top of our list of potential purchasers. His interest in the team had reached the media – where he was routinely and unquestionably described as a 'Greek shipping tycoon' – and we had informed Honda. At that stage I was running a list of people who had contacted us and I reviewed it with Honda on an almost daily basis.

Senior management in Tokyo was represented by Mr Omura, who sat just outside my office. A fluent speaker of colloquial English, who was in his late forties, open-minded, affable and charming, Mr Omura was the perfect bridge between the Japanese culture of Honda in Tokyo and the team at Brackley.

He was committed to finding the best solution to the future ownership of the team and he knew about every incoming call and every meeting we had.

The King of Greece duly got back to Jackie and told him he'd never heard of Kallakis, but he said there were a lot of young Greeks who had made a lot of money since Greece joined the EU, so this was not to say that he was not real. The King couldn't rule him out as genuine.

Kroll, meanwhile, were coming to a dead-end; they could find nothing about him at all. Until, that is, on 23 December they hit the jackpot. To their great credit they found an old newspaper cutting from somewhere in the US, describing how a certain 'Stephan Kollakis' had been convicted in 1995 of selling bogus British feudal titles to hapless Americans and Australians. Suddenly all our suspicions were confirmed.

The first thing I did was call Kallakis's office and turn down his latest invitation to join him at the Royal Ballet. The following day – Christmas Eve – Ross and I phoned Achilleas from my office.

'Is that Mr Kallakis?' I said.

'Speaking.'

'Hi there, Achilleas. It's Nick and Ross from Honda, and I am afraid we have bad news…'

There was a pause, and we could hear a door shutting, before Kallakis replied: 'Yes?'

'Well, Ross and I have been doing some research and we have discovered some details about your past that, unfortunately, mean it will be impossible for Honda to do business with you. We are very sorry—'

'What?' retorted a clearly very concerned Kallakis. 'What on earth are you talking about? What details about my past? Tell me now,' he fumed, going off like a firework display. Eventually we agreed to tell him what we knew and explained what work Kroll had done. Kallakis quickly recovered his poise and then tried to play it all down.

'Oh come on, guys. That was years ago,' he said. 'We all make mistakes when we are young. Why should that stop me now? I'm trying to help you, after all.'

When we countered that Honda had the strictest rules on compliance, he responded in a way that only confirmed in our minds that he was certainly not going to be a credible partner for us.

'Have you told Honda about the report from the agency?' he asked.

'No, not yet because they are all away now for Christmas. But they will see it after the break.'

'Well, why don't we just send them a different report and then they need never know about it?'

There was a long pause. Ross and I looked at each other incredulously. Ross was a making a throat-cutting gesture.

'Look, thanks a lot, Achilleas,' I said. 'It's been great meeting you. Have a happy Christmas, mate. All the best.'

And that was that. I have to say that when we read about his trial and conviction four years later, we were fascinated but not surprised.

The bottom line was that by Christmas Eve – the deadline set by Honda – we had got absolutely nowhere.

Over the holiday period Ross went on vacation, so Nigel and I were left running around trying to sort out the next opportunity. I met someone from Scandinavia at Heathrow airport at the beginning of the first week in January who claimed to have links to people with the sort of money to buy a Formula One team. He came over as having no credibility whatsoever. The funny part of this little cameo was that this chap sent me an email that I forwarded to Ross – who had also briefly met him – and Ross replied: 'Are you still dealing with this idiot?' Unfortunately Ross sent it to both me and the subject of that remark, who was outraged and responded by sending us another email protesting that he was not an idiot.

At the beginning of January we had several meetings with Marcus Evans, the owner of Ipswich Town football club with a background in events management, but that went nowhere. Then towards the end of the month we met the owners of Spyker, the sports car company run by a Dutchman in the Netherlands with Russian financing. Ross and I quickly discovered that there had been several attempts on the life of the man behind the company and so, on the basis of risk evaluation, we came to the rapid conclusion that this wasn't the best idea. We didn't want to get killed.

Then, on 22 January, we had our first meeting with people from Richard Branson's Virgin empire. This encounter will never be forgotten by either Ross or me and is known by both of us – and quite a few others at Brackley – as 'the muppet meeting'.

Branson's representative was Alex Tai, an intelligent and intense ex-fighter pilot who flew planes for his boss and subsequently went on to run the Formula E team for Virgin. He was used to throwing his weight around on behalf of his boss, and at one point during that first meeting with us to discuss possible ownership of the team, he said: 'If Richard buys the team and he finds out you two are a pair of muppets, he will get rid of you very quickly because he does that the whole time and it will be no big deal.'

I have to say that, even though talks with Virgin continued for some time afterwards, those comments coloured all future discussions with them. For Ross, especially, they poisoned the waters and made it difficult for him to want to work with them, however attractive Virgin might otherwise seem. After the meeting both Ross and I, and indeed people in Honda, delved into the unflattering books on Branson by the investigative journalist Tom Bower, and we could see what was likely to happen here. Clearly Virgin saw a good opportunity but it was going to be the usual Virgin deal in which they would use their brand-marketing expertise. They would buy a small percentage of the team for a knock-down price, but have their name on it and try to impose full control. It would be their own Formula One team run by Ross Brawn.

To give Branson some credit, it wasn't just a marketing opportunity for him. The thought process behind it, as he saw it, was that Ross would sit alongside Burt Rutan, the designer of Virgin's *VSS Enterprise*, its proposed intergalactic spacecraft for paying tourists, as two great minds distinguished in their respective fields of design and engineering. Branson also wanted to back British business but additionally he knew he would be able to get hold of something very valuable very cheaply. In the end the deal never happened – it was never likely to, given the way our discussions started – but it eventually morphed into a smaller sponsorship deal that we signed a few weeks later in Melbourne.

Honda deserve great credit because the aspect that was most important to them all along was that they should exit Formula One honourably. What they didn't want to do was hand over the team to someone they didn't have full confidence in. They feared the PR disaster not just of leaving Formula One but of having that exacerbated by selling the team to someone who they believed wouldn't be good owners. In this profit-at-all-costs world I am not sure many companies would have acted as honourably as Honda did.

Neither did they want Branson and Virgin, because in a couple of meetings with Virgin – although Richard was enthusiastic – there were other members of his management team who seemed to be a lot less so. Combining that with the fact that by this stage we'd all read the Bower books, I think there were too many question marks on how this might go. The Virgin approach didn't meet Honda's requirement for getting out of the sport sensibly and taking the pain just once.

Looking for a buyer and dealing with all the approaches we had was an educational experience for all of us because it brought home how many dark forces there are in the world. I had never encountered anyone like Achilleas Kallakis before. Occasionally you got potential sponsors coming along when it was pretty clear they were intent on money laundering, so from time to time you came across people who clearly weren't straightforward, but this situation was completely different in that it demanded that we look under every rock. We had to investigate each of these people as far as we could because we were desperate. We weren't going to do anything dumb or illegal, but we couldn't rule out people just because we didn't like the look of them until we had evidence to conclude – as Kroll gave us in the case of Kallakis – that our feelings were well founded.

The humiliating part of it is that, after you have gone through the process in a case like that, you feel pretty silly and you kick yourself for wasting so much valuable time and money chasing them. But of course we had to investigate each offer as far as possible because, if one of them had been real, it might have been our lifeline.

In retrospect it seems surprising that we did not share our concerns about Kallakis with the police, but at the time we had no grounds to suspect that he was engaged in wholesale criminal activity. It also seems extraordinary, looking back, that we were fairly quickly able to rumble Kallakis and rule him out of doing business with Honda, whereas several major European banks, who lent him hundreds of millions of pounds, failed to adequately investigate him – to their considerable cost.

# CHAPTER THREE

## *NOW IT'S OUR TURN TO BECOME TEAM OWNERS*

The Kallakis debacle had brought home to us not just that it was a big bad world out there but that there might not be a fairy godmother waiting to rescue us after all.

We were beginning to wonder whether it might be impossible in the depths of a dreadful global financial crisis to find someone who was going to be acceptable to Honda from a corporate governance point of view and acceptable to the management as someone who might give the team the wherewithal to be successful.

Ross wasn't threatening to go elsewhere, but I was always conscious that we had to come up with a solution that would keep the most successful Formula One engineer onside because he was a highly desirable asset for any team and he wasn't going to accept any Tom, Dick or Harry as the new owner. I was also concerned about keeping hold of our drivers, particularly Jenson, who was marketable elsewhere.

The idea of a management buyout (MBO) first arose while Ross was away on his post-Christmas holiday. Nigel Kerr and I arranged to meet on 2 January at a Holiday Inn on the M40.

A small conference room on a cold and grey day at a low-budget hotel on Junction 4 of the M40 is about as uninspiring a setting as you could possibly imagine in which to try to sort out a new business plan. But it was halfway between my house and Nigel's house and it would have to do.

I had also invited Gordon Blair to the meeting. When I was at Prodrive, before joining Honda, we had bought a small company represented by Gordon and I knew he was a tough Scots negotiator and someone who knew his stuff when it came to restructuring companies. The idea was that the three of us would spend a few hours brainstorming our options, particularly the whole notion of an MBO.

It wasn't until this point – just over a month after being told by Honda that they were pulling out of the sport – that we had considered this route. It came out of desperation really and the realization that no one was going to save us, so we might have to save ourselves. I would like to be able to claim that we'd had the foresight before Christmas to take this on – and maybe if we had been more entrepreneurial we would have thought of it earlier – but it was only when we couldn't find another alternative that it dawned on us that if we didn't do this for ourselves then it probably wasn't going to happen.

After that meeting we reviewed the possibility of an MBO with Ross to get his buy-in. It did not go particularly well because Ross was very concerned about the financial and reputational risks that team ownership would bring and he was not particularly keen. It was kind of 'OK, let's give it a go because there aren't any alternatives.'

So Nigel and I put together an outline of how this might work. Honda had agreed to give us a little more time – they had originally given us until Christmas to find an alternative buyer – and this document set out that thus far there were no takers we could consider dealing with. We also asked for more money to cover the payroll through January while we continued to work with them to find a solution. We had cut all non-essential expenses and the bill was about £2 million. The document didn't set out an MBO in any detail but it did suggest that management might take on the team in some way.

This was a bad time to be selling anything with the world economy in meltdown. We had a machine shop that was full of tens of millions of pounds worth of equipment but, at the beginning of 2009, there were lots of engineering companies going bust and they were all trying to sell machine tools that were going for two-a-penny. The other issue was that everything we had was bespoke for Formula One. The wind tunnel may have been state-of-the-art, but it was not much use to anyone other than a team trying to make a car go fast in Bernie Ecclestone's global motorsports super show.

Then there were the 700 people who would require paying off. On top of that, you had the potential reputational damage in the UK and elsewhere of closing the business at a time of national crisis. The Honda Formula One team based in Northamptonshire was highly visible and had been proclaimed – by prime minister David Cameron, no less – as one of the crown jewels of British engineering.

We estimated a shutdown cost of more than £100 million, a figure that Honda quite rightly said they needed their own accountants to check independently. They came back and said we could well have under-estimated it, especially if staff contested their redundancy through industrial tribunals and so on.

On the face of it, however, an MBO still looked improbable. It was common enough in European or American business, but in Japan companies preferred more organic restructuring solutions, and MBOs were sometimes associated with management greed, so it happened rarely. Also, we were not experts at this and were finding our way, so we were nervous about what Honda might think. Looking at it from Honda's point of view, we could see why they would not want to give away a company that they had spent a huge amount of money to buy and into which they had invested hundreds of millions of pounds.

The first person we spoke to about a possible MBO was Mr Omura, the senior Honda executive on site at Brackley, on 8 January. To our relief, his view was that this was worth looking at. An MBO was probably not what he expected or had anticipated, but he wasn't against it because we were talking to the facts and the facts were that, at that stage, there wasn't anyone interested in buying the Formula One team.

The initial plan evolved very quickly. Mr Omura organized a video conference the following day with his bosses in Japan. We took part in it but it was a little bit sticky for two reasons. Firstly, what was being proposed was quite clearly not something they were familiar with; secondly, we could see that some senior people in Tokyo were concerned that they were being asked to approve a plan that amounted to a reward for failure. This was a team, after all, that had been patently very unsuccessful, with just one Grand Prix victory to its name in the last three years as a constructor and precious little success as an engine supplier before that. The overriding objective for many of the senior management was to beat rivals Toyota at all costs. We had won one race – and Toyota had not managed that – but we had not backed that up with consistent success, and few could say that the Honda team had proved it was consistently more competitive than Toyota. We had hired Ross a year before but the 2008 season was a write-off. Although it was never said, I suspect that what was going through their minds was: 'Why should we give our valuable Formula One team, which we have spent a lot of money on, to these people who have achieved almost nothing?'

The other element was that, as soon as an organization's management mentions taking over a company, they instantly become the enemy. As the textbooks will tell you, you suddenly become the other side and a negotiator not for the benefit of the owners but for yourselves. We were very conscious of this and felt that switch of emphasis immediately, even if nothing was said. In many ways the discussions were positive, but the emotional balance and negotiating positions changed in an instant.

Under the proposed deal, Honda would hand over the whole company, including all its liabilities, to the management for a peppercorn sum that turned out to be one pound sterling. On the structure of the new ownership, we asked Gordon Blair as an outside adviser to make a recommendation that we accepted. The majority shareholder would be Ross, who had just over half, with the rest split between myself and the other directors, with Gordon taking a share for helping us.

In the meantime Honda agreed to give us enough cash to help us keep racing all the way through 2009, albeit on a shoestring in comparison with our main rivals. At that stage we had no sponsors and no income apart from the money we were paid by Formula One Management (FOM), the owner of the sport run by Bernie Ecclestone. Each year the total income generated by the sport from television rights and other sources was divided between the teams and paid in arrears according to your finishing position in the constructors' championship. Our disappointing recent performances meant we were getting around £10 million from FOM, which was next to nothing in Formula One terms and nowhere near enough to keep us going.

We said to Honda that – based on minimal staffing, and taking into account a small amount of sponsorship money that we hoped to attract, plus monies already in the team bank account – the smallest budget we thought we could operate on for the season was around £100 million. But we knew that if we cut everything to the bone we could work with substantially less than that and make the money last longer. In the meantime, we would work hard to find a way to finance the team.

Honda accepted that figure and it was a seriously good deal with the benefit of hindsight. But at the time Mrs Fry was not as keen as she believed the company would almost certainly go bust a year later. The deal looks good now if you know the rest of the story, but the chance of the rest of the story coming true back in January 2009 was so close to zero that it wasn't even on our radar. Remember, this was an unsuccessful team and the historical precedent was poor. We had the benefit of some good facilities, a reasonable management group and the best designer in Formula One at the helm, so there were some positives, but if you were a betting man there was no chance.

When I discussed it with Kate – and I think Ross had the same experience when talking it through with Jean – there was an element of support and cheerleading. But did she think this was a wise idea? No! And based on the evidence before her, she was right. You could not present any substantial argument that this thing had a cat in hell's chance of being successful. I accepted the MBO was a leap of faith on the part of Ross and me and our fellow directors.

'We've got to give it a go,' I explained as Kate and I sat in the car together on the way to my parents, 'because there is a large team of people who are relying on this who probably won't have anything else to do bar picking up their dole money.'

'Yes, Nick, but what about the risk? What happens if it goes to the wall? You are going to be out of a job and we are going to end up living in a shed before this year is out.'

'I know, I know,' I replied. 'But Ross and I both think it is worth giving it a go. Besides, what else would we do apart from turn off the lights and go home? Then I'd be doing nothing anyway.'

I told her that most people in my position would have said 'let's give it a try', but I am not sure even I quite believed what I was saying at that point. I had, after all, grown used to sounding more positive than perhaps I might admit to feeling.

Bernie was generally difficult all the way through this process. His overall model for running Formula One was that no one should benefit from any major deal unless he got a cut. As the self-styled 'ringmaster' of the paddock, he didn't like the fact that he wasn't involved in this. There was something else too. Bernie did not like Ross. They are such fundamentally different beings, with different beliefs. Ross is very straightforward, while Bernie is a wheeler-dealer. Bernie also felt, as far as I could make out, that Ross never showed the respect that Bernie felt he was due. I don't think Ross ever wanted anything to do with Bernie and never kowtowed to him, and Bernie resented the fact that Ross was one of the few people in Formula One who wasn't beholden to him. At a later stage, for example, he fought tooth and nail to stop the team's name changing from Honda to Brawn – partly, I believe, because of this animosity.

I'm not sure Bernie liked me much either. Typically team principals and team CEOs in Formula One had long backgrounds in motorsport or rallying – people like Tom Walkinshaw, Eddie Jordan, Ron Dennis or Jean Todt – and most of them had had to do deals with Bernie at some point along the way. As a result they all had history both with Bernie and with each other – there were favours owed or prior agreements to be honoured or broken. My background at Ford, and then running the team for one of the big car manufacturers, meant I had been operating largely outside Bernie's orbit. He had nothing on me, as it were, and I felt he didn't like not having leverage that could enable him to control me or intervene in what we were doing.

The negotiations continued throughout January and into February while, in parallel, we carried on talking to other prospective buyers. But it was not a smooth or simple process and those weeks proved far from easy as the negotiations ebbed and flowed. We may have started off with positive vibes from Mr Omura but we then had to go through every level of the Honda Motor Company. Along the way we discovered that there were many executives who didn't like the idea of an MBO because they felt the easiest option from a PR point of view was just to shut the team down and be done with it; any negative connotations could then be hidden by announcing it on a day dominated by big news elsewhere. Others viewed an MBO as a sensible way of getting out but were concerned about what might happen if the management team was successful and 2009 saw us winning races. They knew there was a danger they could end up looking like real turkeys. There was not much we could say to alleviate their concerns on this score except to underline that we would be lucky if we managed to put together even a moderate season, let alone win anything.

In big corporations, full board meetings are choreographed affairs and people don't go into them without having done their homework. In Japan this process of preparation is called *nemawashi*, which literally means binding the roots of a tree together in preparation for a transplant. In business you go round all the decision-makers prior to a meeting, discussing it with them, understanding their concerns and getting their vote. We spent hours and hours every day on the phone and in video conferences – all of us with different interlocutors in Japan. It was difficult sometimes to meet demands or concerns that in some cases were almost philosophical or more about mood than numbers or deadlines. For example, the senior management in Honda wanted it to be seen that they were handing the team over to Ross because he was the big cheese in Formula One. For them it was a much more credible story if they were giving or selling the team to someone who was a multiple world champion as opposed to someone like me. It is unlikely it would have happened if Ross had not been there, but we all played our part in getting it over the line.

We needed to pull all the levers available to us. During my time running Honda's Formula One operation I had completed various pieces of trade promotion work for the UK government. Now seemed to be the time for them to return the favour, and so a phone call was quickly organized with the UK ambassador in Tokyo. Setting my alarm for 2 a.m., I called him and explained our problem. A beautifully worded official letter was soon composed in London and delivered by hand to the chief executive and president of Honda, Takeo Fukui.

It entreated him to preserve important jobs at Brackley and to carefully consider the management's proposal to save the team. I am told the meeting with the ambassador was very awkward and that we were fortunate that Honda was one of the few multi-nationals honourable enough to respond to appeals of this kind from national governments.

The key board meeting for us was on 23 February. In the preceding week discussions had been taking place at senior levels and there was a pre-board meeting on 20 February. This approved selling the team to the management. This was duly rubber-stamped three days later and then the legalities were completed a couple of weeks after that, on 5 March. That was the moment it became a reality that we were going to end up owning a Formula One team. It was just over a week before the final pre-season test at Barcelona – we hadn't been to any of the earlier ones with our new car for 2009 – and it was just over three weeks before the first Grand Prix of the new season, at Melbourne.

However much we tried to sugar-coat it, this was still an embarrassing experience for Honda – a company with a long tradition in Formula One that was now going away with its tail between its legs. Senior management at Honda had presided over an unsuccessful F1 team and now, in the financial crisis, they were not able to continue. It wasn't a good time for them in any area of their business. Their world had been turned upside down, as was the case for most of the other car companies; it was an environment where Dieter Zetsche of Mercedes Benz went to Aabar, the Abu Dhabi sovereign wealth fund, and queued up with everyone else for money. And it was not just Honda and Mercedes. Two of the big three automakers in the US – General Motors and Chrysler – had accepted huge handouts from the government at a cost of $80 billion. It was an environment where not just the survival of a Formula One team was in question but where many of the world's biggest automotive companies were also in serious trouble.

The approach for me all the way through had been focusing on fixing that day's problems. Fire-fighting is another phrase that comes to mind. I would like to say there was a grand plan, but I would be lying if I did.

After the MBO went through, I drove into Brackley – a very substantial facility by any standards – and it occurred to me that 'we actually own this.' It was slightly surreal in the sense that, even though legally I was a major stakeholder, it never really felt like it was ours. I have no doubt that people who have built up a company from scratch feel it is theirs and that they can do what they like, financially or otherwise. Yet I don't believe we ever treated the company as ours in that sense, so we didn't change that much from the way we had been running it for Honda – apart from the fact that we had to be more careful with money. But it wasn't ever a case of 'this is ours, we are now the big bosses; we can do what the hell we like, we can hire and fire and spend money as we wish.'

Although we weren't immediately saying to each other we had to get rid of it, Ross and I were very conscious that the two of us owning the majority of a Formula One team wasn't likely to be a sustainable situation. We knew we'd have to go after outside financial help at some point. It never occurred to us that we might make substantial money out of this. It was the opposite. It was more a case of unless we do very well in nine months, we could be shutting it down.

No one in their right mind – let alone us – could have predicted what was about to happen next.

# CHAPTER FOUR

## *ONE HELL OF A TUNNEL AND GETTING ROSS ON BOARD*

Long before we went racing in 2009, there were a series of progressive developments at Brackley that put us in a position to make the most of the car we had available to us as the new owners of the team following the management buyout.

The first building block had been the last change in team ownership prior to the MBO. This occurred in September 2005 when British American Tobacco sold their 55 per cent stake, meaning BAR (British American Racing) was replaced by the wholly-owned Honda Racing F1 Team. This marked a key shift in the way we went about our business.

One of Honda's great strengths is that it is an engineering company and it understands engineering. The big plus for us was that the team was now an engineering company's engineering project after years of being owned by a tobacco company. BAT had used Formula One as a marketing tool and had little understanding of engineering and no interest in investing heavily in engineering infrastructure. By contrast, Honda had always emphasized an element of self-reliance and investing in its own research, and one of the first benefits of the new ownership was the new wind tunnel at Brackley.

The tunnel had been required since about 2000, but BAT was not prepared to foot the bill and it was a whopper. When we proposed the tunnel – with its £50 million price tag – to Honda, I summarized the project on one A4 sheet of paper: 'This is what we need. This is how we will build it. This is the contractor. And this is the bill.' And that was it, more or less. The only question asked at the approval meeting was: 'Mr Fry, is it the best wind tunnel?' To which I replied: 'Yes, it is.' And I wasn't exaggerating. Most of our more serious rivals were either building or had just built new tunnels, but this one was on another level and still is.

In an era when aerodynamics was becoming the most important discipline in F1 performance, the team had been surviving until then on what was called an open jet wind tunnel. In simple terms, this was a building containing a rolling road conveyor belt in an open chamber. You put a scale model of your car on the conveyor belt – it could only take a half-sized model of the car – and blew air over it from the front, then collected that air from behind and recirculated it. It was an unsophisticated set-up that was considered, even in those days, as nowhere near state-of-the-art. In its place Honda underwrote a dedicated building with a chamber capable of taking not just one *full-sized* car but two, so that we could simulate the airflow interacting on one car and also between the car in front and the car behind. In fact, fairly soon after we commissioned the tunnel, the Formula One rules were changed to ban this sort of testing with two cars in a bid to cut team budgets. Our new tunnel could generate a wind speed of 80 metres per second

– the equivalent of 180mph – and it was driven by a massive fan with a diameter of 5.3 metres.

This extraordinary capability wasn't housed in any sort of building but a structure with huge foundations featuring seventy piles driven through the soil and down into hard rock. The reason for this was not the danger of earthquakes but the requirement for measurements of such accuracy that they could not be made if the building suffered any vibration, which it was very likely to do with a car running at 180mph anchored inside it.

The air being thrust through the tunnel at very precise angles created heat through friction, and that air had to be cooled while the car itself had to be fixed just above the rolling road to prevent it spearing off and crashing full-pelt into the tunnel. A disaster of this nature actually happened during the early running of the new tunnel when a fixing wire broke and the car smashed into one of the huge turning vanes controlling the airflow, causing tens of thousands of pounds worth of damage. Having warned everyone repeatedly of this danger, it was one of the very few occasions when I lost my temper at Brackley. But a faulty wire let us down and there was nothing we could have done about it.

Along with a simultaneous investment in top-quality aerodynamicists, the new tunnel was a monstrous undertaking. It came on stream in July 2006 and, once we had overcome some early issues with how we used it, the RA109 – our chassis for 2009, which became the BGP001 under Brawn GP ownership – was the first car to benefit fully from Honda's investment. It wasn't just the wind tunnel, however. We also had a first-class machine shop that was paid for by Honda, and a huge investment in computational fluid dynamics – the ability to simulate the flow of fluid or air on a computer in order to shortcut physical testing and to speed up development – something that requires vast amounts of computing power. So there was a whole raft of significant expenditure that enabled the team – and still enables the team under Mercedes ownership – to be incredibly successful and that underpinned the design and production of the BGP001.

But with Honda there was always something holding us back and in those years it was their insistence on employing Honda staffers in key positions, regardless of whether they were appropriate for the role. Understandably, given that they were paying the bills, Honda wanted their Formula One operation to have a substantial input from Japan rather than letting the UK-based team just get on with it.

This was demonstrated nowhere better than in their determination that the design and engineering team should be led by Shuhei Nakamoto, who was appointed senior technical director in June 2006. Mr Nakamoto had been with the team in a more junior position prior to that appointment and he was a talented engineer, but his specialism was in motorbikes – a racing discipline in which he had been immensely successful and was again after his stint in Formula One. At Brackley he was a fish out of water; he did not have the experience or technical know-how to lead an engineering team in F1, as his expertise was in a different area, and I am not being unfair if I say he was out of his depth.

His appointment was ordered by Honda at the expense of Geoff Willis, who had been with the team since 2001 and had overseen the installation of the new wind tunnel. Geoff was outspoken and not the most diplomatic when it came to dealing with Honda placemen he regarded as not up to the job, but he was a first-class engineer. He was one of the best assets we had at Brackley, yet there was no way he could stay once Mr Nakamoto had been elevated and he left shortly afterwards and joined Red Bull.

We all knew Mr Nakamoto was in the wrong role, and I had to go through one of the more soul-destroying periods in my management career when having to explain to the media and to everyone in our staff why he was the right man for the job, when they all knew that I knew he was not. I found this incredibly difficult because I was dealing with highly talented individuals who I respected and we all knew what the score was, but we had to accept what was being demanded in Tokyo. In interviews I rambled on and avoided the underlying issue, explaining to *Autosport* magazine, for example, that Mr Nakamoto's appointment was principally an organizational matter, as if the leader of a 500-strong design and engineering team in the world's most sophisticated motor racing formula made no difference. 'The whole nature of this change is spreading the load across more people and not bottlenecking it into a highly paid technical director,' I said. In reality I knew we had made our team dysfunctional and our generally poor results bore that out.

Knowing this wasn't going to work, I started to introduce the thought to Honda during 2007 – and specifically to Mr Oshima – that we should consider someone who was more experienced in Formula One. I was told in no uncertain terms that Mr Nakamoto's future was not up for discussion. Historically the worldwide boss of Honda comes from the engineering and car divisions. The exception that proved that rule was Mr Fukui, who came from engineering but also from motorbikes. So Mr Nakamoto had friends in high places and it was made clear that as long as Mr Fukui was running the show, Mr Nakamoto was going nowhere.

Two things then happened that helped our cause. One was that the performance of the car in 2007 was terrible. Jenson was our top-performing driver but he endured a frustrating season, retiring six times and finishing fifteenth overall, with a total of just six championship points and a best finish of fifth. Despite retiring only twice, Rubens fared even worse and finished twentieth overall with no points at all. In the constructors' championship we were eighth out of eleven.

The second thing was that I declared UDI on the question of who our technical director should be. Despite the fact that I had been told there would be no change, I decided to go looking for someone else to lead our engineering and design team.

'We can't just go on as we are – we will never get anywhere in this sport,' I told Kate one evening as I vented my frustration yet again. 'I think I have got to the point where I am either going to change this – and risk losing my job – or walk anyway. I've got nothing to lose when you look at it like that.'

Kate was sympathetic. She had also had to put up with our years of under-achieving and me coming back from races feeling frustrated and angry that we were seemingly unable to compete and invariably were just making up the numbers.

'Start looking,' she said. 'Who knows what might happen…'

I drew up a list of potential candidates, with the dazzlingly successful Ferrari technical director Ross Brawn and the chief technical officer at Red Bull, Adrian Newey, as my joint first choices on the list. Others were Bob Bell, who led the technical team at Williams, and Pat Symonds, an old stager at Renault.

I sought out Charlie Whiting, the veteran Formula One race director, for some advice because Charlie knew each of these individuals pretty well, going back years. I presented him with my shortlist and asked him what he thought.

'It's got to be Ross, Adrian and then Pat,' he said, 'in that order.'

'Why?'

'Well, Ross is not just a brilliant and experienced Formula One engineer, he is also a brilliant engineering manager and team player. I'm sure he'd know how to get everyone at Brackley working together like never before. I think you've got to go for him.'

Charlie explained that, while Adrian was a first-class aerodynamicist and designer, he operated in a completely different way to Ross as a manager.

'Adrian designs the whole car himself; he keeps it all very close to his chest and tends to be the only person in any organization that he has worked for who knows exactly how the car works. He would be good but I still think Ross is your man.'

Signing Ross would be an incredible coup, a man who had helped Michael Schumacher to seven world titles and had won seven constructors' titles during his time at Benetton and then Ferrari. But at that stage it seemed like a pipe dream; it would be like trying to lure Alex Ferguson away from Manchester United, Ross's favourite club, to one of the lesser lights in the Premier League like Crystal Palace or Newcastle. It seemed far-fetched.

I sounded out the candidates, which included a chat with Adrian at the British Grand Prix in 2007, but I wasn't convinced he was prepared to move anywhere.

Ross, meanwhile, was on a sabbatical during 2007 and was on an extended fishing trip around the world. I knew him a little bit from his Ferrari days, and I phoned him every couple of months to reinforce my interest in him joining our team. I spoke to him in Russia, in the Seychelles and in other remote corners of the fishing universe and he was usually standing in or by water, trying to coax a salmon or trout onto his line. When I couldn't get hold of him, I called his home number and his mother-in-law would pick up. I decided the best strategy was to ingratiate myself with everybody in the Brawn clan, so I would chat away merrily to her or any family member that I could get hold of in the hope that they would pass it on to the man known in the Formula One paddock as the 'big bear'.

Ross was extremely pleasant but he made it clear that if Ferrari made him a suitable offer at the end of his sabbatical, he would feel duty-bound to go back to Maranello. He was very straight up about it. Since he had been technical director there for some years, I assumed that the only post-sabbatical job he would be interested in would be team principal, which was probably not going to be offered as there was no sign at that stage of the incumbent, Jean Todt, going anywhere.

I had reason to believe I wasn't the only one phoning Ross. Toyota – and reportedly Red Bull and other teams – were also interested in him, so it was a competitive process but I was determined to get him.

Although my immediate boss at Honda was aware I was putting out feelers, it was continually made clear in the early part of 2007 that bringing Ross or anyone else in would be unacceptable to Honda because they wanted to take the credit for the success that they felt would come from the existing structure. But I never concealed from them that I was looking around, and they indulged me even as they made it plain that nothing was ever going to come of it.

My logic was that if I could get Ross to a position where he might accept the job, Honda might wake up to the possibility of signing one of the superstars of the sport. On the other hand, as I told Kate, if they still said no I would probably go and find something else to do because it was absolutely apparent that, with the technical structure that we had, we were not going to be successful. If they turned down Ross Brawn that would be the end of the game.

There was never a breakthrough moment as such. I just chipped away. I never discussed it with him directly but I had a feeling that Ross might not want to return to work in Italy for family reasons. He had been away for many years and now that there was a possibility of grandchildren on the way – he has two daughters – it struck me that working from home could be just what he wanted. Also with Jean Todt still running things at Maranello, why would he want to go back to his old job there when I could offer him a step up as team principal alongside me continuing as CEO?

Eventually I got Ross on the hook, as it were, and he came round to my house in Woodstock near Oxford in October 2007 to discuss the detail. He sat in the dining room and in his own quiet way set out his concerns.

'I don't want to sound arrogant about it but I've only got three questions,' he said. 'The first one is: who have you got?'

I had done my preparation and laid out an organization chart showing who was who in the vast engineering set-up at Brackley, which he seemed reasonably satisfied with.

'Two: what have you got?'

I had asked Graham Miller, our head of operations, to draw up a list of all the stuff we had, including the wind tunnel, the vehicle dynamic rigs – on which the car sits and is banged about by thrusters to replicate its experience on the racetrack – and all the engineering and computer resources we had. Again Ross seemed impressed that we had the tools that he needed to be able to do the job.

'Three: what's the budget?'

At that stage our all-up budget for the 2008 season, from which we had to campaign with one set of cars while designing the car for the following year, was around £160 million plus a free supply of Honda engines. Ross nodded. He paused for a second or two and then added a fourth question, and I knew at that moment that this was on.

'I've heard it from you and now I'd like to hear it from the owners. When can we go and see them?'

The following week we got on separate planes to Japan. We had to do it that way for the same reason that our meeting had taken place in my dining room rather than at the factory. Ross was such an iconic, recognizable and highly sought-after figure in Formula One that everyone would have known Honda was to be his destination had we been seen in public together. So it was all very surreptitious.

In Tokyo he was given a reception like a legend of the sport. I'm not sure we met Mr Fukui, but Ross got red-carpet treatment wherever we went, and by the end of it I think he was convinced there was an opportunity with Honda and that being successful with them was not unrealistic.

At the same time the Honda hierarchy was charmed. Having previously not wanted Ross under any circumstances, senior managers were now desperate to get his signature on a contract. One asked me during that visit what Plan B was if Ross did not accept the job?

'There is no Plan B,' I told him. 'It's shit or bust. We either get Ross or we face more years in the wilderness.'

Getting Ross was above all a recognition that we had to evolve to succeed. We could carry on under the old structure and achieve little or nothing, or we could change it. It was clear to me that the fate of the Toyota Formula One team awaited us if we did not have the courage to recognize where we were deficient and then address those issues. Toyota was unlikely to win anything. They didn't have the right people in key jobs, they were based in Germany – outside the main concentration of F1 teams in the UK – and they persevered with two drivers, in Ralf Schumacher and Jarno Trulli, who weren't good enough. We could go that route or we could change it...

Clearly I was putting my own position at risk and I was effectively hiring Ross to be my boss, but I felt that if we wanted to be successful it was absolutely necessary and we were dead if we didn't. (There were some who, once Ross's appointment became known, warned that he would sack lots of people – including me – and bring in Ferrari staffers, but that did not happen.) I also felt he and I had complementary skills: he was far more accomplished than me on the engineering side, and I was more knowledgeable about the commercial side, and we seemed to get on.

Ross was signed as team principal with a primary focus on engineering. After the contract was initialled in early November, I rang Jean Todt and he seemed shell-shocked. They had been setting themselves up for Ross to return to Italy, and Jean appeared to be completely blind-sided by his switch to Honda. It was a Saturday morning and I told him I had to announce it on the Monday, but he asked me for more time so that they could prepare their own response. I was sitting cross-legged on the floor of my study in my house in Woodstock, talking to one of the great men of motorsport and I had to tell him: 'I'm sorry, I can't keep this under wraps. It's going to get out, so we will be announcing it on Monday come what may.'

Two days later we snuck Ross onto the site at Brackley without anyone knowing. Then we got all the staff into the main conference room and I stood on the small stage at the front.

'Good morning, ladies and gentlemen,' I said, trying to stop myself from grinning broadly. 'Thanks for coming. You are probably wondering why we have called you all in. Well, we have something – in fact some *one* – very exciting to announce this morning. I am absolutely delighted to say that we have a new addition to our team and that he will be taking over as team principal from today.'

At this point we should have had a drum roll and some stirring music from the orchestra as Ross appeared from the back of the stage and walked forward to stand alongside me. It was like the messiah arriving. There was a collective gasp of delight and then spontaneous applause and cheers. Ross waved and smiled broadly. The auditorium is not huge, so it was a packed room with people sitting on the floor at the front and most people standing. Several were in tears. It was a moment to remember because the team had gone through so many tough years, and had had to put up with people who clearly weren't experienced in Formula One, and we were at a pretty low point in performance, so they viewed this as a watershed.

Ross was characteristically modest when he spoke to the press later that day, but he expressed the hope that the Honda team under his guiding hand would eventually be able to compete on equal terms with the likes of Ferrari and McLaren.

'I don't think there will be any obstacles,' he said. 'It is up to us to create the tools, philosophies and culture that is needed to win.' Then he added presciently: 'There is not a huge influence I can have on the current car for 2008 because that has been manufactured, but I hope I can start to introduce philosophies and ideas for the future.'

I have to admit that I was seriously excited. Of course, looking back, we can see that this was indeed a watershed moment – when the Honda and then the Brawn team went from being also-rans to world champions – but all that was in the future. I knew Ross had what it took but there were still nagging doubts in some quarters and I noticed the media reception to his appointment was more muted than I had expected.

Perhaps some doubted whether the Ross Brawn who had returned from his sabbatical had the same hunger and commitment that had made him so successful at Benetton and then Ferrari. Or maybe they doubted that Ross would be able to overcome what some viewed as the unbridgeable cultural chasm dividing the English and Japanese elements in the Honda team. If they were right, he would simply get lost trying to make it work and the mediocrity on the racetrack would continue.

It was time to find out.

# CHAPTER FIVE

# *BRINGING THE RA109 TO LIFE AS BGP001*

Ross's arrival at Brackley brought renewed optimism and a spring in our collective step. I had not seen anything like this since our promising season in 2004 in the BAR days, when we had finished second in the constructors' championship. The mood was captured by Jenson, who said he had no doubt that he was in the right team.

'I wouldn't want to be anywhere else in Formula One at the moment,' he said. 'For 2008 it won't be us that wins the championship – it's going to be a McLaren or a Ferrari most likely – but for the future in the sport, I can't think of anywhere better than here at Honda. It's not just Ross – Ross can't do it on his own. Ross knows it's a challenge and it can't just happen overnight, it's going to take a while. But I think we have the facilities to be a front-running team; we have the personnel now – it's just a matter of time.'

The plan laid out by Ross and I to Honda was that 2008 would be what we described as an 'organizing season'. We aimed to build on that and improve during 2009 and then after two years, from 2010 onwards, we hoped to be competitive.

The minimum plan to get towards the front of the grid was three years. But even after three years we never talked about winning a world championship; we just wanted to be there or thereabouts with the top teams.

Ross's influence was felt immediately as he brought order and coherence to the design, engineering and aerodynamics departments at Brackley. We had all the tools in the tool box; we just had not been able to put them together correctly. Ross was able to do that because he had the experience to know what worked and what didn't in Formula One.

The first decision was to write off the 2008 car – the last chassis put together under the direction of Honda. We all knew it wasn't good enough and the decision not to waste time and money on trying to improve it was unanimous. We had to tread carefully with Honda on this because we were spending hundreds of millions of pounds of their money and it cost a lot just to take part in a season, even at the back of the grid. So we presented this as a shift of emphasis to the 2009 cars, not a case of writing off 2008.

The upshot was that we were able to begin work on 2009 very early on in 2008. We could see that there was a nice opportunity to start from scratch with new rules introducing slick tyres for the first time since they were banned in 1998. The new cars would have lower and wider front wings, there would be no more winglets on the sides of the cars, there were changes to the diffuser at the rear, and the introduction of an optional energy recovery system known as KERS, or Kinetic Energy Recovery System, which recycled the energy generated under braking and provided the drivers with a speed boost. (At Brawn we put KERS to one side and did not incorporate it into our cars, viewing it as a complexity that we could do without.) When new design rules come in, the typical experience is that some teams get it right while others do not. We hoped we would be in the former category.

Our 2009 car, which started life under the designation RA109 but raced as the first and only Brawn GP car – the BGP001, was an incredible piece of engineering by any standards. Despite being finished off and then tested during the most precarious of times as we lurched from Honda ownership to a privately owned team, it was astonishingly quick out of the box with straight-line speed, ease of handling and excellent downforce characteristics. Its signature features were its fine aerodynamic detailing that proved spectacularly effective in giving the car exceptional levels of downforce and grip; its stability in cornering; and its novel – some would say rule-bending – rear diffuser design, which also contributed to its stickiness to the track. The car was conceived with a Honda engine in mind, yet would eventually emerge with a powerful but simple Mercedes Benz power plant that gave it the grunt to match the best on the grid.

It is remarkable that this machine proved so potent because, as we went through its design and manufacturing process, we were certainly not trying to win the world championship. We were just taking our first steps under Ross as he went about the first 'Ross Brawn-designed Honda' and the guiding principle was 'keep it simple'. But we were also using that phenomenal wind tunnel with the right person in charge of the engineering for the first time.

The idea for our so-called 'double diffuser' came from a junior Honda aerodynamicist at Brackley. The diffuser is a structure at the rear of the car where the air that rushes underneath the chassis is expelled. As that happens it has the effect of sucking the car to the track. The more powerful a diffuser, the more downforce a car develops, making it easier to drive fast without losing control. The rules for 2009 limited the height, size and angle of the diffuser amid concern that downforce levels were allowing cars to corner at ever-increasing speeds, something that was regarded as becoming unsafe for drivers, track marshals and even spectators.

It was during an early meeting chaired by Ross of the aerodynamic group at Brackley – there were twenty or thirty people in the room – that a young Japanese engineer, Saneyuki Minagawa, spoke up. In halting English he explained his view that we could interpret the wording of the rule in a way that would allow us to build a higher diffuser than appeared intended without contravening the rule. To start with there was a sceptical reception. People were struggling to get their heads around what was being suggested and some implied that his proposal was not possible within the rules. Then, very quickly, the mood changed. This was not only clever, it was argued, but it was supported by the wording of the rule. What's more, other teams were almost certainly going to reach the same conclusion. Ross authorized the aero team led by Loïc Bigois to pursue it.

Ron Meadows remembered Mr Minagawa initially proposing his ideas in a smaller meeting. Meadows believes it was because he was reading the rule literally, through the eyes of someone who knew English as a second language, that he saw the opportunity in the wording. 'He just read it as he saw it,' recalled Meadows. 'Everyone else said no. He said: "It doesn't say that, it says *this*." It was because he wasn't English that he spotted it – he just showed us there was a loophole and then everyone attacked it.'

It is very much to Loïc's credit that we would eventually produce a configuration at the rear of our car that out-performed our rivals to the extent that it did. Loïc was a real character. A Frenchman from somewhere near Nice with heavy bags under his eyes and a hang-dog expression, he was utterly obsessed with aerodynamics and worked all hours of the day and night trying to perfect whichever part of the car he was focused on. He led a team of about a hundred at Brackley and worked with what I can only describe as unremitting determination. We also employed his son Lucien who was part of our marketing team.

We had no idea whether any other teams were going down the same route as us, but because we thought they might be doing it, we did not assume it would be controversial and would lead to protests and attempts to have it banned. It was only when pre-season testing started in early 2009 that we discovered that both Toyota and Williams had followed the same path. And it was only when we began testing our own car in March 2009 that we realized how much of an advantage our double diffuser, in combination with the other innovations on the car, gave us.

In the meantime we took the obvious step of checking with the Formula One technical department, which oversees the implementation of the rules, whether it was legal. Our engineers took our diffuser design to Charlie Whiting, who headed the department, and said: 'Can we do this or not?' If the answer was yes, Charlie would only reply to the team that had made the enquiry and the process remained secret. If the answer was no, then he would publish his findings so that any other team making the same mistake would know not to waste more time and money on it. Charlie said yes.

By the time Ross and I turned up at Heathrow to be told Honda was pulling out of the sport, the design work on the car was more or less complete and the engineers were beginning to put it all together ready for testing in the new year. The major headache we then had was what to do about an engine. We had tried hard to persuade Honda to allow us to continue to use their engines for 2009, but the view in Tokyo was that if they were out, they were *out*. We were told in early January that the supply of engines would have to stop.

It is a deep and delicious irony that if that car had raced with Honda power we almost certainly would not have won the world championship. It was the design work we'd done on the chassis, combined with an engine from Mercedes Benz (which was a match for anything else on the grid), that proved so devastating. But of course we did not know that at the time, as we swallowed the bitter pill of losing our engine supplier and began hunting for a replacement.

You may ask what was wrong with Honda power. Why did it fail to produce the performance associated with Ferrari, Renault or Mercedes engines, for example? The issue we had with Honda was that the emphasis was on the peak power of the engine. We always had a nice figure of what our theoretical maximum power output was but in reality it was a momentary performance characteristic at the top of the rev range that was not sustainable. This is a characteristic of all Honda engines, including their road-car engines – they tend to produce a lot of power but it is at very high rpm compared to other manufacturers. As a result the car felt awkward in the cockpit and the drivers had to change gear more often than would be the case in a car with a broader band of power. When Rubens joined the team in 2006, the first thing he observed was that the Ferrari engine was far easier to drive.

In place of Honda we had the option of either a Ferrari or a Mercedes engine. Both manufacturers would normally keep the details of their engines a closely guarded secret and certainly not share them with rival teams, but both supplied us with drawings of their V8s so that we could assess which was preferable. This was not only unusual but showed a generosity of spirit that Formula One is not known for – both Ferrari and Mercedes Benz could see that we were in danger of crashing out of the paddock and they were happy to step in to help us.

Despite Ross's previous association with Ferrari, it quickly became clear that Mercedes was a better option, firstly from a purely practical point of view. The engine of a Formula One car is bolted directly to the back of the chassis. With the Mercedes engine, the bolts that held it to the chassis were in a similar position to those on the Honda. With the Ferrari engine, the bolt pattern went into fresh air on our chassis – there was no structure to fix it to the back of the car, so Mercedes was a more practical proposition.

The second thing was that, although we could only dream of beating McLaren or Ferrari on the racetrack, we felt that if we did ever get into a position like that, then Ferrari were unlikely to let us beat their works team. With Ross as our team principal, that would have been an embarrassment too far for the Prancing Horse. So we wondered whether we would get the same machinery as the works team.

We assessed our options throughout January and settled on a deal with Mercedes for a supply of engines in early February. Organizing the transfer of €8million for twenty engines for the season – eight for each driver and four for testing – was one of my first duties after the management buyout went through.

Although the Mercedes power plant was a close fit, a miss of a few millimetres is as good as a mile in the precise world of F1 car design. The compromise we had to accept was that the gearbox would now have to be about half an inch higher than it had ever been designed to be, and this also affected the height of the suspension. Any feeling we had that we were benefitting from having a better engine was offset in our minds by the fact that the centre of gravity of the car was higher than we wanted it to be and the whole thing was a bit of a fudge. What had started off as a Ross Brawn-designed thoroughbred was now looking more like a mongrel that had been bodged to accept an engine it was not intended to carry. We felt our best hope, performance-wise, was to sneak into the top five in the constructors' ranking. Even though we felt we had done a pretty good job and we knew the Mercedes engine was superior to the Honda one, we didn't have any aspirations to do better than that until we got the car on the track – if we had got into the top five we would have been pleased with ourselves.

Getting engines from Mercedes was a sensitive issue for McLaren, who were effectively the works team for Mercedes Benz in Formula One. Ron Dennis, their soon-departing team principal and chairman of the company, was not keen on the idea. He didn't try to stop it but there was no doubt that the main proponent of helping us was Martin Whitmarsh, the chief operating officer, who was taking over as team principal and was also chairman of the Formula One Teams Association. Martin was very helpful and was motivated to help another team that might otherwise drop out of the sport. Of course Ron had reservations – he is a motor racing man to his fingertips and racing is in his blood – but no one seriously viewed us as having any chance of being anything other than average.

We may have had Ross Brawn in charge, but on the surface we were a singularly unsuccessful team. However, this was all about to change.

# CHAPTER SIX

## *TESTING THE ROCKET SHIP*

Although we had modest ambitions for 2009, as the other teams completed their first pre-season tests at Jerez in Spain and elsewhere, we started to notice that our car would have been seriously quick if we had been able to attend ourselves.

Looking at our rivals, their cars appeared not unlike our car had looked in its first design phases. We assumed they would be coming forward with big updates and were surprised when they did not. Their machines looked clumsy and inelegant compared to ours.

Andrew Shovlin remembers not quite being able to believe what he was seeing. 'The conclusion we reached at that time was that we could be 1.5 seconds a lap quicker than everyone,' he said. 'We thought this must be a mistake – it couldn't be right. You don't let yourself believe that sort of thing – it sounded too good to be true.'

The first time the BGP001 turned a wheel on a racetrack in its all-white, sponsor-free livery with black and yellow trim, was at Silverstone where we conducted a 'shakedown' test on a bitterly cold and overcast day in early March. It was just a day after Ross and I had formally confirmed to the team, in an announcement to everyone gathered at Brackley, that we would be racing in 2009 under the name Brawn GP. The conditions were not good and we were restricted to the school circuit inside the main Grand Prix track. For our 'pits' that day we put up a small marquee that was just big enough for the race team to change the tyres.

There were probably twenty-five people there altogether and the race engineers stood in the back of a truck, grappling with their laptops as they tried to keep an eye on the performance of the car. It was a case, as one of those present put it, of 'one man and a dog trying to operate a Formula One car'. Only Jenson, whose manager Richard Goddard I had been keeping in close touch with throughout the winter, drove that day.

The bearded Englishman in a red, white and blue helmet had a big smile on his face as he got to grips for the first time with a new machine that he felt more at home with than any that had gone before it during his long years with Honda. After fifty laps of the little track he admitted that he had never got into a car feeling such a buzz. But that test was not of a sufficient scale for us to really understand what we had – that was about to hit us in Spain.

Having missed the first two tests because we were still sorting out the ownership of the team, the following week we arrived in Barcelona for our first run-out with all the other teams on a full-sized track. Apart from a small subsequent test that we attended at Jerez alongside Williams, Renault and McLaren, this was the last big session before the Australian Grand Prix, just a few weeks away, and we blew everyone off the track.

Unleashed for the first time in anger, the car performed spectacularly as Jenson led the timing sheets almost continuously on day one. After four laps on the same tyres we had used at Silverstone, he climbed out of the cockpit to discover to his amazement that he'd gone fastest on old rubber and by quite a margin. Then we put some new tyres on and it started to sink in with all of us. 'I'm not even trying, I'm really just cruising around,' said a delighted Jenson as we all realized we were a leap ahead of everyone else. 'I knew it was a good car – I was 0.6 of a second faster than everyone else,' he said later.

Rubens was even quicker and compared the BGP001 to the lightning-quick Ferrari of 2003 (designed by Ross in collaboration with Rory Byrne.) Both drivers spoke about how easy the car was to drive and especially its stability under braking, a quality not typical of cars produced under Honda management.

Ron Meadows remembers realizing the car was a weapon within a few laps. 'We could see within twenty minutes that this was a piece of kit,' he said with some understatement. He also remembers the reaction of the mechanics. 'After one of the first sessions I looked in the garage and I couldn't see half the staff – they were all in the back placing bets on the internet,' he said. Jock Clear told his wife to get down to the bookies but she thought he was joking. 'Of course I didn't – you say that every year,' she told him when he got home, but we were massive outsiders for any silverware that season so it was worth a long-range punt.

Despite our early hopes and the conclusions we had tentatively drawn about our prospective pace, we were all surprised how good the car was. You always go into these things with a sense of optimism, and obviously with a Mercedes engine we anticipated it would give us a step up in performance, but no one envisaged it would be as dynamite quick as it was. By the end of the three days in Catalonia, the two Brawn drivers were sitting at the top of the timing sheets, a second quicker than anyone else – the equivalent of more than 50 metres on the track – ahead of Nico Rosberg in the Williams FW31, with Timo Glock in the Toyota TF09 in third place.

All of the top four cars featured the controversial double diffuser. The 'official' pre-season favourites – the Ferraris, McLarens and BMW Saubers – filled the lower reaches of the top ten and beyond, with Sebastian Vettel the best of the two Red Bulls in ninth place, and Lewis Hamilton, the reigning world champion, back in eleventh spot in a McLaren that was evidently very poor.

Naturally there was some speculation that we were showboating – running the car light on fuel and trying to impress the motor racing world with artificial speed in the hope that we might attract badly needed sponsors. There were certainly many people in the paddock, including the Renault team principal Flavio Briatore, who felt that that was exactly what we were doing.

One person who knew that our speed and performance was genuine was Fernando Alonso because we had had discussions with him during the latter part of 2008 about him joining the team for 2009. Ross and I had decided that if we were going to attract someone of his calibre then we needed to give him a technical explanation that was honest. So, although Fernando didn't know the finer details, he had a reasonable understanding of the work that had gone into the 2009 car.

'It is real,' said the Spanish two-world champion then driving for Renault. 'The truth is they have a car that Honda began working on in 2007 to use in 2009. That's evident in its design, because it is a very elaborate car with different shapes to the rest.'

The reality of the situation was that, having missed most of the pre-season tests, we had no time for playing to the gallery and in fact our car was consistently and significantly quicker over the longer runs at the Circuit de Catalunya – something that tended to rule out the notion that we were running light on fuel.

One of the pleasures of those heady days was seeing how much our two drivers enjoyed the car. Both men knew what it was like to race in indifferent machinery, and Jenson had become exasperated by some of the cars he was given to drive during the Honda days. But the look on his face throughout the time between first driving the new car and arriving in Australia was like a kid with a new toy. Of course, as a driver he did not want to get too excited in public about it. After all, if a driver says 'this is a brilliant car' then all he is doing is putting the stress on his ability to exploit it. So drivers tend to downplay how good a car is because it places them under a lot of pressure to perform. But Jenson wasn't the only one playing it down. After the Barcelona test there was an air of disbelief in Brawn GP, of not believing our luck, of unspoken optimism. Given what we had been through – not just Honda pulling out in the previous four months but the previous five years of disappointment – the natural reaction across the whole company was to keep our heads down and see how this played itself out.

Jenson is a thoroughly decent guy but possibly someone who was just too nice for his own good in the bear-pit of Formula One. He had joined the team back in 2003 under BAR's colours. He had been with us all the way through, starting as teammate to Jacques Villeneuve. The early high point for him was his first race win – the first and only race win for Honda

– at the Hungarian Grand Prix in 2006, but that was a distant memory by the spring of 2009. By then Jenson had become a well-known quantity within the team. He was regarded as an extremely competent driver even if, ultimately, he had come to us after having been replaced at Renault by Fernando. Jenson and Rubens were treated equally, but in the heart of the team – in an emotional sense – Jenson was probably the number-one driver because we had all been through so much together.

Jenson's strength was his instinctive feel for what a car was doing, which was extremely strong, but the reverse side of that was that he didn't react well to a car that was misbehaving. He wasn't a driver who could take a car by the scruff of the neck and push it to the limits regardless. If the car was behaving well then Jenson would maximize its performance and do an incredibly good job. But when the car was off the pace he appeared less able to cope with that – psychologically perhaps more than physically. I say that because when the car wasn't good there was always a lot of moaning. If he went out on a Friday morning practice run before a race and there was a long list on the radio along the lines of 'this doesn't work properly, that doesn't work properly', then you knew you were in for a long, under-achieving weekend and the issues would probably never be resolved.

On the other side of the garage Rubens had immense technical skill and talent from a driving point of view. One of the reasons that we decided with Honda that we wanted him was that we needed the experience he could bring from a big team like Ferrari. We also knew that he had spent many years in Michael Schumacher's shadow, not just as his number two but also not being able to race him. We felt we could unleash the competitive instinct that, to some extent, Rubens had had to suppress during his six seasons at Maranello.

The Brazilian showed his mettle in the very first test he participated in for us when he drove a Honda car for the first time in 2006. After a few laps he came on the radio: 'There are some vibrations from the engine – I think it's gonna blow up,' he reported.

The astonished engineers looked at each other none the wiser because the telemetry was indicating that nothing was wrong, but they called him in all the same. In the garage they crawled all over the back of the car but could find no indicators that the engine was in danger and Rubens was instructed to go back out.

'Look, if you want me to go out and blow up your engine then I will do it,' he protested, 'but I think it might be more constructive if you took the engine out now, took it to bits and found out what was wrong. Then we might have a chance of identifying the fault so we can rectify it. But if you want me to blow up the engine – feel free – I will go out now and do that for you.'

The pit crew decided to listen to their new driver and, sure enough, a few days later word came back from Japan that Rubens was right; the engine was about to blow. Rubens was a class act and he earned respect among the mechanics and especially among the Honda engineers from Japan who loved his instinctive understanding of their machinery. He was also the most charming of individuals out of the car, which they loved about him too.

Our pre-season testing performance made us highly visible and prompted renewed interest in us from potential suitors – including the most powerful man in Formula One himself.

Our dream start as we finish 1-2 at the Australian Grand Prix.

The team celebrating with Richard Branson after our win in Melbourne.

Jenson, Rubens and the team celebrate our first ever win at the
Hungarian Grand Prix, 2006.

For star power in the paddock no-one beat the Beckhams,
British Grand Prix, 2007.

Pit practice in the old days of the Honda F1 Team. On the fuel hose is Ian Clatworthy, the gentle giant who carried Ross Brawn on his shoulders as we celebrated our 2009 championship victory.

Ross with Saneyuki Minagawa, the young Japanese aero engineer who spotted the loop-holes in the rules for the diffuser.

Nick with Shuhei Nakamoto (*third from left*) on the annual pre-season visit to a shrine in Japan to pray for good performance.

Achilleas Kallakis: the conman who wanted to buy us.

Vijay Mallya: the flamboyant beer-to-airlines tycoon who had a chance to become our owner but passed it up.

Tony Fernandes, the ambitious Air Asia owner, with Nico Rosberg in 2008.

Richard Goddard, Jenson's manager – he always rated Jenson a little higher than we did.

The 2008 team principals gather at Monza – many of them would move on within eighteen months: (*left to right*) Stefano Domenicali, Colin Kolles, Ross Brawn, Christian Horner, Ron Dennis, Luca di Montezemolo, Sir Frank Williams, Flavio Briatore, Adam Parr, Mario Theissen, Gerhard Berger, Franz Tost, John Howett, Tadashi Yamashina, Nick Fry, Martin Whitmarsh.

Bernie Ecclestone lays down the law to Ed Gorman of *The Times*.

*Top*: The Brawn livery at the 2009 pre-season Barcelona test.

*Right*: The fine aerodynamic detailing on the front wing of the new Brawn BGP001.

*Below*: Jenson waiting in the pitlane in Barcelona as his father, John, looks on from the pitwall.

The cat with the cream: at Barcelona, Jenson knew almost immediately that his car was special.

The infamous double diffuser that was instrumental in achieving World Championship glory.

The jewel in our crown: the site at Brackley in Northamptonshire.

In our state-of-the-art wind tunnel, lead aerodynamicist John Owen shows a Brawn GP test model to Michael Schumacher – the Mercedes years proved a tough coda to a remarkable career.

# CHAPTER SEVEN

# *NOW BERNIE WANTS TO BUY US*

It was 9.30 a.m. in London. I was sitting in the spacious ground-floor Knightsbridge office of Bernard Charles Ecclestone, the famed 'ringmaster' of the Formula One circus.

Usually when I met Bernie in London I was with other team principals and CEOs and usually we would sit on the sofas that faced each other in front of Bernie's desk – which itself was in front of a large document shredder. Not this time. This time it was just me and Bernie – Ross was away at the pre-season test in Barcelona – and a chair had been placed right next to his desk. I found myself just a few feet away from the diminutive billionaire with the Paul Weller hairdo, then in his late seventies.

Bernie rarely raised his voice and did not like to beat around the bush. When he summoned you to a meeting there was never any foreplay and this was no exception. It was always straight to the point, but I have to say I was a little surprised by his opening gambit that day, although I did my best not to show it.

'Hello, Nick. Max thinks you're a cunt,' he muttered almost under his breath in his typically deadpan way. He was referring, of course, to Max Mosley, the head of the FIA and the other half of the double act that ran Formula One for decades, known to one and all in the paddock as the 'Max and Bernie show'.

'Yeah, good morning, Bernie,' I replied cheerfully before adding as nonchalantly as I could: 'Why does Max think I am a cunt?'

Quick as a flash, the former second-hand car dealer from Essex who transformed Formula One into the world's richest sport, replied: 'Because you were born a cunt, you are a cunt and you will always be a cunt.'

Hilarious. Yes, I laughed out loud at that. Actually, being treated this way by Bernie was arguably a sign that I had finally made it. (For the record, I never did find out what Bernie was on about and when I checked later with Richard Woods, Mosley's spin doctor – who also did a bit of spinning in those days for Bernie – he confirmed that in fact Max did not think I was a cunt at all.)

What Bernie was after that day was our new Brawn team. But before we get to that, a little history. Whether you liked him or not – and I liked him more than Ross did – Bernie was regarded as something of a legend. He had taken Formula One by the scruff of the neck in the mid-1970s and transformed it from a chaotic free-for-all into a compelling annual global spectacle that entertained hundreds of millions of people, and it had made him – and many of the team principals – phenomenally rich.

He ran the business in his own unique way. He relied much more on his word and a handshake than on documents and lawyers, and he put huge effort into maintaining what was effectively a benign dictatorship. He did this largely through finding, at every turn, ways to divide the teams against themselves so that they rarely presented a united front in opposition to what he wanted to do. It proved remarkably effective and, given the strong personalities involved leading the teams, it was probably the only way to achieve what he did.

When I came onto the scene in the early 2000s with Honda and BAR, Bernie had already been there for years and there were rules of the road that you were supposed to observe in his presence. For example, at team meetings at the circuits there was a clearly established pecking order around the table. Bernie would sit at the head and the big players in the paddock – the principals from Ferrari and McLaren – would be on either side of him, and so it would go in descending order of success and longevity down the table.

As I prepared for my first meeting in 2002 I was warned that, as the representative of Honda, I would be expected to sit way down the room, almost at the end. But I decided this was not for me and I would break with this long-established tradition. I had spent the majority of my career working for Ford, a significant motor company, and in some significant roles, and I was not going to just toe the line and accept the crumbs from the table. I felt that if I didn't demonstrate this from the outset then I would be stuck in the lower orders for good.

I arrived at the meeting early and plonked myself at what was obviously going to be the head of the table, and when Ron Dennis of McLaren and Jean Todt of Ferrari and the others came into the room, they were too polite to ask me to move. You could sense that there was general unease that I was out of my natural position. But, funnily enough, I am not sure that Bernie minded that much – as a natural 'disrupter', he probably found it rather amusing.

That first meeting was an education. I came from a comparatively dull world, where meetings were prepared for, briefing notes were often brought to the table by each participant and there was an agreed agenda. In Bernie's Formula One fiefdom none of those things happened. That day the main topic of discussion was a proposal to change the points system in the drivers' championship – a key element in the overall sporting proposition that you would think would need to be handled with care. Not a bit of it. I was amazed at how the discussion developed. It was a complete free-for-all as the team principals threw out random ideas without basis of fact on what they thought the system should be. Then Bernie made a decision, just there and then.

The other extraordinary aspect of that meeting was that during the course of the exchanges Eddie Jordan, the eponymous team owner and long-time Bernie mucker, decided he did not like the general direction the discussion was heading in. His response was to stand up and start ranting and raving and throwing bits of paper around about the costs of hotels at the circuits. It felt more like a primary school classroom than a board meeting of a multinational business.

Bernie was very much the power in the land in those days and he would be on the phone to team heads – if not every day, then certainly every other day – and he was always working away at his divide-and-rule tactics.

'Flav is saying this about you,' he would mutter in reference to Flavio Briatore, the colourful multi-millionaire head of the Renault team. Or he would say: 'Ron has been telling everyone you think this or that... and he is threatening to do this, if you don't do that...'

He was constantly stirring to make sure the teams did not work together and I learned to take quite a lot of it with the proverbial pinch of salt. The whole environment was designed to keep everyone in a state of perpetual uncertainty and subservience to Bernie.

Meetings were called by his office and it was a three-line whip. Wherever you were, you had to drop what you were doing and turn up, often without knowing what the meeting was about. Frequently, when you sat down, it wasn't at all clear what was supposed to be being discussed and there were never any written minutes of what had been said. The outcome of a meeting was usually down to Bernie's interpretation of what was agreed rather than necessarily what had actually happened. Until late on in the Bernie era, it was a closed society where you were expected to do as you were told and the whole set-up was designed so that Bernie could get his way.

But Bernie was no bully. His perspective on life was based on the fact that Formula One in its modern form was his creation, so the way he behaved was very much that it was *his* business and of *his* making. Most of us had split feelings about this. There was huge respect for him on the one hand because of what he had achieved – and there still is – but, on the other hand, we also knew that we were working under a dictatorship, albeit a largely benevolent one.

Naturally people were nervous of his power because Bernie could make your life difficult if he wanted to. At one stage I incurred his displeasure for some reason and I discovered this when I arrived at that year's German Grand Prix at Hockenheim. At the circuits the drivers and team principals enjoy the significant perk of being able to park in designated areas right outside the paddock gates, with spaces marked out in descending order depending on your performance in the previous year's constructors' championship. In the controlled chaos of a Grand Prix, with thousands of spectators and huge pressure on parking, being able to drive right up to the paddock – as opposed to parking on the outside of the circuit – is a huge bonus and a big help when trying to run long days for sponsors and other guests.

On this occasion I reached the parking area only to find that there was no space allotted to me. To start with, I thought this was some sort of unintended error and checked again, but every space was either taken or going to be taken, and it suddenly dawned on me that this was Bernie's way of sending me a message. I spent the best part of an hour trying to find an alternative parking spot and then began a long walk back to the paddock. All the way, as I made my way through the crowds, I was wondering whether my electronic pass would work and if I would be able to get through the automatic gates into the paddock. Fortunately Bernie had not stopped me doing that.

That was one his methods of keeping the whip-hand. Remarkably, despite running a global business and managing relations with circuits, teams, the media and sponsors, Bernie never relinquished control over who got passes to the paddock and who did not. At every race, he supervised who got in and it was his call when it came to how many guests – often representing sponsors – you could bring in on any day. In a sport when access to the pitlane and paddock was highly prized and was a major element in sponsor entertainment, Bernie had the ability to restrict the scope of your business at any race, so he needed to be treated with a great deal of respect.

But for every negative there were lots of positives. Bernie ran Formula One like clockwork. His staff were excellent, and he never ceased looking for new markets to expand into, even if some of them turned out to be places where motor racing was never going to take off. And he had a great gift for publicity and dealing with the media and promoting the sport. A firm believer that any publicity is good publicity, he never feared bad press and he did a tremendous job of keeping the story going and promoting F1 during the off-season.

When you were talking to Bernie everything was committed to memory, nothing was written down and he was as sharp as a tack. In a discussion he would frequently remind you of previous exchanges that you had had on a particular topic and, in typical Bernie fashion, he would frequently remember them slightly more from his point of view than yours, but he had an incredibly memory. I found dealing with him very straightforward because, regardless of what he said, you knew that he was acting principally in his own best interests and it was never difficult to work out where he was coming from. He always delivered; if you agreed something, and metaphorically shook hands on it, you knew it would happen.

After our colourful initial exchange that day in March 2009, Bernie set out his view that Ross and I were out of our depth in thinking we could not just run the new Brawn team but own it too, and he belittled our decision to share some of the ownership with our fellow directors. I guess he had a point – we were not typical Formula One grandees with a proven track record in this area, like Frank Williams or Ron Dennis, and we didn't have the glamour of Ferrari. But Bernie had other motives; he was also interested in having our team on his side when it came to the ongoing and time-consuming battles between him and the teams over the distribution of the sport's earnings and other matters.

He made clear he was interested in buying the team and seemed not remotely bothered that this might lead to a conflict of interest with him, as the organizer of Formula One, having a stake in one of the players. He didn't say how much he was willing to pay and the discussion was really about what his share would be. He started off implying he wanted to buy a minority share but I told him that if he wanted the team then he would have to buy more than half. I made it very clear that we were not going to roll over and give up easily and, pretty quickly, I could see that he was not going to do it.

Throughout the conversation I was never sure whether Bernie was being serious or not. There was a level of ambiguity about it that was typical of him. Was Bernie really a possible buyer of Brawn GP? Or was he talking on behalf of CVC Capital Partners, the then-owners of Formula One? Or was he just batting it all around to see what my reaction was? Perhaps this was just a fishing expedition and he hadn't made his own mind up, but I never let my guard down.

When our chat came to an end he sent me packing in characteristic Bernie fashion, very much in keeping with how the encounter had started: 'If you think you can fucking do it yourself, then fuck off out of here and do it.'

The Bernie Ecclestone era is now over and the only thing I would say is that it was a pity that he succumbed to the temptation to stick around a bit longer than he might have done. In something as attractive and addictive as Formula One, outstaying your welcome is a particular hazard and even more so when you were the creator of it. While he was certainly within his rights to be in charge for as long as he was, I think it was clear to many of us that in his final years he was not quite the Bernie we had grown to love, respect and occasionally fear. It might have been better if he had called it quits on his own terms a few years before he was finally ushered out of the door when Liberty Media completed its takeover of the sport in early 2017.

People say there will never be anyone like him again. I am not sure that is true. Idiosyncratic, self-made businessmen and women the world over run their affairs how they want and will always do so. With Bernie running the show, Formula One was fun. He kept us all on our toes and I learned a lot from him. At every race and every meeting there was always an element of the unexpected, there were interesting people around and we laughed a lot – and the reason it was like that was because he set the tone.

While Bernie showed interest in us as a buying proposition, it was another idiosyncratic, self-made British businessman who occupied much of my time at the first race of the season in Australia.

# CHAPTER EIGHT

## *BRANSON STEALS THE SHOW AT MELBOURNE*

Melbourne's season-opening Australian Grand Prix was a watershed moment for the new Brawn GP team as we not only won the first race we had entered but scored a one-two, with Jenson leading Rubens home.

That weekend in Australia also featured a remarkable cameo from one of the world's most famous entrepreneurs – a certain Sir Richard Branson – who used the occasion to sweep into the Formula One paddock to sign our first sponsorship deal and slap some Virgin stickers on our almost entirely logo-free white cars.

When the possibility of Virgin buying the team fell through, discussions with Branson's people had switched to the idea of the Virgin Group becoming a supporting sponsor. We needed all the money we could get at that point, and Caroline McGrory and our two sponsorship managers, Richard Berry and Richard Sanders, were tasked with trying to get it over the line. They did a brilliant job. The talks went on for some weeks and in the end a deal was agreed after Ross and I had got on the plane to Australia on the Wednesday evening before the race. Branson's office then informed us that he intended to be with us in person to celebrate the announcement of what was a fairly modest tie-up – and quite a strange one too – and we did our best to prepare to host him.

The Virgin billionaire flew in from a family skiing holiday in the Alps and arrived at the street circuit at Melbourne's Albert Park on the Saturday morning straight from the airport. His trademark shock of blonde hair framed a rather ruddy-looking complexion and his generous girth was attired in a grubby pair of jeans and a white Virgin polo shirt. It was the final day of practice and then qualifying before the Grand Prix on the Sunday. Before the practice session, we organized a small press call at the back of our garage attended by Richard and two models – hastily procured from an agency in Melbourne – kitted out in red shorts and white sleeveless T-shirts with 'Virgin' emblazoned on their chests. Richard gave a typically rambling speech about the synergies between Ross and Burt Rutan and then I set off with him down the pitlane while Ross got on with the racing.

Unless you had seen at first hand the Virgin/Branson effect – at least at that time – it would be hard to imagine the impact he had and the publicity he could generate. Richard watched the practice session and qualifying from the pitwall with me, and after we qualified first and second we were absolutely surrounded. I remember Richard then making his way down the pitlane again and he was completely mobbed by photographers. He was probably only second to the Beckhams (who had been our guests at the British Grand Prix a couple of years earlier) in terms of star quality and the amount of excitement he created.

Richard was straightforward, pleasant, well-spoken and seemed to be a very nice guy. When we subsequently met his two kids they were equally impressive. In my experience, people don't put these personas on – the way they come across is usually a pretty fair reflection of who they really are. Richard had other people around him to do the dirty work while he did the schmoozing and the sweet-talking.

It didn't worry us if there was a perception that Branson was paying more than he actually was for the sponsorship. It helped build on the impression that people had confidence in us, in the same way as good old Achilleas Kallakis had helped us by coming to Brackley in a massive helicopter. What's more, we didn't have any money to do any PR, so having someone else to do it for you – and on a global scale – seemed like a pretty good deal to me.

The sponsorship agreement was a mixed bag. If you added everything up it amounted to about £10 million. But the cash was only part of it, with the balance worked out in kind on a race-by-race basis through separate negotiation each time. We would have much preferred just cash but that wasn't on the table. Instead I used to negotiate – often with Richard himself – on what we could have in lieu, and generally it was great fun as I pitched and he countered. At one race it would be Virgin Airline flights, at another gym memberships through Virgin Active – we settled for just about anything Virgin could provide that helped us reduce our costs.

On the Saturday evening Richard invited Kate and I to dinner with him and several of his colleagues at Nobu, a Japanese restaurant in the casino complex in downtown Melbourne. It was located in the Crown Towers Hotel building where our team, and indeed all our rivals, normally stayed for the Grand Prix weekend. This time we were in the somewhat less salubrious Bayview Hotel, which was cheaper and out of town but had the advantage of being bang next to the track.

After a frantic day at Albert Park, Kate and I arrived late at Nobu and by the time we walked through the door at about 10.30 p.m. Richard and his coterie had been hard at the pink champagne for quite a while. The mood was feisty and uproarious. The champagne combined with jet lag was giving them a big high before they crashed. At the time Kate was keen on yoga, and before long Richard had talked her into demonstrating a few of her moves *on* the table. The place was jumping and it was all good fun.

After a while I noticed that Richard kept disappearing and at one point he visited Jenson's table, where Jenson was eating with his girlfriend Jessica Michibata, his manager Richard Goddard and others. I could see that there was a little bit of a kerfuffle, but I thought little of it. However, according to *Life to the Limit*, Jenson's autobiography published in 2017, Branson had started behaving, in his words, like a 'party-starter' and had begun drunkenly flirting with Jessica, much to Jenson's fury. I only discovered the following day that Jenson was mortally offended by Richard's behaviour. From my perspective I thought it was rather amusing and I certainly wouldn't have felt threatened by a late-middle-aged gentleman approaching my girlfriend if I was a strapping young Formula One driver. My personal view was that this episode was somewhat overplayed.

What I did witness was what happened after Jenson had given Richard his marching orders. On Richard's way back to our table, someone at another table had the bright idea of handing him a baby so that photographs could be taken of the toddler with the billionaire. But Branson was swaying alarmingly as he staggered along laughing with this child in his arms and, while the father seemed highly amused, the baby's mother most certainly was not. I was starting to get visions of a massive PR disaster to follow the more positive mood earlier in the day. We decided it was time to go and soon Kate and I were leaving with Richard in tow, who was also staying at the Bayview.

Before we parted that night, Richard promised to be ready at 7.30 a.m. sharp to go to the track with Ross and me, and he was as good as his word. In fact, hungover or not, he was waiting for us in the lobby when we came down. The Virgin boss was impressively apologetic for everything that had happened the night before and was extremely humble. He told us that he wouldn't be drinking for at least the next month. All in all he was very gracious about what he realized had perhaps not been his finest hour.

During the Grand Prix, Branson sat with me in the garage, watching the race unfold on the screens and standing each time to enjoy the spectacle as the cars came screaming in for their pitstops. When we won there was a huge outpouring of emotion in the team and Branson loved it. His assurance that he would not be touching alcohol for a while quickly went out of the window when he accepted a flute of champagne to celebrate our success.

'I've always been a lucky bastard,' he told the journalist Simon Arron, champagne glass in hand, sporting that huge trademark smile of his.

There was a lot of bonhomie that night and at one point Branson took a call on his mobile from Bernie Ecclestone.

'He wanted to know if I would fly home and accompany him to a casino,' Branson said. 'He wants to stick a million pounds on whatever number I choose.'

Winning at Albert Park certainly relieved the pressure on us, and at least we could enjoy it, but there was no great feeling that we had a long-term solution. I think the huge release of emotion reflected the fact that we had managed to get ourselves into a position where we could do well in a race, even if we did not feel that we were, by any stretch, out of the woods.

When our drivers came back down the pitlane after the podium ceremony all the other teams were clapping. That recognition by our peer group was something that was not just appreciated – we felt humbled that everyone should be happy for our success despite the fact that they were also fighting tooth and nail to get the car that we had developed banned. They recognized that we'd been through a lot and done a good job, whereas we were beginning to realize that, in the BGP001, we had a durable car and a sweet machine to drive.

If truth be told we had only just managed to get both our cars through the race, let alone win it. We were very short of spares, because so many people in the relevant departments had been laid off, and our engineers worked through the night before the race, trying to sort out faulty front flaps on the cars. These were adjusted from the cockpit but the motors and software for them were not good enough and they kept seizing up. By the time we lined up on the grid we had run out of spares, so if either Jenson or Rubens had biffed them we were going to be in trouble. At that race weekend and the three subsequent Grand Prix we had no spare chassis, so it was vital that our drivers avoided big shunts.

Another issue we had were our pitstops, which were not up to scratch all afternoon, especially for Rubens. The reason was that among the large numbers of people who had taken redundancy was Gary Holland, our expert fuel-nozzle hand. It was Gary who thumped the end of the hose into the fuel adaptor on the side of the car as it came to a halt and then wrenched it out again after the fuel had gone in at a rate of about 9 kg a second. It was a skill that required strength and precision acquired over many years, and we had noticed that it was easy enough to pull off in practice but hard for some people to deliver in race conditions. If the hose did not go in correctly first time, it could un-cock and would have to be reconnected, adding precious seconds. The crew also had to be ready with the right hose for each car – red rig for Jenson, blue rig for Rubens – and at Melbourne they got all mixed up. Gary was unerring when the pressure was on, but he had gone off to become a plumber. After that race we persuaded him to come back for each Grand Prix weekend on a day rate and we were able to restore our performance to what it had been the previous season.

As far as the inevitable protests against us went, the drama played itself out more or less as predicted during the early part of the race weekend. We were expecting the Albert Park stewards to be asked to adjudicate on the legality of our rear diffuser – and those of Toyota and Williams – after formal scrutineering of the cars had finished. We then anticipated that the stewards would give us the all-clear and that this would be followed by an application to the FIA Court of Appeal, which would be heard after the race in Malaysia. And that was exactly what transpired, with Red Bull, Renault and Ferrari leading the protest as plaintiffs, while BMW Sauber's application to join them was dismissed because their paperwork was submitted too late.

As this process evolved, it became clear to us that the protesting teams neither understood what we had done nor understood why it was legal nor why the FIA itself believed we were in the clear. When the protesting teams put in their depositions to the Court of Appeal, they were based on what, frankly, were not well-founded arguments. It was hard to avoid the conclusion that the protest was as much a fishing expedition – to try and understand this design opportunity that they had overlooked – as it was an attempt to get it outlawed. In short, they didn't seem to have the foggiest idea how it worked.

The teams who had missed this trick were not only suffering on the racetrack but also knew they faced a huge job catching us up. The intricate way our diffuser was incorporated into the rear of our car meant that copying it was going to involve an almost complete redesign of the back their cars, which would be expensive and time-consuming.

At Melbourne, and in the early races that followed, we made it as hard as we could for our rivals to see what our cars looked like at the back. Although we were not allowed to cover up any part of our chassis on the grid, we adopted the common practice – though rather more enthusiastically than we might have done had we been running at the rear of the field – of instructing our mechanics to stand in a ring around the back end of the cars to try to stop photographers getting close-up shots of what we had done.

The fact that no one, either at the track or at the subsequent tribunal in Paris, seemed to understand how this thing worked was brilliant from our point of view. Later, when we were going through the Court of Appeal, we had a scale model of the back of our car made specially for the hearing. I remember sitting with the engineers and our QC and turning it around in my hands and studying it from all angles. But even then it was difficult to see how the bloody thing worked. It was an inspired piece of engineering.

There were concerns in some areas – and the media played it up – that we might lose at the hearing, set for 5 April, and that our performances in the first two races could be thrown out. We were not taking anything for granted – we knew a hearing in Paris could go either way – but we also knew what Charlie Whiting had thought at the outset and nothing had changed since then. Jenson batted the question away in his post-race interviews in Melbourne.

'It's not something I have any control over,' he said. 'It doesn't change anything for me. I can't do anything about it.' In the meantime we pressed on into the Formula One unknown, trying to make ends meet and continue our form on the track.

# CHAPTER NINE

## *WINNING WITH NO MONEY*

Ross and I flew back from Australia on the Monday night after the race – Ross to supervise on the engineering front for our next Grand Prix in Malaysia in just six days' time, and me to get on with the practical realities of where the hell we were going.

We were exhausted after an intense few days in Melbourne but we were buzzing with the excitement of winning, and we quickly refocused on the next stage of what was really a journey into the unknown for all of us.

My main task was to sort out the practical side of making so many people redundant. Going through the formal process required the staff who were losing their jobs to have the chance to argue their case as to why they should be retained. We conducted reviews to make sure the process was done properly and brought to a solid conclusion, which it was.

The second thing I focused on was getting more money in the door. The big sponsorship deals in Formula One are generally done at the latest by the autumn because that's when companies set their budgets. So getting a title sponsor with huge amounts of money after the start of the new season was extremely unlikely, even though we were winning and likely to continue to do so at least in the short term.

Our strategy was to try and sell packages on a race-by-race basis. To prevent our limited cash reserve from diminishing too quickly, we had to raise about £1 million a race. That was approximately what it was costing us to compete at each circuit, so if we could hit that target we would be running in cash-neutral. Our approach was to target companies in or near each race market, and it proved immensely successful. For example, for Spain we signed the Swiss bank MIG and Sony Pictures; in Singapore we were sponsored by Canon cameras; and in Brazil we had Banco do Brasil, a Brazilian insurance company, and a beer manufacturer. Alongside these deals we had our Virgin tie-up for each race and we signed a small season-long cash sponsorship with the British sailing apparel manufacturer Henri Lloyd and with the Swiss watch manufacturer Graham. It was a hand-to-mouth existence requiring a lot of energy and man-hours per deal but we got it to work.

My other job was to be Brawn GP's official scrooge. We reckoned we were going to have enough money to keep us going throughout the 2009 season, but if possible we wanted to avoid going bust at the end of it. The only way to do that was to eke out the money and turn the flood of outgoing expenditure into a trickle.

The normal way of running a company is to set a budget, give the various departments their own spending limits and then everyone works to those figures for the rest of the year. The plus side of that arrangement is that you are delegating responsibility for financial management to the people who are actually spending the money. The problem with it – and it's a problem for all companies – is that if departmental heads have a budget, they tend to spend it whether they need to or not. They also tend to be aware of the danger that if they don't spend it all, then the following year's budget will be diminished by the amount of their underspend, so there is very little incentive to save.

Ross and I, together with Nigel Kerr, decided the only realistic way to approach this was to have no budget at all and instead try to control every outlay as if our life depended on it. The rule we came up with was that Ross, Nigel or I had to sign off any expenditure by any department that was above £75 – which was effectively everything. Now that is a draconian measure by any standards. And to stop the system completely seizing up, the people who were making the approval decisions had to make them quickly. That meant one of Ross, Nigel and I had to be available at all times, and we had to keep up.

This ran completely counter to anything anyone in the team was used to. Under Honda's ownership there was almost too much money sloshing around and so making the effort to limit expenditure was never a particularly important consideration. We were going from one extreme to the other.

It was bizarre to find ourselves quibbling over what in Formula One terms was the change in our pockets and there were some amusing moments. One of the first to test the new regime was Ron Meadows, who popped into my office looking for approval of a bill of about £120. He made his case – it was for some widget or other to do with the car – and he was doing a good job until he made the mistake of pointing out that this was a relatively small amount of money.

'It's only 120 quid, Nick,' he said.

To which I replied: 'If it's only 120 quid Ron, then you won't mind paying it from your salary…'

We didn't have to say that too many times to too many people before word got around that we were running an incredibly tight ship.

One of the big expenses in a Formula One team is the cost of sending people to races – and when you start to win, everyone wants to go. Another of my tasks was going through the travel list for each race and deciding who could go and who we could do without. I was usually Mr Nasty in this triage process, while Ross was probably slightly more reasonable, but we ended up with the minimum number we thought was doable. We got it down to about forty people altogether – including mechanics, pitwall staff, logistics people and caterers. In our Honda days we would routinely have up to 120 people at each race. The way we selected who could travel was a fair process, though, and I can say that with my hand on my heart because among the people I dropped off the travel list for the next three races was me.

So I was not in Malaysia when Jenson put his still-very-white Brawn GP001 on pole for the second race in a row. This time he did it in the sweltering tropical heat of Sepang in the hills outside Kuala Lumpur, and he was grinning from ear to ear as he prepared for the race start the following day.

The Grand Prix was threatened from the beginning by an intimidating weather forecast of thunder, lightning and heavy rain. That made it particularly interesting for us because, due to the fact that we had missed half of the pre-season tests, we had yet to run our cars in the wet. The race was going to be our first experience on that score.

On race day I went mountain-biking early in the morning with my brother to try to take my mind off what was coming up. Like everyone else in the team, I was on tenterhooks, wondering how we would do after our spectacular start in Australia. We knew the other double-diffuser cars – the Williams and Toyotas – were on the pace and we also regarded the Red Bull cars as a real threat, so it was a relief to see Jenson back on pole.

When the red lights went out the following day, the 'Frome flyer' made a bit of a mess of the getaway. As they roared down to the first corner, Nico Rosberg in the Williams came charging through on his inside. Jenson tried to squeeze the young German driver and the two cars very nearly touched wheels, but Jenson had lost track position and he was forced wide, dropping to fourth.

From then on he drove a solid race and showed his class and speed when asked by Ross to lay down a couple of super-quick laps after Rosberg and then Jarno Trulli in the Toyota pitted in front of him. Jenson turned up the engine, opened up the throttle and hammered round the circuit, setting fastest laps as the clouds grew ever more menacing behind the grandstands.

When the rain eventually came it did so in dribs and drabs to start with, and Ross and the pit crew made the right calls to keep Jenson and Rubens on the right tyres for the conditions on the track at any time. While others lunged for wet tyres too early, our drivers stayed out on slick dry-weather compounds, maximizing their performance, until it was wet enough for intermediates and then eventually full wets. It was a pitwall team and driver pairing showing confidence in their machinery and their decision-making, and it was a great example of why Ross was invaluable not just for running engineering and design but for race strategy too.

As the rain came hammering down, cars started sliding off all over the place but our boys kept their machines on the tarmac – aided no doubt by the extra downforce from the diffuser. When the safety car came out on lap 32, Jenson was tiptoeing around the circuit ahead of Timo Glock in the other Toyota and Nick Heidfeld in the BMW Sauber, with Rubens fifth and Rosberg seventh. The race was suspended and then eventually stopped, leaving Jenson to discover he had won his second Grand Prix in succession while sitting in his drenched cockpit on the start–finish straight with his personal trainer, Mike Collier, doing his best to keep the worst of the deluge off him with an official Brawn umbrella.

It was fortunate for us that the race was canned because Jenson's steering wheel had become completely waterlogged and our mechanics could no longer restart the car. We were so short of staff in Malaysia that, as the race team scrambled to try to prepare for a restart, Ross was tasked with wheeling the tyre barrow for Rubens's car to the grid – he was the first team principal to be seen doing that at a Grand Prix since Ron Dennis and Frank Williams in the late 1970s and early 1980s.

Under the rules, the cars needed to have completed 75 per cent – or forty-two laps – of the fifty-six-lap race distance for it to count as a full-points Grand Prix. In the event, the results were decided by the order at the end of lap 31 (the final full lap before the appearance of the safety car), so only half-points were awarded for just the fifth time since 1950. This gave Jenson a total of 15 points after two races as championship leader, followed by Rubens on 10 and Jarno third on 8.5 points.

We had survived our test in the monsoon and our first two 'fly-away' races had produced two wins even if – remarkably – we had yet to take the chequered flag in full racing conditions, having finished under the safety car in Melbourne.

Watching the coverage from home, I tried to enjoy it almost as an ordinary fan would. But I hated the feeling of being out of place. I had been to every race for years when I was running BAR and then Honda, and I found it almost more stressful being thousands of miles away, watching events unfold from my armchair. I say 'from my armchair' but in fact I found it almost impossible to sit down and instead paced up and down in front of the TV, texting people at the circuit for instant updates and all the background detail and gossip.

Despite the cost issues, I can see that it might look odd that, as chief executive, I was not at these races. But my answer to that is that I did not travel because it was not absolutely necessary for me to be at any of them. I also felt that I had to set a good example to all the other people in the team who were told they could not go. There were much more important things to do at the factory, trying to ensure that we had a future, than hanging around at circuits.

Being at home, I sensed the excitement we were generating. There was a fairy-tale quality to everything we were achieving and people who loved motor racing were clearly enjoying every minute of it. After the win in Malaysia was confirmed, Jenson's father John was on hand at Sepang in his trademark lucky pink shirt to sum it up.

'Yeah, funny victory but we'll take it,' he said just after what his son called a 'crazy race' was finally called off. Then Button Snr reflected on the uncertain times he and Jenson had been through during the winter as the team teetered on the brink of collapse: 'We tried to be as positive as we could. Honestly, we didn't know until one month ago whether Jenson would be driving in F1 again or whether he'd be sitting at home, watching it on television. And now we've got this dream start to the season – let's hope it goes on,' he added with a knowing smile.

John was in many ways the perfect motor racing dad. He was instrumental in getting his son to Formula One in the first place and then he played a masterly role behind the scenes. He completely understood that Ross and I were running the team, and he never took issue with what we were doing. He kept in very close contact with me and I would brief him on stuff that perhaps Jenson was not forthcoming about. Equally, when we needed Jenson to do things that he might otherwise have balked at, John proved a wise and persuasive intermediary. John was discreet and chilled out, and he never dropped the ball through years in Formula One that included the ultimate high point in 2009 as well as some tough times in earlier seasons.

Midway through the two-week gap before the Chinese Grand Prix in Shanghai, Ross and I decamped with our lawyers to Paris for the FIA Court of Appeal hearing on the diffuser issue. This was now being portrayed in the press as a case pitting the 'diffuser three' against the rest, which was nice because it gave it the feel of a miscarriage of justice and, in that reading of it, we would be the wronged party who would triumph on the day.

Going to Paris for FIA meetings or tribunals was a fairly well-worn path for Formula One teams in an era when battles on the track were more than matched by internecine warfare between the promoter (Bernie), the regulator (Max) and the teams. On these trips we always stayed at the same hotel around the corner from FIA headquarters on the Place de la Concorde where the hearings took place. We always sat in the bar of the hotel the night before, chatting through the case, and the next day we always took the same route on foot to the FIA. And invariably it rained.

Although we were confident of our case, the backdrop of infighting and Max's unpredictable nature meant the outcome was never considered to be a given. To start with, all the cards were held by the FIA. In most professional sports the independent adjudicator on rules disputes is the Court of Arbitration for Sport in Lausanne. That's where you go if you think you are being hard done by. Max and the FIA always fought against giving the court in Lausanne a role because they wanted to keep the whole thing within their own framework. Despite the fact that the judges they called upon to sit in the hearings were professional people who clearly were independent, it was always felt by team managers that the outcomes were delivered at the behest of Max and Bernie.

On the positive side of the balance sheet, we had gone through all the right steps throughout the process, starting with consulting Charlie Whiting, and we knew that both Max and Bernie were keen to see our fledgling team prosper. I did not give a positive result more than a 60 per cent chance because we also knew we probably weren't being judged entirely on the merits of that particular case, but on whether we had been good boys or not.

Our QC, Paul Harris, was absolutely brilliant and set out our case in masterful fashion, but his fee made a big dent in our limited financial resources and we had to be careful that we did not come across as being too clever by half. At one point in the hearing, for example, the Ferrari silk, Nigel Tozzi, described Ross as a 'person of supreme arrogance', which seemed a bit far-fetched. They were trying to portray our interpretation of the rules as destructive to the health of Formula One because, while the FIA was trying to drive costs down, the double diffuser was an unnecessary technical innovation that was having exactly the opposite effect. Of course, that was rubbish.

When we won the case, it was a huge relief because by that time we had fully come to appreciate that the double diffuser was critical to our chances of doing something astonishing in 2009. With it our cars were the fastest on the track by some distance; without it we suspected we would be fighting in the upper midfield. Winning the case that day in Paris did not just mean that we could keep our car as it was, it also meant that our rivals had no choice but to commit thousands of hours of work and a huge amount of money to redesigning their cars in a bid to try and catch up.

Fernando Alonso was always a step ahead on this subject – he was one of the most astute drivers when it came to understanding what went on under the bonnet – and he summed up the challenge facing most of the other teams, now that we had prevailed. 'It's difficult because you have to work on the whole car,' he said. 'It's not just adding the diffuser and suddenly the car is a second quicker. The diffuser makes you go fast if you have a new front end, new sidepods and a new engine cover. You have to rebuild the whole car and that would take a lot of months.'

For us, getting the diffuser row off our desks was a major relief because it had been such a diversion from all the other stuff we had to deal with.

For the next race – the Chinese Grand Prix – I followed my recipe for Malaysia and went cycling on the Saturday during qualifying and spent race day working, off and on, in the garden at home. That race was held, from start to finish, in a downpour outside Shanghai and it proved the first little warning sign that this was not going to be a pushover by any means.

Starting fifth on the grid behind Sebastian Vettel on pole in the Red Bull, then Alonso (Renault), Webber (Red Bull) and Rubens, Jenson finished third. Rubens was one place behind in fourth, on a day when there were spins, crashes, aquaplaning and woeful performances from Ferrari, Williams and BMW Sauber. The race confirmed the emergence of a new and outstanding talent in Vettel, who did not put a foot wrong in atrocious conditions that even Jenson – a wet-weather specialist – found 'very, very scary'. Vettel had become the youngest winner of a Grand Prix in 2008 when he drove his Toro Rosso (Red Bull B-Team) to victory at Monza, and now he had secured Red Bull's first Grand Prix win at the age of just twenty-one. He had put a marker down – there were comparisons in the press with a young Schumacher – and he reminded us that, even with the diffuser, we were not going to have things all our own way.

That race also stood out for a different reason: a hissy fit by the Renault boss, Flavio Briatore, who completely lost his temper during the Friday press conference at the track when he was asked about the diffuser ruling in Paris. The flamboyant Italian had something of a reputation for losing his rag and he certainly did that in Shanghai. He said the ruling had ruined a championship which, as far as he was concerned, was already as good as over.

'It is impossible to recover the ground we have lost,' he fumed. 'In three or four races the championship will be decided and I don't know what the interest of the TV viewers will be when Button has 60 points and [Kazuki] Nakajima [of Williams] has 50. It will be better to listen only on the radio and watch something else.' Then he turned his fire on our drivers: 'And then you have a Brawn driver who was almost retired,' he said in a reference to Rubens, before describing Jenson as talentless and irrelevant and 'a *paracarro* [roadside concrete bollard] fighting for the championship.'

I have to admit I had a quiet chuckle when I heard about this. Flavio always wanted Formula One to be an entertainment formula rather than a technical one – he is a marketing person not a techie – and what we had achieved was, for him, the antithesis of what he thought the sport should be about. Besides, after several years of being successful with Fernando, his team was under big pressure to get back to the top and he could see the chances of that happening rapidly slipping away. Before the end of the season we would discover exactly what lengths Flavio had been prepared to go to, to try to restore his glory days, but for now I had to commend Jenson for his restraint when responding to Flavio's diatribe.

'He's obviously a very angry man after the diffuser issues,' Button said of his former boss at Benetton when asked about it in China. 'It's very unfair [of him] to say that. The team has worked very hard in difficult circumstances and it's very unfair of Flavio to comment as he has, just because he is a little bit bitter. Instead of getting angry, people need to concentrate on improving and catching us up.'

Rubens was less diplomatic: 'There are plenty of good people in the paddock and plenty of bad losers,' he observed.

It was back to normal service the following weekend in the scorching heat of the Sakhir circuit in the desert on the outskirts of Manama, the Bahraini capital. Jenson started from fourth on the grid – behind Trulli, Glock and Vettel – in a car that was looking quick but not quite as quick as it had been relative to everyone else. His qualifying was all the better because we had problems cooling the engine in the desert heat and he could only do one quick lap at a time before easing off again.

On race day he drove a stunning opening lap, easing round the outside of Vettel at Turn 1 and then taking on Lewis

Hamilton, who had jumped him in an improved McLaren Mercedes from fifth on the grid. While the cars sped past the half-empty main grandstand, Jenson got alongside as Lewis hit his KERS button, accelerating from 185 to 190mph. Jenson, not having the benefit of KERS on the Brawn, calmly dropped in behind, picking up a tow from the McLaren, and then outbraked Lewis on the inside at Turn 1 on the second lap. As the challenge from the lightly fuelled Toyotas of Trulli and Glock fell away, partly due to a flawed tyre strategy, Jenson drove faultlessly to his third win in four races. This put him on 31 points at the head of the drivers' rankings, with Rubens in second place on 19 and Sebastian third on 18.

On the Saturday of that weekend – still staying at home to preserve our meagre budget – I went to see Fulham play Stoke City in the Premier League at Craven Cottage and was delighted to see Fulham win 1-0 through a goal from the Norwegian striker, Erik Nevland. On the Sunday – race day – I went cycling early in the morning, feeling superstitious about changing that habit.

My chance to get back to the track came with the fifth race of the year, and the first in Europe, at Barcelona, where we had had such a successful pre-season test. For this race we made a technical upgrade to the cars but it was small fry compared to the money we knew our rivals were spending. In the period up to the Formula One summer break after the tenth round – the Hungarian Grand Prix at the end of July – we spent a total of just £600,000 on development. We estimated Christian Horner's Red Bull team was spending more than that on each race. Our upgrade for Spain gave us a small step forward but we all felt the net position amounted to a slight erosion of our pre-season advantage.

True to the theme of scrimping and saving, I flew to Barcelona on the easyJet service from Luton on the Thursday before the race and then spent my entire weekend looking after the sponsors we had engaged for Spain, among them executives from the Swiss bank MIG and people from Henri Lloyd. In Barcelona we had also signed a deal with Sony Pictures Releasing International to help them launch one of the biggest Hollywood movies of the year, the blockbuster *Terminator Salvation* starring Christian Bale. We carried the film's name and imagery on the cars' rear wing endplates, and for the PR shots we had a life-size Terminator figure on hand outside our garage at the Circuit de Catalunya to lend the whole thing a touch of authenticity. I waxed eloquently about the synergy between the film – featuring a post-apocalyptic story set in 2018 – and Brawn GP's battle for survival: 'The Terminator brand promises exciting action and high drama as machines and human ingenuity battle for supremacy,' I told *Campaign* magazine. 'It's a perfect match for Brawn GP and Formula One.'

The build-up to the race in Spain was full of talk about the sleeping giants of the paddock – McLaren, Ferrari and BMW Sauber – and whether they would arrive with cars that could get on terms with ours and those of Red Bull. From our point of view, we had won races in the dry, the wet and in the heat of the desert. The question we faced now was whether we could carry on winning in Europe, and Jenson got the first part of the answer resoundingly right when he clinched pole with a beautiful lap, which he started just two seconds before the third and final qualifying session ended. It was his third pole position of a season that would only deliver four in total, and he had Sebastian sitting alongside him on the front row of the grid, with Rubens leading the second row just ahead of Felipe Massa in the Ferrari.

In the race itself, once again Jenson did not get away well and he quickly lost the lead to Rubens at the start of a first lap that saw a big crash at Turn 2 as Trulli's Toyota took out Adrian Sutil's Force India and the Toro Rosso cars of Sébastien Buemi and Sébastien Bourdais. This brought out the safety car, and when the race restarted it was Rubens who led the charge ahead of Jenson.

What happened next caused the first outbreak of tension in our race team that season as Ross took a decision to switch Jenson from a three-stop to a two-stop fuel strategy, while Rubens was left on a three-stopper. The way it worked out was that, with Jenson piling on the speed when he needed to, he drove to another convincing win while Rubens was left smouldering in second place, thirteen seconds adrift. The Brazilian was furious and said in post-race interviews that if he suspected there was a policy of favouritism towards Jenson he would 'hang up his helmet tomorrow'. For him this felt like a replay of all those races at Ferrari when Michael Schumacher was top dog while he was little more than a warm-up act.

Ross was adamant afterwards that Rubens's fears were entirely unjustified. The switch in strategy had been dictated entirely by concern on the Brawn pitwall that Jenson was going to get stuck in traffic unless they switched him to a two-stopper. There had been no premeditated plan to favour one driver over the other. *Autosport* magazine – something of an authority on contemporary Formula One racing – judged that Rubens had lost because he was unable to drive a lighter car faster than Jenson when the Briton was carrying more fuel.

Of course, it is absolutely critical that both drivers feel that they are being treated equally and in our team they were. If you have a veteran driver and a beginner, it makes sense for the younger driver to fall in behind the more experienced one. But when you have two world-class drivers of the calibre of Jenson and Rubens at the top of their game, their expectation, quite rightly, is that they are going to be treated equally. However, 'equally' does not necessarily mean that they are both going to be treated in exactly the same way at each and every race because, invariably, one driver gets into a stronger position than the other and consequently does rather better out of it. It is completely natural in that situation – because they are intensely competitive individuals – that one driver thinks he has been hard done by in comparison to the other. The reality is that, in most teams, this run of the green evens out over the course of a season. What tends to happen is that one driver will have a bit more luck on one occasion, and be given preferential treatment in terms of pitstops or whatever, and on another the opposite is true.

Where teams run into difficulties – and this has happened a couple of times at Red Bull under Christian Horner – is when drivers haven't got the confidence that the favour will be returned or the balance of advantage will swing back in their direction. And that's the beauty of having someone with the experience and natural authority like Ross running race strategy. Under his management at Honda and then Brawn, a driver could be angry at one moment but – once he had sat down in the peace and quiet of the transporter, gone through the data and the situation had been explained to him – he could have confidence that if the same thing happened again in reverse, the balance of advantage could swing back to him. And that is exactly what happened in Spain with Rubens.

When a championship is at stake, this balance will change as eventually it becomes clear to everyone involved that one driver has an opportunity to win that the other driver does not have. In that situation it is entirely rational and sensible to support driver A over driver B. But reaching that threshold cannot be a matter of debate because driver B is still one of the best in the world and it is his career that you are playing with – the situation has to be allowed to reach the point where it is self-evident that this is the right thing to do from a team point of view.

After Spain, Jenson talked openly about the dream and how it was coming true. 'Even when times are tough, we seem to be able to get the wins,' he said immediately after the finish. 'When it goes well, it goes well; last year when it went bad, it went bad. I feel on top of the world at the moment. The team has done a great job and with this package you could see we have got our advantage back again, and thanks to Mercedes as we couldn't do it without them.'

Ross and I flew home on the late easyJet flight from Barcelona to Luton arriving at 11.55 p.m. and we were sitting way back in about row 26 in a plane full of British race fans. It was great because they loved the fact that we had just won the Grand Prix but were travelling home with them in the cheap seats. There were lots of congratulations coming our way and again you sensed the excitement around our little project.

And there was something else: the fun we had chatting to people on the plane made it abundantly clear that they regarded Brawn GP as first and foremost a British team. This was hugely enjoyable for me. We had spent years brainwashing our staff at Brackley that they were part of a Japanese team and a Japanese family, showing them videos of the birth of Honda and how Mr Honda himself had established an international perspective from the start. It was always hard work but now we didn't need to think like that any more and the fans could sense that.

The transition to a British team was very easy and natural. We had a British driver in Jenson; we had a major UK-based company on board in Virgin, and another British family-owned sponsor in Henri Lloyd. We reverted to type easily and quickly. While we weren't waving the flag in an overly nationalistic way, it was clear that this was a very British effort.

Now, with five races under our belts, our next appointment was the most famous of them all.

# CHAPTER TEN

# *A NIGHT TO REMEMBER IN MONACO*

It is race morning in Monaco – the most glamorous Grand Prix of the Formula One calendar. The weather is perfect: a warm, sunny day and a deep-blue, cloudless sky. The grandstands around the tight and twisting circuit in the principality on the shores of the Mediterranean are packed. Thousands of people are heading to their seats overlooking some of the most iconic corners and straights in motorsport – Sainte Devote, Beau Rivage, Mirabeau and La Rascasse. In the harbour, the gin palaces and yachts are packed in and the race-day parties are just getting underway – the place is buzzing with excitement as the cars whip round, ready to line up on the grid for the start.

The V8 engines are loud at any circuit; at Monaco the noise is amplified by the buildings and the banshee howl of the F1 herd is almost overwhelming for spectators sitting just yards from the action. For the drivers this is the ultimate contest – the supreme test of nerve and concentration once described by Lewis Hamilton as 'like driving a rocket round a car park'. For them, this is still the one to win above all others; a chance to write your name in the most sought-after winner's roster in world motorsport.

After four victories in five races, we had come to Monaco full of hope and some confidence. But we all knew that, more than at any circuit on the F1 calendar, things could go wrong here in an instant.

The first thing was to get on the front row. Jenson did that with a beautiful drive in qualifying on Saturday to put his car on pole alongside Kimi Raikkonen in the Ferrari, while Rubens led the second row alongside Sebastian Vettel's Red Bull. It was one of the finest drives of Jenson's career on a track where it is difficult to pull off the perfect lap. But when his tyres 'switched on', meaning they reached their optimum working temperature, he made the most of them.

That day – in a small but interesting detail – the fluorescent yellow front wheel fairings, or hubcaps, on Jenson's car were back to front. This was because the guy building them at the factory did not understand the aero concept we were after. The result was that a small dink in them – a feature helping to control the flow around the wheels – was facing backwards instead of forwards. It was a minor cock-up that the aficionados might have spotted and an example of how staff shortages could lead us into error. In this case we had not had the time to write the manuals in sufficient detail to ensure these components were built correctly at the factory. When we asked Jo Bauer, the FIA technical delegate at Monaco, if we could change them round for the race, we were told we could not.

Race morning had been hectic with sponsor engagements and lots of guests to chaperone on a busy grid. By the time the start sequence began I was sitting in our team garage in the pits feeling knackered, watching it all unfold with our mechanics on the live television feed and with the onboard car data from our engineers on my laptop. We knew that if we could get off to a good start, then – assuming the car had no technical issues – the race was probably won because at Monaco it is hard to overtake.

The howling crescendo just behind us on the start–finish straight gradually built to a deafening wall of noise as the lights came on and we all sat transfixed by the image of Jenson's white car sitting on pole. He'd had a few poor starts in recent races against opponents who utilized the extra boost from their KERS systems; he could not afford one now.

When the lights went out he launched perfectly, moving almost serenely, and led the stampede into the right-hander at Sainte Devote. Behind him Rubens made an excellent get-away on the right-hand side of the track and stole ahead of Kimi. Within seconds the Brawn cars were running first and second at Monaco in scenes recorded by thousands of cameras on smartphones all around the circuit.

I followed the action for the first four laps but by lap 5 I had succumbed to the temptation to catch up on sleep. Looking back, it seems impossible that anyone could drift off in the middle of that noisy pandemonium. But I managed it, slumped over my computer, oblivious to the progress of our drivers on the most famous street circuit of them all.

Then I felt a tug on my arm. It was Nicola Armstrong, our PR director. She was shaking me awake.

'Nick? Nick…'

'Errr… yeah?'

'Nick, there are only three laps to go and Ross wants you to go and get the trophy.'

\*\*\*

Monaco was always a high point in any season but also arguably
the most challenging and stressful Grand Prix of the year for
the teams. Ron Dennis, the McLaren boss, used to say the
Monaco weekend was the only time he and his former wife –
they divorced in 2011 – used to argue (they must have done
quite a lot of it there, then, I guess). The teams are compressed
into tiny physical spaces, the garages are a fraction of the size
that they are at any other circuit, and you are trying to work in
an environment where everyone is tripping over themselves.

On top of that, Monaco is the place to be on race weekend,
so you have more guests and sponsors to look after than at
any other race. The practicalities of doing that are tricky
because the garage is in the middle of the circuit, while the
sponsors and guests are usually seated in the main stand on
the opposite side of the track. They may be only 60 metres
away as the crow flies, but getting people from one side to the
other is a 20-minute mission on foot, no matter how important
a VIP you may be.

In our typically exotic fashion, I flew out on the Wednesday
evening from Luton to Nice with our old friends from easyJet.
One of the first things I had to do when I got to Monte Carlo
– and this is something that I look back on with no pride
whatsoever – was to remove our Austrian test driver Alex Wurz
from our books. In my role as Mr Scrooge I had reluctantly
concluded that we could not afford Alex and I had to find a
way out of his contract. The way I did it – which, as I say, I am
not proud of – was to release him on the grounds that he had
signed up for that year's 24 Hours of Le Mans endurance classic
with Team Peugeot Total. Technically Alex was supposed to
have informed us before he signed a contract with another
manufacturer, and he had not done that. I knew I was being

mean-spirited because, if he had asked us before he signed for Peugeot, we would almost certainly have said yes. But this was the only way to achieve my goal and that is how it was done. I guess in desperate times, desperate men do desperate things. I am glad to say that Alex, who had previously raced in Formula One for Benetton, McLaren and Williams, went on to win at Le Mans that year, alongside David Brabham and Marc Gené, in what was one of the highlights of his career.

Removing Alex meant we were going to tackle the remaining twelve races of the season without a reserve driver, but this was a risk Ross and I were prepared to take. The reality was that, in my entire twelve years in Formula One, we only used a third driver twice so we didn't lose too much sleep over our decision to dispense with Alex on that score.

The cash-strapped theme was all too evident in Monaco where you can burn through money faster than any city in the world. Hotel bills could be crippling so everyone in our race team, except Ross and me and the drivers, were put up at a cheap hotel that was a long way out of town and from where they were bussed in each day. This made their long exhausting days just that little bit longer. Ross and I got a good deal at the Columbus Hotel on the seafront in Monaco, where we normally stayed. But we were there reluctantly and only because, with our extensive sponsor obligations, we felt we had to be in town.

On the Thursday night after practice – when our cars either led or were in the top four in both sessions – I went to the annual Grand Prix party on Vijay Mallya's boat anchored in pride of place in the harbour. This wasn't just any sort of boat but a huge superyacht called *Indian Empress* that had previously been owned by the prime minister of Qatar. On board the 312-

foot palace on the water, which was sold in 2018 for €35million, were hundreds of the Formula One glitterati jostling to see and be seen, while Vijay sat, rather like a modern-day Indian emperor, receiving his subjects.

The following day I was on another monster boat – this time Flavio Briatore's *Force Blue One*, which checked in at a mere 207 feet – for a team owners' meeting, and I followed that on the Saturday night with dinner at the Louis XV restaurant at the Hôtel de Paris in Casino Square. Owned by the celebrated chef Alain Ducasse and boasting three Michelin stars, this was about as high-end and expensive as you can get. I was there to meet the chief executive and two senior directors of an online poker and casino company who had been in touch with us with plans to get involved on the sponsorship side.

Full Tilt was a hugely successful money-making enterprise based in Ireland, where they had hundreds of computer programmers working on new poker-derivative games to keep their customers happy, or should I say hooked. The top guys were all Americans and I found them at our table in the opulent baroque dining room that glittered in gold, each wearing black suits, dark glasses and sporting slicked-back hair.

To start with, the conversation was very slow and stilted and it seemed quite a threatening atmosphere for some reason. I remember thinking 'thank God my mum can't see me now.'

Over dinner it emerged that they were interested in taking the title sponsorship of the team for the following season – in 2010 – and we discussed this plan at length over the most expensive alcohol I have ever drunk. The chief executive stunned even the restaurant sommelier by ordering the best champagne on the menu followed by one of the most expensive red wines from a cellar containing 400,000 bottles.

I have no idea what the bill came to, but it would have made a serious dent in our team budget for the whole race weekend. I chuckled at the contrast: at Brackley we were fretting over every £75 outlay, and there I was sitting at a table with a basket of bread that probably cost at least that amount.

Following that dinner we mocked up designs of our cars in matt black with playing cards scattered all over the chassis. It was eye-catching in a tacky sort of way and the Full Tilt people seemed quite impressed. However, this initiative hit the buffers when we later began ownership talks with Mercedes Benz and they were not remotely interested in a tie-up with an online gambling firm.

\*\*\*

After Nicola had successfully woken me, I found myself in a garage full of jubilant mechanics and team staffers as they watched Jenson cruising to his fifth victory in six races. When he stormed over the finish line we cheered and hugged each other, enjoying an ecstatic moment in our lives. We had won the 2009 Monaco Grand Prix.

Even though we had arrived at the principality a few days earlier hoping we could continue our devastating early-season form, none of us was prepared to bet on us winning on the streets around that famous harbour and it really did seem like a dream. Jenson had driven a perfect race and had led from start to finish, with Rubens third behind Kimi in the Ferrari.

It was a kind thought by Ross to select me to receive the constructors' trophy, and alongside him I made my way through the throng to the start–finish straight. This is where the three podium-finishing cars park in front of the royal viewing stand, ready for the presentations to the winning team and driver by Prince Albert. It was one of many unique features of the Monaco race because at every other Grand Prix the top-three cars head for parc fermé in the pitlane and there is a dedicated podium for presentations nearby.

We got there in good time and were all ready and waiting, but where was Jenson? It was possibly my fault, but no one had thought to remind him that if he won at Monaco he was not to go to parc fermé but carry on going and stop at the finish line on the main straight in front of the royal stand. I am sure the reason for that omission was that we were all far too superstitious to dare to even think of it before the race started.

In his moment of glory Jenson did indeed head for parc fermé with all the other cars, where an FIA official pointed out his error. Soon word came through that our boy was now running down the start–finish straight in his white and black race overalls and still wearing his fluorescent yellow helmet towards his appointment with royalty. It was a unique and very funny moment in the history of this great race and the crowd lapped it up as Jenson made his way towards us, waving and laughing with delight as he did so. When he reached me he launched himself into a bear hug as we celebrated in style.

During the trophy presentation Prince Albert, who found Jenson's 'mis-parking' highly amusing, was immensely congratulatory. He seemed genuinely pleased and that really came home to us that night as we enjoyed the special formalities that follow winning in Monaco. In another unique feature, there is a black-tie dinner in honour of the race winner hosted by Prince Albert at the Sporting Club de Monaco on the night of the race. On that occasion he was accompanied by his then-girlfriend – and now wife – Charlene. Only the winning driver and members of his team are invited from the paddock and you sit at the top table with Prince Albert.

There is an old Formula One superstition that you must not pack a dinner jacket for this race because, if you do, you will definitely not win it. So straight after the podium Ross and I had to scrabble around, trying to borrow a dicky bow and dinner jacket while Kate hunted for a suitable dress. Kate and I got what we needed from Gareth Griffith and his wife. Gareth was a software developer and a supplier to our team, and he had a flat in Monaco. He was about six inches shorter than me and somewhat more barrel-chested, so I wasn't looking my best. But that is part of the tradition – you win the race and then turn up for one of the smartest dinners you will have ever been to in someone else's clothes, looking rather dishevelled.

For pre-dinner drinks we were shuffled into a small VIP area with Prince Albert and the other hoi polloi. Dinner was then called and we showed our inexperience again as we headed for the main ballroom with everyone else, only for a flunky to come up and politely point out our mistake in perfect English: 'No, it's not time for you yet.'

Prince Albert and Charlene, Ross and Jean, Jenson and Jessica, and Kate and I were then held back for a few minutes before being taken through, two by two, into the main ballroom where 500 people were standing and clapping us in. 'Oh my Lord, we've really hit the highlights here,' I thought to myself.

During a hugely enjoyable dinner with the royal couple, we reached the stage when dessert was being served. Almost imperceptibly, and like something out of a James Bond film, the roof of the Club began to open so quietly that, as we sat talking, we barely noticed it. Above us was a starlit Mediterranean sky that exploded into life with the most enormous firework display.

The part that really sticks in my mind was watching Jenson looking up at these fireworks like a five-year-old boy, wide-eyed with amazement and wonder. I wasn't the only one to notice this. Prince Albert put his hand on Jenson's arm, looked at him and said: 'This is for you, Jenson.' It was a really nice touch. Despite his incredible wealth and the royal trappings, when something like that happens, no matter how used you are to these things, it cuts right through and it's something I will never forget. Inside F1 it is sometimes said that Monaco is the only race that gives more to Formula One than Formula One gives to it, and it is quite true.

After the dinner we went to the Amber Lounge with Prince Albert and had the surreal experience of being on the dance floor with him while surrounded by security men. We were supposed to fly home on the 10 p.m. easyJet service to Luton that night which, given the circumstances, we did not make. Instead, after one more night at the Columbus, we took the easyJet flight to Bristol of all places the following morning. Someone from the factory came and picked us up and I got home at 6 p.m. in time to mow the lawn.

That trophy presentation was the only one that I took part in during the entire 2009 season. The reason for that was that Ross used the presentations to share the enjoyment and thrill of victory throughout our team. He had learned in his early days in Formula One, with Flavio's Benetton outfit, how disappointing it was when a team principal insisted on attending every podium himself. Ross had no plans to repeat that. Even though his name was on the door, he generously asked people from all over the team to do the honours when we had trophies to collect.

From one of the oldest races on the calendar at Monaco, it was time to head east for round seven of the championship at one of the sport's newer tracks.

# CHAPTER ELEVEN

## *KEEPING OUR HEADS AS RON CALLS FOR THE AERO NUMBER*

I did not go to Turkey, where Jenson swept to victory ahead of the two Red Bulls of Sebastian Vettel and Mark Webber. We didn't know it at the time but this proved to be a watershed in our season and the last race that Jenson would win in 2009.

On this occasion Jenson started second on the grid behind a more lightly fuelled Sebastian who then ran wide at the fast kink in the track at Turn 10, presenting our boy with an opportunity he took with both hands. Despite the fact that we got our gear ratios all wrong that day, Jenson was imperious during fifty-eight ultra-smooth laps at a scorching Istanbul Park, while Rubens underlined why he had slipped firmly into the supporting role. Having stalled his car on the grid for the second time in seven race starts, Rubens dropped from third to thirteenth and then drove like a man possessed trying to make up the ground lost. After a spin and then a tangle with Force India's Adrian Sutil early in the contest, he eventually retired with gearbox failure, making his the first car in Brawn livery not to finish a race in 2009.

Flying back from Istanbul, Jenson was on top of the world and sitting pretty on 61 points at the head of the drivers' standings. Rubens was a distant second on 35 points, with Sebastian third on 29.

'I would love to win every single race this year,' said Jenson as he celebrated victory number six out of seven starts. 'But I've got another nineteen guys on the circuit that want to stop me. I'm in a good position, for sure,' he went on. 'This race showed that we do have the best car, but I think we have the best package too.'

In winning six of the first seven, Jenson had managed a feat achieved before him by only four legends of the sport – Alberto Ascari, Juan Manuel Fangio, Jim Clark and Michael Schumacher – and all of them went on to become world champion in those seasons.

For us the danger was that we would get overconfident, and we had to try and keep our heads down and just focus on what we were doing. In the build-up to Turkey, Donald Mackenzie of CVC Capital Partners, the Formula One owners, was reported as saying that Brawn's supremacy was not doing the sport 'any good', and Bernie Ecclestone was heard bemoaning the predictability of the title race. Meanwhile the media was starting to treat the championship as a walkover. Jenson was variously described as a driver who could now 'do no wrong', who was propelled by the 'certainty of success' and who could 'walk on water'. His rival drivers were coming to the same conclusion. After Turkey, Sebastian was quoted as saying the Brawn cars were 'on a different planet'.

The question was not if he would win but when, and how many races would turn into dead rubbers, something that was bad business for the circuits concerned and for Formula

One's attractiveness to its global audience of over 800 million people. Yet it wasn't just that we had enjoyed a spectacular run of success – our rivals had not stepped up to the plate. Ferrari was having a woeful season, as were McLaren, while Toyota and Williams had faded after showing early promise. Red Bull were the main threat but they were showing signs of tactical naivety at times and, although Sebastian was a quick and brave young driver, he was still inexperienced at this level.

We had been batting away predictions of inevitable victory for several weeks, even by the time we raced at Istanbul. During a team principals' meeting back in Barcelona a month earlier, Christian Horner had joked with me that we would have the drivers' and constructors' titles in the bag by the summer shutdown in August.

It's a tricky thing to deal with, but what you need to remember in Formula One is that your rivals always say what they do for a reason. There may have been a degree of factual truth to what Christian was suggesting, but what he and the other team principals wanted us to do was to relax and start believing it ourselves. It all sounds very Machiavellian, but in top-level sport – especially in Formula One – you learn to take almost nothing at face value. It's a wonderful environment to work in, in terms of clever people and exotic places to travel to, but the paddock is the only world I know of where being paranoid is a prerequisite for success because they are all out to get you, including the sport's promoter.

As far as the media coverage was concerned, our team had been through so many ups and downs over the years that we had become almost immune to it. We tried not to get too excited about the plaudits and not too down about the criticism. My approach was not to ignore what the press was thinking, because you have to understand what people are saying about you, but to take it all with a pinch of salt whether it was good or bad.

We were aware from the start of the season that we had to get as big a lead as possible in the early races because we knew the others were going to catch up. No one at Brackley saw us winning race after race all the way to the end. We enjoyed it while it lasted but we were under no illusions about how long it would continue.

McLaren's form was a big bonus for us. Lewis had come into the season with high hopes of defending his hard-won first drivers' title the year before but, sadly for him, his new car was a dud. After Turkey he was down in a lowly eleventh place in the drivers' standings with just 9 points to his name, while his teammate Heikki Kovalainen had just 4 points in thirteenth place. We knew this was causing a lot of pain in their proud team – after all, they had a glorious history to live up to – but the phone call I received one morning from Ron Dennis (who was chairman of the McLaren Group at that stage, having handed over day-to-day control of the race team to Martin Whitmarsh) still came as something of a surprise. In fact, for a second or two I was completely knocked off balance by what I heard him saying.

I was standing by the window in my office, looking out on the car park – the very same one where Achilleas Kallakis had landed in that humongous helicopter – when I heard my mobile ring on my desk. I turned and picked it up and saw 'Ron Dennis'. I thought this was a bit odd, because it was unusual for Ron to call me direct, but I answered and returned to the window.

'Hi Nick, it's Ron.'

'Oh hi, Ron. How are you?'

'Good. Good, thanks, although the circumstances could be better…'

'So what can I—'

'Yeah, look, Nick, I wanted to ask a favour.'

'By all means, go ahead.'

'Well, I know this is highly unusual and you can tell me to get lost if you want. The problem is that our car is totally underperforming, as you have no doubt noticed, but my engineers say our aerodynamic package is on the money. The thing is I just don't believe them.'

'Right, yeah, I know that feeling…'

Ron carried on talking about the problems at Woking and I gradually realized that he was about to ask me – as he had suggested – something very unusual indeed. Ron wanted to know just how good our aero package was and exactly what numbers we were seeing in our testing in the wind tunnel. These were the closely guarded crown jewels of Formula One racing.

Ron was facing a difficulty that all team principals come up against. As the person in charge, you are very much at the mercy of your engineers when it comes to understanding your relative performance because there are no points of comparison that you can use to evaluate where you are in technical terms versus where your competitor is. Although you can win or lose on the track, it's not like soccer. If you are about to play Chelsea, as a rival manager you will have a wealth of data about them to mull over – you will know how they play, their players' strengths and weaknesses, and how their performance changes during the course of a game. You can do a huge amount of analysis of how they approach the game and why they are successful or not.

In Formula One, as team principal, you have to supervise the design of your own car, which has to be unique to your team, but you have no detailed idea how other people's cars work. You know they have got an engine and they have four wheels, but you don't know the weight distribution or the strategy behind the aerodynamics. You don't know the balance of the car front to rear or how the brake system works and you have no way of finding out except through simple observation of their machine in operation. There will always remain a whole bunch of unknowns as to why one car is quick and another car is less quick, and you can't just copy what you see on a rival car without understanding why their design team arrived at that solution. You have to understand how the whole thing works before trying a similar approach.

When it comes to summarizing a car's performance, the fundamental statistic – the one that everyone dreams of knowing above everything else – is the figure that measures its aerodynamic efficiency. Why? Because when you are already at the limit of the performance of the engine, to make a car go faster, the area of principal return – the way to go even quicker – is through the aerodynamic treatment of the chassis. Within the paddock the performance of a car in this respect is expressed by a single number that represents the relationship between aerodynamic downforce and resistance through the air, or drag. Everyone in the sport knows approximately what a good number is and what a less good number is. The numbers are not directly comparable from one car to another because each team has its own measuring tools and wind tunnels with different calibrations. But if someone gave you their number you would be able to broadly equate it to where you were.

Ron and I were on reasonable terms and he was someone who deserved immense respect for what he had achieved. He wasn't in the same team as us but he was on the same side, in that he was also running a team that was partnered with Mercedes Benz, so we were in the same extended family. What's more, he had been instrumental in agreeing to let us use Mercedes engines. He had agreed to it and had waived his veto even though, as the main customer, McLaren had the right to stop Mercedes linking up with anyone else. Clearly he assumed Brawn GP would be an also-ran in 2009 but, nevertheless, he was someone I felt we owed a favour.

Ron's description of what he was hearing from his engineers certainly rang bells with me, from years of underperformance with Honda cars. The engineers know the car is not up to scratch but they refuse to accept the blame. As far as they are concerned, the reason the car is not as good as the others is because their rivals are cheating or they are getting some level of help that is not available to them. They quite naturally feel they are doing a good job and will try and argue away why the car is not going well, or argue that there is a performance gap that they can close in a specific period of time because they know what the solution is.

Requesting the aero number from a rival team is just not a question you would normally ask. Even if you did ask, you would never expect anyone to tell you the truth. The first thing you would expect them to say – politely – is 'fuck off'. If they did tell you their number you would have no confidence that it would be real.

During that call I don't think Ron made any caveats or said he wouldn't tell anyone what I might tell him. It was just understood between us that this wasn't going to be a conversation that was to be repeated. The bottom line was they were all at sea and he was being told they were in good shape, but clearly he was not convinced.

After the preamble I had guessed what was coming, but I was still completely conflicted for a minute or so when I heard him actually ask for it. On the one hand, I felt that if I told him, I would be a traitor to Brawn GP; on the other hand, I felt that if I didn't tell him I would be being unfair to someone who had helped us a great deal.

I decided to tell him. When I did give him the number there was stunned silence. Clearly our figure was significantly better than theirs. Ron was impressed and frustrated all at once but it also confirmed his suspicions – he was being told things by his engineers that simply did not bear comparison with what we were doing. He was extremely grateful and I sensed that, armed with this information – or should I say ammunition – he was impatient to find a use for it and so we said our goodbyes.

As soon as the call was over, I went and told Ross what I had done. He was completely cool about it and just shrugged it off. I think he understood that we owed a lot to Ron and, although I had helped him by giving McLaren a target to shoot for, they clearly wouldn't have any idea how to get to the performance level that we were at. The McLaren engineers were probably going to react with disbelief to what Ron was going to tell them, but we had given him a very big stick to beat them with.

I never regretted telling him, although the McLaren cars – the MP4-24s – got significantly better as the season progressed. In upgraded form, the car that Eddie Jordan had described in the early part of the campaign as 'possibly the worst McLaren ever designed' went on to win two races, in Hungary and at

Singapore, with Lewis at the wheel. McLaren eventually finished third in the 2009 constructors' championship.

Their dramatic improvement demonstrated just how quickly a well-resourced rival could make up ground on us during the course of a season, and that our initial successes were no guarantee that we would maintain that form and competitive advantage right to the end.

# CHAPTER TWELVE

## *THE BUYING GAME: MERCEDES, THE GLAZERS AND AIR ASIA*

The management buyout had given us a platform on which to take the team through the early part of the season, but we all knew that our commercial situation was not tenable in the long run against teams owned by big companies like Ferrari and Red Bull. We could continue for the 2009 season, but we had insufficient money for 2010 and we would have to get outside investors in to put us on a firm footing.

A breakthrough in this respect had come in early May, just a few days before the Spanish Grand Prix. Nigel Kerr and I had flown to Germany that morning for one of our regular meetings with Norbert Haug, the head of motorsport at Mercedes Benz, our engine suppliers. This was a run-of-the-mill update session with Norbert. Mercedes had considerable control over us as part of the engine deal. This included them having a right of review of any potential new sponsors to ensure they were compatible with the Mercedes brand image. We were also required to give prior notice about any prospective investors in the team, for the same reason. These were elements of control that you would not normally give away to an outside company but the situation early in the year, when we concluded the engine-supply arrangement, was exceptional and these strictures did not seem unreasonable to us. In fact, we had little or no alternative.

At that stage Mercedes was also a part-owner of the McLaren Formula One team. That meant we were potentially informing one of our main rivals about our commercial dealings that normally would be kept secret. After all, if McLaren got wind of a new sponsor we hoped to sign through Mercedes, they could easily steal that company from underneath us before we got approval from Norbert. So our relationship with Norbert was unique and based on a great deal of mutual trust from the beginning; and I suspect we were a lot easier to deal with than Ron Dennis at McLaren. We got on well with the heavy-set, gravelly voiced, former motorsport journalist who presided over Mercedes's racing activities for twenty-two years.

Under Norbert, Mercedes won championships in various formulae all over the world. He was a highly influential figure in motorsport at the time and he was an entertaining character who was always up for a big celebration after a race win. At Mercedes, as we were to discover, they did that sort of thing with the same commitment to excellence and thoroughness as they approached their engineering, and the company's expenditure in this area was huge.

Norbert was a proper racing man and luckily for us he had the foresight to realize that, in order to maximize the aims of its brand, Mercedes needed its own team, as opposed to continuing as a minority partner with someone else. However, prior to that meeting on 5 May, we had seen no hint that

Mercedes Benz might be more than just interested in us as an engine customer. We had no idea they might be thinking of a bigger commitment and it never crossed my mind that it would happen. Mercedes is a giant in the automotive world, whereas we saw ourselves as a minnow trying to survive. What's more, the iconic German automaker had been with McLaren for fourteen years and not in our wildest dreams did we think they might drop their allegiance to Woking and pair up with us instead.

We flew in the morning and reached the futuristic and extensive plant at Stuttgart at lunchtime. It is quite some place and Norbert's office had a grandstand view. I have seen what the Ford Motor Company has at its main factories, and the facilities at Subaru and a little of BMW, but Mercedes is on another level, with a scale and depth of research and production that is mind-boggling. It is an engineering company through and through that has invested its money in the finest wind tunnels, climatic chambers and engine-test facilities, and it's a step up from anything I have seen anywhere else.

Nigel and I opened the meeting by running through where we were in terms of getting sponsors and the general financial shape of the company. We were transparent about what was going on and how much cash we had. We wanted to keep Norbert abreast of the situation and part of that was helping him feel confident that we were under control at least for the 2009 season. It wasn't the focus of discussion, but we also intimated that there were several people who were interested in investing in the company, and that was when Norbert, who was accompanied by a colleague from the finance department, piped up out of the blue:

'Well, Nick, we might be interested too.'

'Oh... OK... well, that's certainly an interesting idea,' I offered rather meekly in response as my pulse quickened.

Then they quizzed us in even greater detail on the current state of the team, and it became clear to both Nigel and I that they had come to the meeting with a mandate from the very top to go after us.

It was an exciting moment, to put it mildly – we had been dealing with some flaky would-be buyers up until then and there we were, at the heart of one of the finest automotive engineering companies in the world, being told they might be interested in investing in us. It was as casual and unexpected as that, and Nigel and I did our best to make it look as though it was no big deal.

For a while not much happened, at least on the surface. The races continued and the lawyers and financial people at Mercedes worked away in the background, assessing what we had and how a deal might look. In the meantime we became even closer to our friends in Germany as a result of the huge row that was raging in the sport at that time over plans by Max Mosley to enforce a budget cap on the teams, with the aim of restricting spending during the following season. Max would eventually fail in that endeavour and leave the FIA by the autumn. But before that happened there was great pressure on the teams to stay together and present a united front in opposition to both him and Bernie, who was also fighting his corner.

As the battle continued during the early part of the summer we were tempted at one stage to break away from the other teams. This was partly because Bernie owed our company over £10 million in television revenue from the Honda days. We needed to get our hands on that money, and he tried to tempt us by saying we would get it if we renounced our alliance with the other teams. However, during a team principals' meeting devoted to this issue Dieter Zetsche, the chief executive of Mercedes Benz, made clear to both Ross and me that if we stayed the course with the others then Mercedes would try to help us. When the CEO of one of the biggest and best brands in the world says to you 'we will try and help you out', or words to that effect, it certainly has an impact. Even though it was not a binding commitment, it was another clear signal from Stuttgart that a deal could be done.

There were numerous telephone calls and discussions that went on right through July as the Mercedes lawyers sized up an offer. At the same time, as we had made clear to Norbert, we were conducting discussions with other serious potential buyers. We had noticed that the calibre of potential investors and buyers had markedly improved since the start of the season in the light of the succession of wins we had achieved on the track.

There were two other parties looking at us. The first was the Glazer family – the American owners of Manchester United and the Tampa Bay Buccaneers in the NFL. In March we began discussions with Ed Woodward, who was then running Manchester United's commercial and media operations. Woodward is now executive vice-chairman and the top operational executive at Old Trafford. We were introduced through the London bank JP Morgan – the daughter of a senior executive at the bank was working for us as an aerodynamics engineer – and they told us they thought they knew someone who might be interested in buying the team.

It was a bizarre time at the beginning of 2009 if you were in the mergers and acquisitions department of a merchant bank in London because there was nothing to do – no deals to be done – as the world financial crisis continued to bite. And there we were, the figureheads of a team that was winning races and the value of which was increasing all the time. We presented ourselves on as many doorsteps as would let us in, and we had ready access because we were an interesting proposition and they had nothing else on.

While our negotiations with Mercedes Benz were time-consuming, analytical and detail-orientated – exactly what you would expect in a big corporate organization – our discussions with Woodward at his office in London's Pall Mall were more casual. He was someone we could quickly see was on our wavelength, and he was smart and financially orientated.

Even at that stage the commercial organization of Manchester United was very impressive, with about forty people in London alone working on sponsorship projects. Ed was fun to work with and he had a strong vision for the team and how it could work alongside the football part of the Glazer portfolio, which we found attractive. His idea was that if you already have a big sponsorship team and management structure at Manchester United, why not use that to run a Formula One team too? He was excited by the prospect of having Ross Brawn, a Formula One legend in his prime, alongside Sir Alex Ferguson, then still very much at the top of his game, as two icons of British sport in the same stable. It also just so happened that Ross is a big Manchester United supporter, so that fitted nicely too. Indeed, at one point Ross went to Old Trafford to see a match and met members of the Glazer family to discuss this proposition.

Another person showing interest was Tony Fernandes, the ambitious and impressively successful owner of the no-frills Malaysian airline, Air Asia. He had been involved in Formula

One in various ways for some time and had been a real fan of the sport. He was interested in buying our team and, like Richard Branson before him, saw this as an opportunity to take a big step up from being a past sponsor of other teams to a team owner. He was a serious option for us. He knew what the sport was about, and our discussions with him started at the British Grand Prix in mid-June when he and I had a drink at the Bear Hotel in Woodstock near my home.

Later I spent an afternoon with Tony at his head office at Kuala Lumpur airport. He took me to their flight simulator where, with a training captain sitting alongside me, and Tony standing behind me, I 'flew' an Airbus. Taking off and flying it seemed easy enough, but I am sure they had the absolute beginner's settings on so it wasn't that hard. Landing was a bit more difficult. Simulators move around like real planes, and my landing was bad. Appalling, in fact. I came in nose down, too fast and got everything in the wrong order. We slammed into the runway and the impact was so heavy that Tony – who was giving a running commentary and laughing out loud – was catapulted over me and virtually landed in my lap.

After we'd dusted ourselves down, he took me around the Air Asia flight school where legions of carefully selected, attractive young Asian women were learning the ropes as cabin staff and other roles in the airline. Tony was referred to within the company as 'boss', and in every classroom we went into they would all stand up, turn around and chant as one: 'Hello, boss!' Tony was clearly living the dream.

After that meeting in Kuala Lumpur, we continued to run discussions with Tony in parallel with the Glazers and Mercedes Benz. While Norbert knew there were other bidders, he did not know, as far as I am aware, who they were.

When it came to price, we asked Gordon Blair, who had helped us structure the MBO deal, to lead the negotiations with Mercedes and the two rival bidders. He was tasked partly because he was experienced at doing that but also because he was one step removed from us. Negotiating this kind of thing is invariably a fractious and difficult process. We were trying to sell for as much as possible; the would-be purchasers were trying to get it for as low a price as possible. So it was good to have someone separate from us – a lightning rod – who the other side could battle with, without any of the ill-feelings generated affecting our ability to work with them in the future.

In terms of value, there were several elements to consider. One was our performance on the track and our likely performance going forward, which looked pretty healthy – six wins in the first seven races had convinced many that the 2009 championship was as good as over, though of course we didn't see it that way. But with each race win, our stock went up.

Then there were the staff and facilities at Brackley. We had had to get rid of a lot of people but those still with us were top quality. The same could be said of the physical assets, not least the wind tunnel.

The other element was our potential future revenue. This was influenced by what happened on the track but also depended on what sponsorship contracts we had and, on that score, I enjoyed a massive slice of good fortune.

It just so happened that at the end of July, on the day that Mercedes' big German rival BMW announced that it was following Honda in pulling out of Formula One, I happened to be in Singapore for meetings with potential investors. I got wind of the BMW decision and, as soon as I had completed my commitments in Singapore, I got on a plane to Kuala Lumpur and made my way to the imposing Petronas towers where the Malaysian national oil company is based. Petronas had been BMW Sauber's main sponsor for four years, but the German car manufacturer had evidently informed them very late in the day that they had decided to leave the sport and executives at Petronas were hopping mad about it.

That morning – it was later that day that I visited Tony Fernandes and the Air Asia flight school – I sat with the marketing directors at Petronas, led by Anita Aziz, and we more or less agreed the outline of what would turn out to be the second-biggest sponsorship deal in Formula One at that time, behind only the Philip Morris Marlboro cigarettes tie-up with Ferrari. I was able to tell Petronas that Mercedes was very interested in buying us and they responded by saying that, if that deal went ahead, then they would like to come on board. Petronas made it clear that they had no interest in doing a deal with a privately owned team, and as I left the building I knew more than ever how vital it would be to successfully complete our negotiations with Norbert.

The coincidence in the timing of my visit to Singapore and the BMW decision was extraordinary, and another example of how fortunate we were in so many ways during our charmed season of 2009. But it is also true that you have to make your own luck, and I was there and ready to capitalize while our rivals – among them Williams, who were also after Petronas (I'd actually seen pictures of a mock-up of the Williams car in Petronas livery) – were not in Kuala Lumpur that day.

The next step with Mercedes was the announcement and signing of a Memorandum of Understanding in early August, summarizing our plans to sell the team and their plans to buy it. This was not a legally binding document but it moved the deal closer to reality. In fact by that stage Ross and I and our fellow directors were clear in our minds that Mercedes was by far the best option. It was interesting because we all felt much happier with Woodward and the entrepreneurial Glazer culture and, in one of our final board meetings at Brackley to discuss our options, we held two votes in a semi-serious spirit.

'Who in our hearts would we prefer to own the team?' asked Ross. 'All those in favour of Mercedes raise their hands.'

There was no response.

'And those in favour of the Glazers?'

All five directors raised their hands.

'OK, so who in our heads do we think should get it? Those in favour of Mercedes?'

Once again, all five hands pointed skywards. It was clear that, although we all wanted the team to go to the Manchester United stable, it was a no-brainer in motor racing terms that it would be owned by the people in Stuttgart. The German car giant produced one of the most consistently powerful engines in Formula One and held out the prospect of us becoming a 'silver arrows' works team. This would put us in a strong strategic position. There was huge capacity for further investment by Mercedes and we knew that Norbert understood what would be required to keep the team at the front end of the grid.

Mercedes was prepared to pay a decent price but it is likely that we would have got even more money from the Glazers. That was because Ed Woodward was offering a much more performance-orientated deal that would have paid out handsomely as a result of the team's subsequent successes. We never got into this level of detail with Woodward, but what was clear was that he and his team at Manchester United were more interested in working *with* us than us working *for* them.

The Air Asia option was less appealing when set against the sporting advantages of teaming up with Stuttgart. Fernandes's offer was in a similar price range to Mercedes' but it was never going to beat what Stuttgart could offer us.

Another deciding factor was the increasingly strained relationship between Mercedes and McLaren, which made it easier for the German company to switch horses. (When the sale was announced, Mercedes also revealed its decision to sell its 40 per cent stake in McLaren.) At that time Ron Dennis was trying to develop his own road cars, and Mercedes Benz was not interested in being part of a company that was going to manufacture cars that competed with its own range. On our side, we were a successful team; Ross was an outstanding technical mind in Formula One and I was an automotive guy who spoke the sort of language Mercedes understood.

In our slimmed-down form, we were also of the scale that was being touted at the time as the right size for a Formula One team in the post-financial crisis world. We pushed that aspect, of course, conveniently ignoring the fact that our car was the fruit of hundreds of millions of pounds of investment by Honda.

These things always take much longer than you ever anticipate or want. We couldn't let ourselves get over-excited until it actually happened because there were so many hurdles in the way. Ultimately it could rest on whether we won the championship or not – it wasn't a requirement of the deal but we were well aware that people can change their minds. And on that score our fortunes were about to change quite dramatically.

# CHAPTER THIRTEEN

## *THE DIP*

The run-up to Silverstone always filled me with dread. We had never done well there. It was almost a sort of bogey track for us. If you look through the team's record, we had never been any bloody good there and we never really understood why. So I always had a sense of foreboding, and this year it was exacerbated by the fact that we had done very well until that point. I almost felt it was inevitable we were going to trip up, and Silverstone was always the event where Jenson appeared to be under the most pressure.

The local teams are under the microscope at the British Grand Prix. When you are away from home, you take a small number of people with you and you are a self-contained group that is just allowed to get on with it. But the British Grand Prix is a huge event and this year it was bigger than normal because we were going into it leading the world championship, and everyone and his wife wanted to be there, including all our employees.

For Jenson, Silverstone was always the Grand Prix where the full posse turned up, which made things more complicated than perhaps they might have been. As well as his trainer Mike Collier, his manager Richard Goddard, his personal assistant Jules Kulpinski, his mate Chris Buncombe, his dad and a few others, he also had his mum and two sisters on hand. In that situation Jenson was left to mediate between his divorced parents and look after both of them – not an easy setting for a young man trying to focus on winning his seventh race of the season.

When you don't do well at a track you tend to go into it plagued by doubts. Even though we had every reason to believe the car was good – it had been outstanding until that point – there was always a nagging worry that then fed on itself. It felt like we were on a knife-edge, and just because we had been dominant it didn't mean we would continue to be dominant. A lot of this was to do with confidence and I never felt we had much confidence in doing well at Silverstone, ergo we didn't do well there.

Jenson came to the Northamptonshire circuit, desperate to show what he could do in front of his fans and to join the long list of British drivers who had won on home turf – among them Lewis in 2008, David Coulthard, Johnny Herbert, Damon Hill, Nigel Mansell, John Watson and James Hunt. But the narrative of a difficult three days on a track, which at that time was facing being dropped from the calendar in favour of Donington Park (a switch later scrapped by Bernie), was all about tyre temperatures on a relatively cold and windy weekend in late June.

We had seen in China – the only one of the first seven races that Jenson did not win – that the Brawn GP001 struggled in lower temperatures. In the cooler weather the car never managed to get its tyres properly 'switched on', which translated into poor grip on the tarmac. At Silverstone for qualifying, the air temperature – on what Ross called 'a typical English summer's day' – was a lowly 16°C and Jenson only just made it into the third session before lining up sixth on the grid for the race. It was becoming clear that a new front wing for the weekend was proving to be a backwards step. Afterwards Jenson complained that the rear end of the car was 'skating around' and he had no grip in either the high- or low-speed corners. Ahead of him Rubens was in second place, splitting the two Red Bulls of Sebastian Vettel on pole and Mark Webber in third place.

Despite this unpromising build-up, Jenson still went into the race as the overwhelming favourite. Commentators were talking of a new British sporting hero delivering a 'demonstration drive' to glory in front of his adoring fans. But my own fears were to prove right on the button (forgive the pun), as he struggled through a largely uneventful race on a day when overtaking proved extremely difficult.

When the cars roared away from the grid in front of over 100,000 fans on the Sunday afternoon, Jenson fell back in the rush to the fast right-hander at Copse Corner and dropped to ninth place. Thereafter he toiled in the midfield, especially during a long middle stint when he initially carried a heavy fuel load. Having been stuck behind Trulli in the Toyota early on and then Rosberg in the Williams in the later stages, after 191 miles and sixty laps he ended up where he had begun: in sixth place. It was his worst performance of the season by some way.

At the time we put it down to the Silverstone bogey and the temperature issue, and both Jenson and Ross emphasized afterwards that Brawn would be back on form at the next race, in Germany, assuming it was held in fine summer weather. While Jenson struggled, Rubens drove well to finish third. This left him just 2 points ahead of Sebastian in second place in the drivers' rankings, while Jenson was still 23 points to the good at the top of the table.

The race at Silverstone featured a masterful drive by Sebastian, who claimed his first career hat-trick of pole position, fastest lap and race win, with his teammate Webber second. The young German was looking like a serious contender in a Red Bull that featured no fewer than sixty-five new parts, the result of a thorough upgrade that weekend as Christian Horner's outfit continued to close the gap on us. Our own work in that area had been frustrated because our engineers could not properly evaluate whether new parts were improvements or not on a car that wasn't performing properly on its tyres.

Despite the fact that we had next to no money, we kept to the team tradition of putting on a party at the factory on the day of the British Grand Prix for all our employees and their families. We organized a pig roast and hired clowns, entertainers and a bouncy castle plus a huge screen to watch the race. Then, after the Grand Prix, we all went back to the factory to greet the staff and have a few beers with everyone.

The big event between Silverstone and the German Grand Prix three weeks later was that Kate and I got married. On top of all the racing, and the hunt for sponsors and buyers for the team, we managed to get this organized at a hotel near Stratford-upon-Avon.

We chose Ettington Park because everywhere else had strict rules that were rather off-putting. At Ettington Park, an imposing country house in its own grounds, the management said we could do whatever we liked. If we smashed the place up – which we certainly had no plans to do – it was no problem, we would just have to pay for the damage. When we asked what time the bar staff had to go home, they said that if we stayed up all night they would too.

We took over the whole hotel and Jenson did the superstar thing, arriving on the front lawn with Jessica in his helicopter. We did the formal bit in the hotel, then moved to a small chapel in the grounds for a blessing and then had one hell of a party in the main hotel. It was extremely drunken and jolly and a lot of the team joined us for drinks and dinner. The nicest thing was that when the bar staff did eventually go home, Ross Brawn became the barman. He was told to note down what he had served and they left him to get on with it. He managed the situation with his usual calm authority. The next day we laid on tours around the factory for wedding guests, or at least those among them who were up in time.

The following weekend in Germany, it was more of the same as cool conditions put paid to our dreams of bouncing back after Silverstone. Once again the cars were sluggish and, although Rubens qualified second and Jenson third, we finished the race with them in reverse order, but in fifth and sixth places.

The mood in the garage afterwards was gloomy and tense at a racetrack where we were naturally keen to impress Mercedes as they continued evaluating us as a buying target. From my point of view, not doing well at the Nürburgring was a worry, to say the least.

Once again the Red Bulls were imperious, with Webber this time taking the spoils – his first win at his 130th attempt – and Sebastian second. The sinking feeling in our team was exacerbated by Rubens, who believed that we had not only been outperformed by Red Bull but out-thought by them too. He was convinced that Ross had thrown away a possible race win for him by requiring him to stick to a three-stop fuel strategy that did not work.

'I'm terribly upset with the way things have gone today because it was a very good show of how to lose a race,' fumed Rubens. 'I did everything I had to do. I had to go first into the first corner and that's what I did. The team made me lose the race basically. If we keep going on like this we'll end up losing both championships [constructors' and drivers'] and that would be terrible.'

In the all-important standings, Rubens had slipped to fourth place on 44 points, with Webber just ahead of him on 45.5, while Vettel was now second on 47. Up ahead Jenson was sitting on 68 points but his lead over Sebastian, which had stood at 32 points after the Turkish Grand Prix, was now down to 21 points. The alarm bells were ringing a little more loudly.

Again we pinned our hopes on the next race, arguing both to ourselves and to our fans in media interviews that the almost invariably scorching temperatures at the Hungaroring would come to our rescue. This was where Jenson had scored his one and only race win for Honda in the rain in 2006, and we felt confident he would be back on track this time round in a car with further aerodynamic upgrades after Germany.

But it all went completely against us on a dramatic weekend outside Budapest when Brawn GP was in the headlines for the wrong reasons. During the third session of qualifying, Felipe Massa in the Ferrari was injured in a freak incident when a suspension spring fell off the back of Rubens's car and hit him on the head. On the pitwall Ron Meadows spotted what had happened immediately, saying: 'I think it's come off our car.'

Our subsequent investigations revealed that a damper shaft had broken when the car hit a rut in the track, overloading the structure. This released the heave spring that sits above the gearbox and supports most of the weight of the car. We discovered that a similar suspension failure had occurred at exactly the same place on one of the Ferraris the previous day.

Slow-motion replays of Felipe's accident showed that initially the spring looked to be heading away from Felipe but it then bounced back in towards him. Weighing about 700 grams, it penetrated Felipe's visor just above his left eye as he was accelerating to around 175 mph. He immediately lost consciousness and his car speared straight into the tyre wall, where the medical staff at the track stabilized him before he was airlifted to hospital. His condition was described as 'serious but stable' and he would spend his first night in hospital on a respirator and under sedation.

I was stunned by this. I found it hard to believe that something like that could happen. Components rarely come off the back of cars, but then to have a relatively small part hit a driver on the head was shocking. Considering the potential nature of Felipe's injuries – which I am delighted to say he went on to fully recover from – his family were very gracious. No one made an overly big deal about it. It wasn't as if people were pointing fingers at us, accusing us in some way of being culpable. Everyone in the paddock at the Hungaroring felt the same – it was just a case of incredibly bad luck.

We carefully prepared our cars for the remainder of qualifying to try make sure something like that could not happen again. But the incident influenced our final grid positions because our drivers fell out of their planned sequence on a day when the timing system failed at the track. The next day

Jenson started in eighth place, his worst starting position of the season to date, while Rubens was back in twelfth.

The race proved another disappointment. As Lewis stormed from fourth on the grid to his first victory of the campaign in a much-improved McLaren, Jenson drove another indifferent race after contending with severe tyre wear from the start. He managed to gain one place over the course of seventy laps around the tight and twisting Hungaroring, a circuit that should have suited our car. But the bigger worry was that the track was hot and yet still we struggled to get on terms. On lap 32 Jenson was heard complaining to the pitwall: 'Guys, I'm already getting oversteer. How can this car be so bad at the moment?'

Perhaps the only bright spot on our horizon was that Lewis had taken points off the Red Bulls, with Vettel retiring for the fourth time in the season – this time due to front suspension damage on lap 29 – and Webber finishing third.

What this contest in Hungary had done was prove that the track temperature issue, which had served as a useful explanation for our lack of competitiveness at Silverstone and in Germany, could no longer fully account for our predicament. In the aftermath of the race in Hungary, with his lead over second-placed Webber now down to 18.5 points, Jenson came to the conclusion that something had gone wrong with the car.

'It's disappointing because we had high hopes for this race,' he said afterwards, 'but we were fortunate to come away with two points. We've had two different updates on the car and they shouldn't unbalance it in any way. You can say the others have stepped up their game, but our car is not what it was to drive a few races ago.'

Even Ross was beginning to think he and the engineers had taken a wrong turn on the development curve and spoke of needing to 'work back' to try to identify where the car had gone awry.

It was time for the month-long, mid-season summer break. The team was required by the rules to close down for two weeks, and Ross and I shut the factory and the email system at the earliest opportunity.

We all needed a breather to try and get our campaign back on track.

# CHAPTER FOURTEEN

# *RUBENS ON A CHARGE AS JENSON STRUGGLES*

Refreshed after the break, we returned to the racetrack more confident that we had solved some of the underlying issues with the car. Both Jenson and Ross were talking about a breakthrough.

'In the time available to them, despite the holiday, the engineers now say they know what the issues are. I trust them. I think we understand the car much better than we did one or two races ago,' was how Jenson summarized the position on arrival in Valencia for the European Grand Prix.

Ross echoed those sentiments and welcomed the scorching temperatures on Spain's Mediterranean coast, where one of the least successful – read dull – new street circuits had been laid out around the America's Cup harbour and the commercial docks: 'We are back to dealing with a normal car again,' he said.

During Friday practice the team worked hard to try to verify that the work done in the break had been in the right direction. Rubens's car was set up as per the Spanish Grand Prix as a control, while Jenson's was tweaked this way and that. Despite focusing on this, our cars ran first and fourth in first practice and second and third in second practice. It looked promising.

In qualifying, Rubens was on song in third place behind the McLarens of Lewis and Heikki Kovalainen, while Jenson had to settle for fifth after making a small mistake at Turn 4 on his quick lap.

The race proved one of the least interesting of the season. Jenson got swallowed up in the midfield and finished seventh. Rubens, meanwhile, showed all his experience – out-driving Kovalainen and then pouncing when Lewis's last pitstop went wrong – to take the chequered flag for the first time since China in 2004. It was a great result for him and for us as a team because the Red Bulls misfired, with Webber ninth and Sebastian's blown engine meaning he failed to finish again.

It was stinking hot that day and Rubens, in his late thirties, was not as fit as some of the other drivers. This was something we had been aware of from the start of a season that featured more than its fair share of hot races, but his shortcomings on the fitness front were not helped by the fact that he fell out with his physio early in the campaign.

The hero of the hour in Valencia was Jock Clear, Rubens's race engineer, who for the last dozen or so laps was coaxing him to the end. We were seriously worried about whether Rubens had the stamina to keep going. I listened to Jock cajoling and urging him on as Lewis came rampaging up the track into his mirrors: 'Go Rubens! You can do it!' yelled Jock as the Brazilian charged for the line, crossing it 2.3 seconds ahead of Lewis's McLaren.

The race in Valencia underlined that Rubens was becoming a factor in the title race in the second half of the season. He was back to second in the drivers' rankings and he had no doubt that he had could win it, even if he was still 18 points adrift of his British teammate. For him this was his chance to fight back. He also knew that he was out of contract for the following season, so he was not only taking advantage of Jenson's wobbles but trying to secure his future in the sport as well. He had put his early difficulties with clutch control behind him, and a change in brake pad material by his mechanics had given him more confidence, so he could now drive more aggressively and his class was beginning to show.

Personally, it never struck me that Rubens could, or would, prevail. For me, Jenson was always the one who was going to win the title. That conviction was based partly on what Jenson had achieved in the early races but also on the emotional attachment we all felt towards him. The truth of it was that he was *our* driver. We had been together for such a long time. His progress that season wasn't as pretty as it might have been, but he was always our number-one driver. He had been that from the get-go with BAR and then Honda, beating all his teammates starting with Jacques Villeneuve back in 2003, then Takuma Sato in 2004 and 2005, and then Rubens in 2006, 2007 and 2008. He had stuck with it through the dark days of Honda when we had coaxed him to give his best performances regardless of the fact that we were no-hopers. So in my mind he was our man and we were going to do our best to get him there.

I didn't go to Spa for the Belgian Grand Prix because we were still saving money and so I was not going to races unless it was absolutely necessary. Spa is one for the aficionados, in any case. It is a fantastic place if you are a Formula One fan, but from a commercial point of view it is a disaster because it is in a difficult area with few good hotels. Unless you like beer and chips, the local cuisine might not be the best and the weather is unpredictable. It is great for people who are mad about motor racing but it is not a good place to take most commercial sponsors.

On race morning I went mountain-biking in the Surrey hills south of London, as I had done on the other weekends I hadn't travelled to races, but this time I went over the handlebars and bashed my head. It proved a portent of things to come because Jenson also crashed that day.

In the build-up to the race Jenson got together with the British press contingent in the motorhome, as he regularly did at Grand Prix weekends. Unusually – albeit briefly – he lost his cool when asked by the correspondent from *The Times* whether he really wanted to win the Formula One world championship or not. The implication was that he seemed almost too calm in the face of adversity, to the point where it looked like he wasn't trying and as if winning the title just might not be the be-all and end-all of his life.

The question stung Jenson. He had always had to put up with the legacy of early assessments of him in Formula One that he was more playboy than serious contender, and this hurt. In response he dropped the smooth-talking, happy-go-lucky persona that he used to deal with the media – mickey-taking of journalists was always his 'go-to' mode under pressure – and revealed the torment of frustration and desire that he was contending with. The debonair Englishman even swore.

'I don't think people are saying that seriously,' he shot back. 'Who could possibly say that? "Does Jenson want this title or not?" Why the fuck am I here?' When told it was good to hear him spell it out in such unequivocal terms, he was not so sure: 'This is not what I have to say because that is not a [proper] question – it can't be. "Does he want the title?" No, I want to finish second or third,' he added in sarcastic disgust.

Andrew Shovlin – then Jenson's race engineer and now the chief race engineer at Mercedes AMG F1 – sympathizes with Jenson's frustration. Looking back, Shov says he and his colleagues have since learned a lot more about how to help a driver deal with the stresses of trying to win a championship.

'Jenson had a small group of friends and family and would confide in them rather than spend a lot of time talking to us about it,' Shov told me. 'We probably didn't understand the engineering enough to help him be better prepared. He knew deep down he wanted the championship more than anything but he didn't know what to do to get it, other than train hard, sleep properly, get to the tracks early to prepare and be in the right frame of mind. A lot of his frustration was born out of his feeling that, of course, he wanted to win but a lot of it was out of his hands,' he said.

Jenson's hopes for a solid race at Spa, after a poor qualifying session on Saturday, were quickly dashed, however. He made a good start from fourteenth on the grid, but then tangled with Romain Grosjean in the Renault and ended up in the gravel at Les Combes halfway through the first lap. Three other cars joined him, including that of Lewis. There is a great photograph of the two Englishmen standing side by side, waiting to be picked up by motorbikes, looking a bit embarrassed and apparently not quite sure what to say to each other.

This was Jenson's first retirement of the season but it would prove to be his only one. Despite not being able to sustain his early dominance, he was a model of consistency in this season of all seasons and this was critical in ensuring that he prevailed in the end. Rubens started fourth in Belgium and finished seventh. The race was won by Kimi Raikkonen for Ferrari, leaving an astonished Giancarlo Fisichella for Force India in second place, and taking advantage of the ultra-low downforce settings for the iconic track in the Ardennes forest.

That weekend in Spa will also always be remembered for what happened on the evening after the Grand Prix, when the so-called 'crashgate' scandal erupted over the sport like a filthy volcano. It emerged that the FIA was investigating allegations that the former Renault driver, Nelson Piquet Jnr, had been asked by his team management to crash his car on purpose at the Singapore Grand Prix a year earlier. The 'accident', on lap 14 of the sixty-one-lap race, had the effect of bringing out the safety car and enabled his teammate Fernando Alonso, who was not involved in the conspiracy, to win.

'Crashgate' became a huge global scandal. It was widely regarded as one of the most egregious examples of cheating in sport because it involved not just achieving success by underhand methods but also endangering the lives of Piquet, other drivers, and marshals and spectators. In the end Flavio Briatore, the colourful Renault team principal who denied involvement, and Pat Symonds, the engineering director who admitted his part in the plan, were banned from working in Formula One (though the bans were subsequently rescinded).

While the media were stunned by these revelations, I have to say that when we saw the crash happen in real time in Singapore, most of us involved in the sport suspected something odd had happened. An incident like that – a crash out of nowhere in isolation on the track – doesn't happen fortuitously. There was a general feeling in the pitlane that night that it was all a bit too coincidental. I remember smiling wryly as I watched the drama unfold on the monitors.

On the other hand, we all had difficulty getting our heads around the idea that someone had deliberately crashed a car. In any company, when you are the boss, you have the potential to persuade people to do things they might otherwise not want to do – and in Formula One everyone wants to win and they will do almost anything to retain their job and be successful. But another important role of a boss is to know where to draw the line. You can lead people – or coerce people – to do things that are inappropriate, but this was an example of a team doing something that was completely reckless and irresponsible.

Without wishing to condone it at all, it was also an example of what people under pressure are forced into doing. You can have the same discussion about Volkswagen and the scandal over covering up diesel emissions from road cars. Were they right to do what they did? Clearly not. But I think it demonstrates that if people are under that much pressure from above to deliver results – and they feel that they are in danger of losing their livelihood – then people can do dumb things.

I guess ultimately something like this comes down to moral values in terms of what is right and what is wrong. Formula One is a sport where you have to push the limits. Unless you do that you won't be successful. So you are always coming up against the boundaries, and sometimes you get it right and sometimes you get it wrong. But you don't mess around with people's safety and fundamentally that is what they were doing.

Flavio is a rogue and loveable rogue in some ways. Pat, I believe, is a decent human being who was probably led into the plan misguidedly and probably found it difficult to say no for obvious reasons. Someone had to take the rap and at the end of the day it is right that it was the boss, so Pat went. But Piquet's career was totally wrecked. He was a young driver battling huge insecurity and a more famous father – Nelson Piquet Snr – who had had a stellar career in Formula One himself and who, it seemed to me, almost did not want his son to succeed. I had interviewed Nelson Jnr with a view to him driving for us a couple of years earlier. His father was present for the interview and I remember feeling that the older man was there to sabotage his son's career. He was just undermining him at every turn, which I thought was completely extraordinary. Sadly Nelson Jnr never made it back to Formula One.

After Spa, Jenson was quoted as saying the 'sweet spot', where his car produced its best form, had 'shrunk' and he admitted that he had made errors in qualifying at both Valencia and Spa. By this stage – with thirteen of the seventeen races completed – it was pretty clear that when the car was not quite right Jenson was struggling more than Rubens. In fact the 'tortoise', as Rubens was known by his critics in Brazil, was clearly out-performing his British teammate in qualifying and in races. The gap in the points between them at the head of the drivers' rankings was now down to 16 points.

We had been blaming everything except our number-one driver. It took an intervention from Felipe Massa, now well on his way to a full recovery at his home in São Paulo, to articulate what many of us were beginning to feel. He told a local journalist in no uncertain terms that Jenson was choking.

'Jenson has gone down [in performance] because of the pressure – it's the only reason,' said Massa, who was rooting for his Brazilian friend Rubens. 'At the start of the season, everything was nice and easy. He was in a new team winning six out of the first seven races. That's different to fighting hard for the championship. Now he has a different kind of pressure,' added the man who had lost out so narrowly in the championship battle with Lewis the year before. 'In the earlier races he was almost half a second quicker than some teams. You win the race easy and is not much pressure. But now we have races where things are more difficult. So, for me, the pressure has had a big impact on his mind and he needs to deal with it. If he does not cope with the pressure, he will not win the championship.'

Harsh words, and at the time I certainly was not prepared to admit anything of the kind. In my interviews I kept to the mantra of taking each race as it comes and reminding journalists that we had always expected a dip in our form as a team and we were dealing with it. But, of course, Felipe was right. Jenson was creaking under the pressure to close out his championship. The car had been challenged by Red Bull, and now by McLaren and Ferrari, but there was no doubt that Jenson had tightened up, especially in qualifying.

His comments about the sweet spot were no excuse. In any season, the perfect competitive set-up of a car is going to be harder and harder to find as you refine it towards its limits and as your rivals gradually catch up. And as you reach the optimum state, performance-wise the cliff edge on either side gets steeper and steeper. I think the great drivers realize they are on the limit the whole time and can operate on that edge. The slightly less good drivers always expect their car to be on song – or benign – which is increasingly rarely going to be the case.

In agreeing with Felipe's assessment, I would point out that it is important to understand the context here. No one is saying Jenson was not a great driver. The point is you have to be unforgiving in your assessments because we are talking about the very best drivers in the world. When you are at the absolute apex you have to be evaluated on harsh criteria. There are the icons – the Hamiltons and Sennas of this world – whose driving is fairly fearless, but if you are even 1 per cent off that then you are not as good, and that is the comparator base.

Monza and the Italian Grand Prix was a big weekend for us. Alongside Monaco and possibly Barcelona, it was always one of the busiest races because everyone wants to be there. The atmosphere at the Pista Magica is always electric. The circuit is superb and the fans – the famous *tifosi* – are everywhere.

From a corporate point of view, it is the complete opposite to Spa – a glamorous race close to the hotels and nightlife of Milan – so we were busy with guests and sponsors. I flew out on the Tuesday before the race for a team principals' meeting on the Wednesday, which proved to be one of the last get-togethers of some of the iconic figures in the paddock – men like Frank Williams, Luca di Montezemolo and Ron Dennis, almost all of whom have now left the sport.

This was also the race weekend that Max Mosley formally retired after having run the FIA for sixteen years, a period during which he oversaw huge improvements in safety for drivers and fans alike. But he was also an arch-manipulator who schemed endlessly alongside Bernie, ensuring that the paddock was always a den of intrigue if not occasionally scandal.

Max had suffered the indignity of being exposed by the *News of the World* as a secret exponent of sadomasochistic sex with prostitutes in 2008. His departure from the paddock was marked by a dinner – which I did not attend – at which Jonathan McEvoy of the *Daily Mail*, on behalf of the Fleet Street F1 press corps, presented him with a whip purchased from Swaine Adeney Brigg, the Queen's purveyors of riding crops, much to Max's amusement.

I have thought quite a bit about Max's legacy to Formula One. Although everyone feared him to some extent, they respected his first-class intellect. In hindsight, it is easy to see that he was a good guardian of the sport, and when you got him outside the work environment he was bloody good fun to be with. He showed remarkable courage in the way he fought back from the exposé of his private life while also having to cope with the loss of one of his two sons, who died of an accidental heroin overdose. I was impressed that he was able to use what had happened to him to good effect with his campaign for new rights of privacy in Britain and elsewhere. I know others may disagree and he remains a controversial and complex figure but, as they say, you should say it as you see it not as you hear it, and that is my view of him.

At Monza we ran a heavy fuel load in qualifying for a one-stop race strategy, and lined up with Rubens just ahead of Jenson in fifth and sixth places on the grid. After the session we experienced another moment of real intra-team tension when Jenson found out that Rubens had been running more camber on his rear wheels (which governs the angle of the wheels in relation to the ground) than we had agreed would be the case. Jenson went to Ross and complained that, in his view, this was not fair. Rubens's mechanics were bemused by his reaction and took it as a sign that the Englishman was still concerned that the Brazilian could yet beat him over the season.

In a largely incident-free race on a beautiful late-summer's day, both drivers produced flawless performances and finished one and two on the track in the parkland of the Royal Villa of Monza, with Rubens on the top step of the podium. The game was all about beating the cars ahead of them on two-stop fuel strategies – among them those of Lewis, Kimi and Heikki – and they executed Ross's plan to the letter. Rubens was very emotional after winning on a track that was particularly special to him, following his long years at Ferrari.

The real significance of this race was that the Red Bull challenge had fallen away as Vettel struggled for pace and finished eighth, and Webber found himself in the gravel after just two corners. For them, as Ron Meadows put it, this race had been a 'dagger in the heart', and it left the championship now just between our drivers who were 14 points apart. Of course, we never admitted as much and Sebastian did recover some ground at the end of the season, but it now looked almost inevitable that we would win both the drivers' and constructors' titles. The only question was: could Jenson hold off Rubens over the final four races?

Jenson was clearly relieved to be back on the podium for the first time since Turkey three months earlier. He knew he had a serious contender to deal with in Rubens, who was full of confidence about his ability to take the battle right to the wire. Immediately after coming off the podium at Monza, where thousands thronged the track below them, the 'Frome flyer' tried a little joke at the expense of the Brazilian who could yet deny him his dream: 'I don't know, I've put on a brave face lately, but I absolutely hate this guy and he doesn't know his arse from his elbow when it comes to racing cars.'

All in all, Monza had been a red-letter day. Ross and I celebrated by taking the easyJet flight from Bergamo that night, arriving at Luton at midnight. We stood for an hour waiting for the lone passport officer to check our documents before we wearily made our way home.

We knew where we were heading; we were just not quite sure when we were going to get there. At last the pressure was starting to come off.

The issue between Jenson and Rubens was not settled at either the Singapore Grand Prix – where they finished fifth and sixth, with Button ahead and extending his overall lead by a single point to 14 points – or the Japanese Grand Prix at Suzuka a week later. There Sebastian produced a spectacular performance, leading from pole to chequered flag, to reignite his slim championship chances. With Button anonymous in eighth and Rubens one place ahead of him, the ranking had closed up again: Jenson was now on 85 points, Rubens on 71 and Sebastian on 69.

There were just two races left and, though Jenson was still the favourite, Rubens had grand plans for the next race at his home track at Interlagos, and Vettel was in a mischievous frame of mind.

'I will fight until the last breath,' Sebastian said after his victory at Suzuka. 'Two more races like this and it's looking better. Our task is straightforward: try to win. Get as many points as we can and then everything else is out of our hands.'

It was interesting that as Jenson seemed to stumble towards his moment of glory – in some ways advertising his weaknesses in the cockpit as much as his strengths – it was his British rival Lewis who spoke up to urge him on. Out of contention himself, the then-reigning champion, who would go on to become one of the greatest the sport has known, enjoined Jenson to take his prize and try to enjoy it on the way too.

'It is an overwhelming experience and for many of us drivers it is a dream since we were very young,' said Lewis after winning the race in Singapore. 'It is something that you wake up with and you live and breathe it, day by day. You live to get to that dream and now [Jenson] is in a great position to take it.'

Lewis knew that the British public was behind our man. 'I can only guess what will happen,' he added. 'But I know Jenson has a huge amount of support back home and it's the same for me. It is going to be great for Britain, for England. They are very proud of their sportspeople back home, so it's going to be great for them.'

Easy really… all Jenson had to do was go out and get it. He had two races left in which to do just that.

Jenson wins his second race sitting in a tropical downpour at the Sepang circuit in Malaysia.

Jenson gives Nick the full bear hug in his moment of glory at Monaco.

There's nothing quite like winning on the streets of Monte Carlo.

Celebrating Jenson's fifth win with Jessica Michibata, Jenson's girlfriend, and his father, John, in his lucky pink shirt.

The stampede after the start at Istanbul where Jenson pulled off his last victory of the season.

Rubens confers with engineers Jock Clear (*centre*) and Andrew Shovlin (*right*) on the grid at the Nürburgring for the German Grand Prix.

How did that all go so wrong so quickly? Jenson and Lewis compare notes after crashing out on lap 1 of the Belgium Grand Prix at Spa.

Sebastian Vettel (*left*) and Fernando Alonso (*right*) on the grid at Singapore. Vettel was a threat all season long in the Red Bull.

The showdown at Interlagos: Nick shares a joke with Jenson in the garage.

Felipe Massa waves the chequered flag in Brazil as Jenson finishes fifth to clinch the driver's title.

The spoils of victory.

*Left*: Party mode: Nick and wife Kate at the FIA end-of-season gala dinner.

*Below*: We did it – the shareholders (*left to right*): Gordon Blair, John Marsden, Nick Fry, Ross Brawn, Nigel Kerr and Caroline McGrory, with Jenson and Rubens.

*Opposite above*: Launching the new car for 2010 – the Mercedes chief Dieter Zetsche is second left.

*Opposite below*: The new world order: Ross, Michael, Nico, Norbert Haug and Nick with Petronas staff in Kuala Lumpur.

MERCEDES**GP**PETRONAS
FORMULA ONE™ TEAM

Niki Lauda with chief engineer Paddy Lowe – Niki was instrumental in us signing Lewis.

Lewis gives Nick's son Rafferty his first driving lesson at the Mercedes HQ in Brackley.

# CHAPTER FIFTEEN

# *BRAWN GP SCALES THE HEIGHTS IN BRAZIL*

In the years since we won both the 2009 drivers' and constructors' championships on a tumultuous afternoon at the old circuit at Interlagos in the suburbs of São Paulo, I have read various accounts of what happened that day, including Jenson's own.

In *Life to the Limit* he makes it pretty clear that he arrived in Brazil feeling edgy and unsure, and worrying about whether his critics, who accused him of bottling under pressure, were right. His pre-race nerves were not helped by having a dream the night before qualifying – or maybe a nightmare is a better description – that he would have a terrible session and end up way down the field. And on a day of heavy rain and thunder, when his side of the garage was caught out by changing track conditions, his premonition came disastrously true as he found himself lining up fourteenth for possibly the biggest race of his life.

One compensation, after the much-delayed session that became the longest in Formula One history, was that Sebastian was even worse off in sixteenth. But the real threat was Rubens, who was inspired on his home track as he approached the end of his seventeenth season in Formula One and took pole.

Rubens described his drive that day as the 'first phase' in achieving his dream. 'The job is only half-done and I'm keeping my feet firmly on the ground,' he said, having by no means given up on his own championship-winning chances. 'I'm not going to watch what's going on anywhere else. I'll go as hard as I can and then get on the radio at the end to see where Jenson and Sebastian have finished.'

While Rubens nestled in home comforts and drew strength from the roars of the partisan crowd, Jenson had to put up with the boos and jeers at one of the more ramshackle but also most atmospheric circuits on the Formula One calendar. Even off the track he had to be on his guard. On a night out in the city during the build-up to the race, a local TV station pulled a prank on him, placing a ladder outside the door of the restaurant where Jenson and his retinue were having dinner. Their hope was that he would walk under it and they would film him, inviting bad luck as a consequence. Jenson and his crew were not falling for any such tricks and they knocked it over before he could come under its spell.

At the time, my own view of his prospects in that race were more positive, especially after his disaster in qualifying. That was because what was happening to him was uncannily similar to events at that track three years earlier. On that occasion, driving for Honda, Jenson had also qualified fourteenth. But on race day in 2006 he drove like a man possessed. He scythed his way through the field – out-braking rivals at the famous Senna Esses, the corkscrew left–right downhill sequence at Turn 1 – and finished on the podium in third place behind Felipe Massa's Ferrari and newly crowned world champion Fernando Alonso in a Renault.

That day was one of the only times in my career when I intervened to a significant extent in our race strategy. When you qualified below tenth, the computer programme that analysed outcomes invariably advised a one-stop fuel strategy. You would load the car up at the start and hope to gain a few places by being out longest, and then fuel to the end.

Our chief engineer at the time, Craig Wilson, quite legitimately argued that we should do exactly that. But I felt, as did Jenson, that we should throw the dice and so I overruled Craig during a very bad-tempered discussion. The question was: 'Jenson, can you overtake at least six cars in the first few laps because, to make this work, that is what you've got to do?' And Jenson said: 'Yes.' And that's what he did in what was an outstanding drive.

Jenson has not specifically mentioned the comparison, but my guess was that the events of 2006 may well have been on his mind in 2009 as he prepared on race day. It was noticeable that he turned up at the Autódromo José Carlos Pace on Sunday morning fired by a new and steely resolve to sort this seemingly unending battle out once and for all. When our engineers told him in the pre-race briefing that he should aim to finish fifth, he was in no mood to accept it, and replied: 'No, I'm going for the podium.'

His father, John, who ended up watching most of the race through his fingers, picked up the same vibe. Jenson had told him he was intent on finishing the thing off. 'I knew the mood he was in,' John recalled later. 'I said to the mechanics: "You can fit a rubber bumper on the front because I think he might need it."'

Jenson himself was starting to talk up his chances. He pointed out that you could win from fourteenth on the grid, or even sixteenth, on a track where overtaking was on the menu and on a surface that might suit what he called his 'fussy' car. 'I will be right in the middle of the pack but I'll make the most of it,' he said confidently.

That is always a nervy situation, because in the midfield you are much more likely to get knocked off than you are at the front, but I at least had the confidence that he had done it before and I felt that history might repeat itself.

I think for Jenson it really was a case of now or never. He did not want to risk playing out the final drama at a brand-new track at Abu Dhabi two weeks later – much as the locals there wanted that to be the case – and he knew he had Rubens on his shoulder and could still not write off Sebastian, so this was the time to go for it.

Andrew Shovlin remembers the general feeling that we needed to get this done right there in São Paulo and make up for the disappointment of Saturday with a strong performance on Sunday. 'Jenson and the team were very much focused on not taking it to Abu Dhabi because funny things happen at the last race of a championship quite often,' he said.

The mathematics were that in the constructors' championship we were almost home and hosed. Red Bull could only catch us in the unlikely event that both their cars finished first and second in both of the final two races and we failed to score in either of them.

In the drivers' championship, it was more complicated even if a successful outcome for Brawn GP was almost guaranteed. If Jenson and Rubens finished in the positions that they started the race in Brazil, then Rubens would go to Abu Dhabi within 2 points of stealing a championship that Jenson regarded as his own. Other than that, Jenson needed to finish within 4 points of Rubens to win in Brazil, while Sebastian needed to be first or second to keep his own hopes alive.

I arrived in São Paulo on the Wednesday morning before the race and spent most of the day doing media interviews. The whole world, it seemed, wanted to talk to Brawn GP and reflect with us about how we had got to this point in our remarkable journey since that meeting with Honda almost twelve months earlier at Heathrow.

We had also become popular with the British government. Diplomats were keen to fly the flag and remind everyone that this was very much a British effort based at a factory in Northamptonshire, albeit fuelled for many years by Japanese money.

That night there was a reception and a big dinner in our honour at the British Consul General's residence in São Paulo attended by directors of British companies doing business in Brazil. The following morning I gave the group a short speech on the wonders of doing business in the UK. It was a useful way of taking my mind off what was coming up next, because from then on we were all focused on the build-up to the Grand Prix.

The race was a nerve-tingling affair – to put it mildly – because Jenson was playing an aggressive game and at any point his charge for glory could have come to a sticky end. At the same time we wanted to see Rubens do well at his home track, but I have to admit my heart was following Jenson's progress and the car with No.22 on its nose.

As the drums beating in the stands reached a crescendo on a warm and sunny afternoon, the cars stampeded down the start–finish straight, heading off anti-clockwise towards the crunch point at the Senna Esses.

Rubens led from the front. Jenson got away well and then benefitted from mayhem in the first sector as seven drivers were involved in shunts behind and ahead of him, including a heavy collision between Jarno Trulli in the Toyota and Adrian Sutil in the Force India. This also took out Fernando Alonso's Renault and resulted in Sutil and Trulli grappling together on the infield after getting out of their wrecked cars.

Among those who subsequently pitted were Heikki in the McLaren, who had spun at the Senna Esses, and Kimi in the Ferrari, who had hit Webber. Heikki was first to leave his box but he did so with the fuel hose still attached to his car, resulting in petrol spilling onto the pitlane. This briefly and spectacularly ignited as Kimi drove through it. Ahead of him Heikki came to a stop outside our garage and our mechanics rushed out to get the hose off his McLaren before waving him back into the race.

Jenson, meanwhile, had nipped through the pandemonium unscathed as the safety car came out and he found himself promoted to ninth place. From that point on, he drove with more fluency and aggression than he had all season in what he would later describe as his finest race.

He made four top-drawer passing moves, including an inside-outside overtake of Romain Grosjean in the Renault through Turns 4 and 5 immediately after the resumption, and three out-braking manoeuvres at Turn 1. The first was against Kazuki Nakajima in the Williams. The second was on F1 debutant Kamui Kobayashi in the Toyota, who defended like an old pro. Jenson was growing increasingly exasperated by Kobayashi's tactics and complained to Shov about him on the radio. The first time he tried to get through, he could not make his move stick and our hearts were in our mouths as he slipped back again, but the second time he did it for keeps.

His last big move was against Sébastien Buemi in the Toro Rosso. Jenson's car almost collided with the Frenchman's as the rear of the Brawn twitched under acceleration – again we watched on the edge of our seats.

Jenson climbed through the field and ran second for several laps in the later stages, before the final round of stops saw him settle in fifth place.

Meanwhile, Rubens had been struggling to hold the pace to stay in the lead. Having slipped back to third, he was being harried by Lewis in the McLaren in the closing stages. As Hamilton got past, the cars touched and Rubens picked up a puncture in his rear-left tyre that required a pitstop that dropped him to eighth. At that point his dream was over.

The race was won by Mark Webber for Red Bull. But the only thing that mattered was that Jenson had done enough to clinch the title as he swept past the finish line, where a smiling Felipe Massa was waving the chequered flag.

Our boy was ecstatic in the cockpit and pumped his fists in glee. Over the radio we could hear Jenson singing the Queen anthem 'We Are The Champions'. 'We are world champions, world champions,' he roared as Rubens came alongside to congratulate him, raising his hands from the wheel in applause.

On the pitwall Ross and Andrew Shovlin shook hands and slapped each other on the back. There were tears aplenty too and Ross became very emotional as the mechanics and the Button retinue – led by John Button, who was over the proverbial moon – began the celebrations.

Many of the key players in the team would go on to win more championships in Formula One with Mercedes, but few would later say any of those titles were more satisfying or emotional than this one because of the unique circumstances that led up to it. I watched the final stages of the race more or less hiding from what I was seeing on the monitors by crouching behind a tyre stack in the paddock, a bit like a child hiding behind the sofa during *Doctor Who*. When it was all over I felt a surge of relief and sheer joy as the pressure to complete the job suddenly evaporated.

After climbing out of his car, hugging Rubens and his physio Mike Collier, Jenson, with his crash helmet still on, threw himself on his teammates who were gathered behind the railings and cheering him to the rafters. Then he faced the mass ranks of the Formula One photographer corps and bowed as if to say 'that was my virtuoso performance'. In contrast to Lewis a year earlier, who seemed almost broken after the ordeal of trying to close out his championship at Interlagos, Jenson loved every minute of his success and went charging around the cramped paddock in a sort of ecstatic reverie, shouting: 'I am the world champion.'

He was still high as kite when he sat down at his own championship-winner's press conference. 'I don't really think that there has been a season like this in Formula One, so it is great to be sat here as world champion,' he said. 'And personally, I think I thoroughly deserve it. I have been the best over sixteen races and that's what world championships are.'

As a team manager you are always slightly conflicted in these situations because you want to celebrate for one but sympathize with the other at the same time. One of the things that I remember most about that extraordinary moment in all our lives was how well Rubens handled it. He had started on pole position and ended up eighth, while his teammate had started fourteenth and got fifth and the world championship. And this had happened at Rubens's home track in front of his own fans.

He was incredibly gracious in defeat. When Jenson and his engineers missed their scheduled plane back to the UK that night as they celebrated long into the small hours, Rubens offered them the use of his private jet, which I thought was magnanimous in the extreme. Not only had he lost, he also volunteered his pride and joy to take his rival back home. It was above the call of duty.

Rubens was mocked at the beginning of the season – people thought he was finished at thirty-seven – but he showed flashes of brilliance and in the second half of the campaign he was the better driver, out-qualifying Jenson in the last eight races. If he hadn't started so badly who knows what could have happened. Sadly, history will show him not winning the world championship, but the reality is that Rubens was an outstanding driver of racing cars.

Like a lot of South American drivers, he perhaps had a slightly more balanced view of life and the importance of family than British, European or American drivers. This is something that arguably takes the edge off the single-minded determination and selfish focus required to be successful. To win at this level you have to dedicate yourself to it 100 per cent and to the exclusion of everything else. I always felt that Rubens was a bit too sane to do that. In many ways he also ended up in the wrong place at the wrong time, up against someone of uncommon dedication in the shape of Michael Schumacher. In Brazil he was following on from Ayrton Senna, so he was in an invidious position there too, but he achieved a huge amount.

We all partied in downtown São Paulo that night, courtesy of one of our Brazilian sponsors for that race, the Itaipava beer company, who put on a big bash with half the paddock in attendance. Everyone was delighted for Jenson and especially for his father who had been there for his son at every step of the way.

The evening's highpoint was watching Ian Clatworthy, one of our IT guys. He was a big man and, like Ross, was also nicknamed 'the Bear'. His party trick was to carry someone around the dance floor on his shoulder, holding them up with one arm, and this time it was Ross's turn to get the Clatworthy treatment. But a lot of us were feeling almost as tired as we were elated, and even Jenson left early to think it all through.

The following morning I took a flight to Rio de Janeiro, where I checked into a hotel near the beach to chill out for a few days before it was time to head back to the factory and prepare for the final race at Abu Dhabi.

I think, for most of the team, what we had achieved really only sank in the night after the Grand Prix in Abu Dhabi. That was the first time when everyone truly went berserk. You often see people on TV saying that a remarkable event 'hasn't sunk in yet'. Well, it was the same for us. It is difficult to explain how that can be the case. After you've achieved something that you have been working towards for such a long time, all you really want to do is go to sleep because you are so emotionally, mentally and physically overwhelmed. It only starts to become real in your mind some time afterwards. It's one of those moments where you are pleased, you are satisfied, but you can't take in the magnitude of what you have achieved.

Back in London I got a glimpse of what it must be like to be Jenson when the whole world wanted a piece of him. I was travelling on the Underground one morning when someone recognized me from the television coverage of the race in Brazil and asked me for my autograph. Others cottoned on to who I was and soon there was an orderly queue of strangers waiting for my signature. It was a bizarre experience but one that brought home to me what we had achieved and what it had meant to so many people back home.

We may have been world champions in both categories but that did not change the reality of life for us as an independent team with extremely tight budgets. At Abu Dhabi we were forced to stay in self-catering apartments in a tower block in Dubai. We were all based there, including Ross and me, and each morning we had to get up at the crack of dawn for a one-and-a-half-hour bus ride to the gleaming new Yas Marina circuit in the administrative capital of the United Arab Emirates. This was not without its risks: one evening on our way home we had a scary moment when our driver fell asleep on the motorway. Luckily Simon Cole, our chief engineer in charge of reliability, sitting immediately behind him, was eagle-eyed and woke him just in time.

With our work done in Brazil, that weekend in the Gulf was a lot more relaxed. Kate and I went sailing off Dubai on a huge trimaran run by Oman Sail on the Thursday, and that night Emirates airline – who were sponsors of McLaren but who I spent some time wooing – organized a 'dinner in the desert' for the whole team. We all went out and sat on cushions in tents, with camels and belly-dancers in attendance – the whole nine yards. On Friday night there was another reception by the British government at the ambassador's house in Abu Dhabi. I was guest of honour alongside my boyhood hero Jackie Stewart. Suddenly we were everyone's best mates.

The race itself had a slightly flat feeling. It was the first dead rubber in a Formula One season since 2005. Lewis looked on course to win it, but retired with brake damage early in his second stint after being chased by Sebastian. The young German star then led his teammate Webber home to secure Red Bull's fourth one-two of the season. A newly emboldened Jenson drove a confident, controlled race to finish third, with Rubens fourth.

The final championship ranking made it look easy. With 95 points, Jenson was 11 clear of Sebastian in second place, with Rubens 7 points further back in third.

That night was when we went for it. The Virgin Group hosted a dinner for the whole team in Abu Dhabi and then we invaded the Amber Lounge. During the early part of the evening we were in a very crowded bar, where you could barely hear yourself think, and we were all jumping up and down with joy. Everyone was just so relieved and so happy. We were like a bunch of kids who you couldn't tie down. It was a spontaneous outpouring of relief, satisfaction and pleasure at having achieved our goals. There were no speeches from either me or Ross – there was no need and no one would have heard us anyway.

The team coach left the Amber Lounge at 5 a.m., and on the way back to Dubai Kate and Caroline McGrory regaled their fellow coach passengers with Irish rebel songs. Caroline had been brought up in Northern Ireland and was stunned to discover that my American wife knew many of the same ballads as she did, a reflection of her upbringing in an American-Irish community in the States. There was just enough time for our inebriated mechanics and staff to dash up to their apartments in Dubai, grab their bags and then make their way to the airport, feeling more than slightly the worse for wear.

Kate and I stayed on in Dubai and had dinner with friends who live there, before flying home with Emirates – who upgraded us to first class. This was the ridiculous-to-the-sublime. Just a few weeks earlier we had been travelling on easyJet or taking the bus back from London and now we were being treated like royalty.

We got back and decamped to the Seychelles for a few days of rest. Just over a week after the race in Abu Dhabi we exchanged contracts with Mercedes, and a week after that their purchase of the team was announced.

Until we actually signed the document, there were no guarantees. I don't remember the pressure being off until then. There was tension right up to the very end as to whether everyone was going to agree to it. In the end, everyone did and by then it was less a cause for celebration than a feeling of complete relief.

The day we exchanged contracts, I went to Cheltenham races and backed two winners and finished £16 up. Then, in December, a sponsorship contract between Petronas and the new Mercedes Formula One team was finalized that was valued at more than £50 million a year. This was a good year, there was no doubt about it.

There was an understanding with Mercedes that we could continue to run the company in the way that we had been doing. Our new owner did not want – at least initially – to turn it into something very different from what it had been. So the existing management team could continue in their roles and we would continue to be based at Brackley (where Mercedes-AMG Petronas Motorsport can still be found today). But I found it surprisingly difficult emotionally to let go. This was our team, five of us had been running it successfully – with little paperwork and with instant decision-making – and it had been a lot of fun.

When you sell any company, and especially when you are selling to an organization as big as Mercedes Benz, you know the world is going to change dramatically both for better and for worse. For better because you've got security, you've got access to resources and you've got the brand name that goes with it. But you also know – as I did from my time working for Ford Motor Company – that it comes with a lot of corporate process and a lot of paperwork and bureaucracy, and that someone else is ultimately making the decisions.

# CHAPTER SIXTEEN

# *SPLITTING WITH JENSON*

You would think that, having won the Formula One world championship with Jenson, our relationship with him would have been stronger than ever. We might even have gone on to greater things with him, as the team switched to Mercedes ownership, with perhaps more titles awaiting our dashing English driver. But real life is not quite like that and, even as the champagne corks were flying after Jenson secured the championship in Brazil, I knew and Ross knew that we were almost certainly going to lose him.

We didn't want to – far from it. We both admired and liked Jenson. I had worked with him at Honda since he first joined the team from Renault back in 2003, and we had been through a lot together. Both Ross and I felt that whatever his shortcomings as a driver – and there were some – Jenson was the man we wanted to lead us into 2010.

Jenson knew the team inside out. He had a strong working relationship with his key mechanics and advisers – especially Andrew Shovlin, who knew exactly how he liked his car set up. Similarly, we all worked well with 'Team Button' – his father John and manager Richard Goddard. Most important was the sum of our collective experience. Together we had worked our way up from the bad old days of uncompetitive cars with Honda, to a first race victory in 2006 and then the most unlikely of fairy-tale championship wins three years later.

From my perspective, keeping Jenson made a lot of sense. While I was keen to replace Rubens, who seemed to us to be reaching the natural end of his long career, twenty-eight-year-old Jenson was still at the peak of his powers and he was world champion. Having the current Formula One top dog in your team certainly makes winning over sponsors easier and it opens doors for coverage. It also gives you leverage in all that you do when it comes to negotiating with other team principals and Bernie.

Jenson was easy to get on with, the British media seemed to have a great rapport with him, and I was clear in my mind that keeping him was high on the list of our priorities.

It was in early September 2009 that I began to realize our relationship with him was starting to unravel. All other things being equal (which they weren't, of course), we appeared at that stage to be on course to win the drivers' title and it was time to open formal discussions with Richard Goddard over Jenson's future. Richard invited me to his home in Guernsey to thrash something out. But even as I boarded the plane, I was already aware that things might not be easy. The mood music from Team Button was all about Jenson's enhanced value now that he was finally on his way to achieving his dream.

A stocky, bearded individual who has never been afraid to speak his mind, Richard is one of the rocks on which Jenson built his career. He welcomed me warmly to his home on the island. It was a sparsely furnished house and had clearly barely been lived in by a man who was almost always on the road with his star driver – either at races or testing. We settled down with a cup of coffee in the lounge, where there was a sofa, a couple of armchairs and a television in one corner – hardly the most conducive atmosphere for what could have been a cosy chat by two long-standing colleagues.

Almost immediately it became blindingly obvious that we were a country mile apart. The reality was that Ross and I regarded Jenson as a £10 million-a-season driver – which is roughly what we were paying him in 2009 – while Richard thought Jenson was on his way to becoming a £25–30 million superstar. He was hinting at the sort of remuneration being enjoyed at that time by the sport's highest-paid driver Fernando Alonso, who was reputed to be earning around £30 million. Although Richard probably was not going to go that high and we were prepared to go a little higher than £10 million, I could see that this was hardly a bridgeable gap; we were talking different languages.

I guess it all came down to the tricky question of how much was down to the car and how much to the driver. There is no doubt that you need a huge amount of self-belief to drive a Formula One car, and drivers are always going to believe – regardless of the truth of the matter – that it was them that did it. It is a trait that the very best drivers must have in order to operate at the level they do. In Jenson's case, there was no doubt in his mind that it was his brilliance that was the defining factor. He and his team had to believe that.

However, Ross and I took a more detached view. We knew we had the fastest car and we were, at that stage, watching Jenson make heavy weather of winning the title. While he would go on and get the job done – and he certainly did a great job in 2009 – we had no illusions about his form over the years and where he stood in the F1 pecking order. In our minds, Jenson was a good driver, but he was not a Fernando or a Lewis – or a Sebastian Vettel, for that matter.

So what's the difference? Well, for example, Lewis can take a car that is not the best and still win with it. He can't take one from the back of the grid to the top of the podium, but he can take a machine that is destined for second or third to the chequered flag through his sheer driving brilliance, his bravery, his stunning confidence in his own ability and his skill at overtaking other drivers. And the key is that the other drivers know this, which is at least half the game because then they start worrying about a competitor like Lewis. If they are looking in the rear-view mirror and see someone else, then they will know all about that driver's weaknesses and know how to deal with them. But if they see Lewis in their mirror – and Michael Schumacher had the same effect – they instantly start thinking that they are going to be outdone because he has established a reputation for winning.

By contrast, Jenson was a driver who, if given a great car, would make the best of it but he struggled in less good machinery – something we saw time and time again during his long career at Honda. I can completely understand the point of view of Jenson's fans, many of whom rate him rather more highly than I do, but again I would point out that it is important to remember that we are talking about arguably the twenty best motor racing drivers in the world. They are all incredibly good and, when I say Lewis is better than Jenson, we are talking in such tiny percentage terms that it almost seems unfair to split the difference. But this is not a game; this is top-level sport and these drivers are paid huge amounts of money to do what they do. The reality is that there is a difference and if Lewis were a footballer he would be scoring goals when Jenson would not be, and that is why one is paid much more than the other. At that time, in my view, Lewis, Fernando and Vettel were in the top tier, whereas Jenson was among the best of the rest, alongside the likes of Kimi and Felipe.

I stayed the night with Richard in Guernsey and in the evening we went out for dinner, an occasion at which we might have continued our discussion about Jenson's future with the team. But in the event there was not a lot to talk about on that front and we chatted about almost anything else. I left the island the next day knowing that there was a big gap to bridge; I wasn't certain at that stage that Jenson was leaving but when I got back to Brackley I told Ross that we might have to think about a replacement for him.

It was at the Singapore Grand Prix – the second edition of Formula One's first night race – that we let Rubens down gently. He came to see Ross and me in our team chalet in the paddock, and we informed him that it was unlikely we would be working together in 2010, much to his evident disappointment. Rubens had wanted to continue but Ross and I both felt it was time to give his seat to a younger driver. I had noticed that the Brazilian veteran had become overly superstitious and was in the habit of carrying all sorts of good-luck charms under his driving suit. That sort of thing always sets the alarm bells ringing.

In the meantime, we had begun negotiating with Nico Rosberg, who I first sat down with at that year's Goodwood Festival of Speed in May where our host, Charlie March, found us a quiet room in the main house to have a chat. At that time Nico had a poor reputation in the British press, with some prominent commentators writing him off as an also-ran who had only made it to the Formula One grid because of who his father was – F1 world champion Keke Rosberg. But I immediately formed a different view. Nico struck me as sensible, bright and logical, and self-assured – in that meeting his father was nowhere to be seen and he represented himself more than adequately. Nico had served his apprenticeship well during four seasons at Williams, where he had done a decent job. He may not have had the potential to be an out-and-out number-one driver in a top team, but I saw him pushing a top driver close or working as a strong number-two, and we had him earmarked for one of our race seats for the season ahead.

Relations with Jenson developed in parallel lines. On the one hand, we forged ahead together in pursuit of Formula One's greatest prize, but on the other hand our future commercial or contractual relationship continued to fall apart. For me this was oddly reminiscent of what had happened with Richard Burns when I was managing the Subaru rally team in 2001 for Prodrive, and I felt a little twinge of déjà vu.

Richard had never quite believed he would win a title with Subaru and, so convinced was he of the team's frailty that halfway through what turned out to be his British Rally Championship-winning season in 2001, he signed a deal to move to Peugeot. The only way we could keep him was if he won the title. As that reality began to dawn on him and us, I convened a management team discussion when we briefly considered (and then just as quickly dismissed) the possibility that Richard might throw the title race solely to keep his post-season move alive. But neither he – nor any other elite sportsman, for that matter – is ever likely to do that.

In the end Richard went on to win the title at the Rally GB in Wales and we all went out and got seriously the worse for wear in Cardiff. Then the following day – and with the sorest of heads – I met his manager, Julian Jakobi, at a hotel near Heathrow to discuss what would happen next. They wanted out and presented a long list of claims against Subaru and Prodrive. We had failed to honour our own undertakings to him in this and that respect, and so on. I presented some hastily assembled figures showing that Richard would owe us millions for leaving as world champion because he would be depriving Subaru of the opportunity to maximize the PR value of its victory. Jakobi looked at the figure I presented him with – which was something in the region of £75 million – and nearly fell off his chair. Ultimately Richard went anyway, but sadly he never won another rally.

The remarkable aspect in both situations was that there was complete separation between the two elements. Both Richard and Jenson continued to drive at full intensity in pursuit of sporting glory, and their focus on the championship was not affected by uncertainties over where their career was leading next.

In the case of Brawn GP, the fact that Ross ran the engineering and racing side with the drivers, while I worked separately through Richard Goddard on the business side with Jenson, was a definite strength. We were neatly splitting our responsibilities and, although I always felt I had to be the bad boy doing the nasty stuff, Ross did the smoothing-over and the combination worked.

In Jenson's case, the ongoing negotiations that Ross and I were conducting with Mercedes to buy our team were also contributing to the breakdown of trust. Richard wanted a piece of the action – he wanted to be a shareholder in Brawn GP and Jenson may have wanted that too – but neither of us were prepared to countenance that idea. In theory it was an option, but the practicalities looked unmanageable. How, for example, do you fire someone as a driver when either he or his manager is also a part-owner of the team? Jenson would have become much more than just an employee and Richard much more than just his manager. This would have affected relations between Jenson and his teammate, and Richard would probably have expected an even greater say in how the team was run. We realized this was likely to introduce a whole raft of difficulties that we would prefer to do without.

It all came to head when Jenson came to see me at Brackley at the end of November 2009. It was just over a month after we had won the title and not long after the announcement of Mercedes' purchase of the team. To his credit, Jenson came to say goodbye and confirm what by then had become inevitable. He was leaving to go to McLaren to drive alongside Lewis and his time with us was over. He came to the meeting not with Richard but with his lawyer, a solicitor based in the east Midlands with a limited track record of handling the contractual negotiations of sporting royalty.

Jenson has described elsewhere a tense encounter at which I lost my temper and told him in no uncertain terms to wipe the smile off his face. He described his expression at that moment as the involuntary reaction of a nervous thirty-year-old who is being shouted at. I would agree – it was partly 'I'm going', partly 'I'm a bit nervous about telling you', which he certainly was, and partly 'I don't really want to be here.'

In general I am not a shouty type of person. However, I do believe that deliberately putting on a bit of a show, as if you're very upset, a couple of times a year can send an effective message to an organization because you so rarely do it. It is a way of conveying a message that you have thought through in advance – and in this case I *had* thought it through, and at the end of the meeting I sent Jenson packing and shouted after him: 'And you can take your high-street solicitor with you.'

Caroline McGrory was also present but I hadn't discussed with her what I had been planning, and she was stunned. 'Wow!' she said. 'That didn't last very long.'

In an amusing coda to that dramatic encounter, Jenson's lawyer – who shall remain nameless – wrote to me afterwards, complaining that I had called him a high-street solicitor and then proceeding to enumerate his professional qualifications in a letter that made me laugh out loud (which I am sure was not his intention). He had been OK in the meeting – it was just wrong place, wrong time.

The truth is I *was* annoyed. I was annoyed because over many years Jenson and I had been through one hell of a lot and I had made a big effort to look after him, financially and contractually, and this seemed a very poor return for my efforts. For example, back in 2004 Jenson had got himself in a huge mess when he signed a contract to return to Williams from BAR Honda. The deal was referred by David Richards, then our team principal, to the FIA's contracts recognition board, which concluded that Jenson's existing commitments to BAR took precedence. This was a very expensive error by Jenson's then management team led by John Byfield. We eventually got round it by persuading British American Tobacco to loan Jenson the money he needed to escape his obligations to Frank Williams against his future earnings. This was well over £10 million, and I subsequently persuaded Honda on several occasions to write off parts of that debt, allowing Jenson to escape with minimal financial inconvenience.

That was not the only time that we helped Jenson on the money side because when Honda pulled out of Formula One at the end of 2008, we persuaded them to honour the remaining year of his contract and then topped it up with extra money from Brawn GP.

Throughout my career I have never tried to stop anyone from leaving my staff if I thought they were doing the right thing – going to a better job or a better opportunity that I couldn't match. I have never tried to dissuade anyone from doing something that had good logic behind it. But with both Richard Burns and Jenson, I had no hesitation in believing that they would have been better staying where they were. In Jenson's case we were in a situation where we had just won the world championship, we had Ross leading the team and we were well on the way to getting a significant car manufacturer and a big sponsor on board; it seemed a really dumb time to leave, considering he had stuck with us through years of poor performance.

In the event Jenson went to McLaren where he performed creditably against Lewis in his first three seasons – out-scoring him in total points – and he finished second in the championship in his second year there. But in his seven years at McLaren, Jenson managed just eight race wins and spent much of his time in the mediocrity of the middle of the grid, ultimately at the wheel of a McLaren with a Honda engine.

It is easy to posit what-ifs, but had he stayed with us and done well – and Mercedes had a lot of time for Jenson – Michael Schumacher may never have come back from retirement and Jenson could have been battling Lewis in the car that has made Lewis the multiple champion that he is.

The greatest irony of what I think of as a sad break-up with Jenson was the fact that he probably moved to McLaren for less money – reportedly £18 million over the first three years – than he would have earned had he stayed with us, something that underlined how badly Richard had overplayed his early demands.

The final instalment of this saga came when McLaren announced Jenson as their new driver without doing us the courtesy of informing us first. When Ross joined us after his sabbatical, I made it my business to call the Ferrari team principal, Jean Todt, before we announced it, knowing that Jean was hoping that Ross might return to Maranello. Ron Dennis at McLaren made no such efforts and the whole thing had the feeling of a backlash about it.

I sensed there was a lingering resentment in Ron at the way we had taken the Mercedes engines his team was using and had then run away with the championship when McLaren could manage only third in the constructors' standings. The decision to let us use Mercedes engines had been taken principally by Martin Whitmarsh, although Ron had gone along with it. My feeling was that Martin had pushed for it, arguing that it was in the best interests of Formula One, but Ron was not happy about it.

I found out that Jenson had been announced as a McLaren driver while I was driving up the M40 one morning not long after my tumultuous encounter with Jenson and his lawyer at Brackley. I had been to Heathrow to drop Kate off for a flight to the States, and my secretary called to say that McLaren had issued a press release naming him. It felt premeditated – a Putinesque-style attempt by someone intent on getting their retaliation in first. I was furious not because they had caught us on the hop but because neither I nor Ross – who was also away that day – were at the factory where we could quickly address the many questions we knew our staff would have.

I stopped at the next services and tried to call Ron and then Martin, both of whose phones went to voicemail. So instead I called the McLaren head of communications, Matt Bishop, and I know I was probably less than politically correct in what I told him about the way I believed his team had behaved. For my outburst I was subsequently admonished by Norbert Haug, our new boss at Mercedes, who undoubtedly had a point but I needed to let off steam one way or another.

We may have lost Jenson but that opened up an opportunity I never imagined I would have as we hunted for a replacement driver for 2010.

# CHAPTER SEVENTEEN

# *MICHAEL*

Drunken and joyous parties aside, the moment when what we had achieved in 2009 finally hit me was several months later at a pre-season test at Silverstone.

By then under our new owners, we were testing the new car for 2010 – the 'silver arrow' – and we had our two new drivers on hand for the first time. Nico Rosberg had done his laps and now it was the turn of our other driver, a man who was regarded as a living legend of the sport.

Michael Schumacher left the garage and went out and did an installation lap, checking that all was working correctly on the car before heading back into the pits. As he made his way through the final few corners, our headphones came alive – it was our sporting director Ron Meadows, issuing the standard time warning to the pit crew so that they would be ready to receive the car outside the garage.

'Michael Schumacher, thirty seconds,' said Ron in the detached and practised way these messages are delivered.

'Holy camoly, we have got Michael Schumacher in our car,' I muttered to myself.

It was in that instant that all that we had achieved crystalized in my mind – hiring Ross Brawn as team principal, surviving the Honda pull-out just over a year earlier, winning the world championship, getting Petronas on board and selling a majority stake in our team to Mercedes. It was as if Schumacher's presence at last confirmed that this fairy tale *had* all happened and it was not the stuff of fantasy – we were now a strong outfit in the peak formula of world motor racing and a good enough team to have a seven-time world champion in our car.

Less than half a minute later my eyes confirmed that my ears had not been deceiving me, and the man the whole sport referred to simply as 'Michael' came down the pitlane in his silver arrow. Then, with practised ease that belied his three-year absence from the grid, he expertly positioned his car in the tight pitlane so that the mechanics could wheel him back inside the garage.

The whole thing sent a shiver up my spine. The team that Ross and I had managed to save from oblivion just over a year earlier was now in safe hands with a strong and committed new owner, and we had 'Michael' in one of our cars. I guess you could say we – and I – had finally arrived in Formula One.

\*\*\*

I had never been a Michael Schumacher fan. Probably like most people in England who followed motor racing, I was brought up on the caricature of him as a dastardly German who beat Damon Hill in an unfair way to win the world championship in 1994 and was involved with an Italian team, Ferrari, that was regarded as being occasionally 'liberal' in their interpretation of the rules.

Nevertheless, Michael's resignation from the Scuderia in October 2006 – or should I say his retirement – is clearly etched on my mind. I remember sitting transfixed, watching the press conference as he brought his controversial but glittering career to an apparent close after an unprecedented seven world championship titles. On the one hand, I was thinking 'thank God he is going and now the rest of us have a chance,' but I also felt sad for him. Ferrari was bringing in Kimi and I couldn't help but feel that Michael was being pushed out – that he was going against his will and that he was hanging up his driving boots reluctantly. It was one of those dramatic moments in the sport that stays with you – a driver who had redefined success in Formula One, and whose achievements may never be equalled, was leaving the pitlane. Little could I have known that three years later we would be the ones to offer him another contract to drive in Formula One, this time for Mercedes Benz.

As our 2009 championship-winning season drew to a close and we prepared for life under Mercedes ownership, we were short of a second driver. Jenson was jumping ship to McLaren and we had already decided to replace Rubens. We had Nico waiting in the wings, but who else could we get?

It was the wrong end of the year to be signing anyone at the front of the grid; most drivers were already committed for the following season, and we were really stuck. We looked at the German driver Nick Heidfeld, then with BMW Sauber, but he had not won a race in ten seasons and he was hardly the superstar that Mercedes were looking for. It was pretty clear to both Ross and I that we were being asked to find a potential world champion or an existing world champion, and Heidfeld didn't fit that bill.

People often assume that there was some sort of grand plan to bring Michael back, harnessed to a returning Mercedes as a full works team in Formula One for the first time in fifty-five years. But the truth of it was that we never anticipated ending up with two German drivers and nor did Mercedes particularly want that. Obviously from a marketing point of view, having two drivers of the same nationality is not as advantageous as having two people who could be used for different purposes, and this was especially so for a global company like Mercedes Benz. So there was no pressure on us from them to hire Michael.

The key moment came as Ross and I were celebrating our championship win with everyone else at the after-party at the Amber Lounge in Abu Dhabi. Both of us had had a few beers and we noticed that Michael was there, enjoying meeting old friends and looking very relaxed. It occurred to me, then and there, that he might well be interested in driving for us – after all, we had just won the championship and we had a new and ambitious team owner on board.

'Why don't you go over and have a chat and see what he says?' I shouted in Ross's ear over the din of the music on the dance floor.

Ross and I hadn't discussed it before; it was just one of those things – Michael was there and we thought 'let's talk to him'.

Even though it was going to be a somewhat abrupt initial approach, I expected Michael to be interested at the very least. Everyone knew that during his time away from Formula One he had continued to do the type of things that adrenaline junkies get drawn to, like motorbike racing – he had fallen off and hurt himself quite badly doing that – and skydiving and skiing. You sensed he was still keen to test himself and get back in the cockpit.

When Ross broached the subject, the vibes were immediately positive. Ross returned to the dance floor from Michael's table with a big grin on his face.

'He's interested,' he shouted.

'Wow!' I said.

It was from that encounter that the deal to put Michael in a Mercedes Formula One car for 2010 and the two seasons following was done. Getting Michael would dig us out of a huge hole. Looking back, I regard it as a coup to rank alongside saving the team, winning the world championship, selling the team to Mercedes, or signing Petronas.

For us it was instant stardust and brought the benefit of Michael's years of experience, his racing knowledge and his unrivalled expertise at setting up a car. For Michael it was far more risky. He was trying to make a comeback after three years out of the cockpit, but also add to his tally of seven championships, ninety-one race wins and sixty-eight pole positions. And there was a big question mark over his physical fitness as he continued his long recovery from serious head, neck and rib injuries incurred nine months previously while testing and crashing a Honda superbike at 140 mph. Those injuries had prevented Michael from making a comeback at Ferrari several months earlier following Felipe Massa's nasty injury at the Hungaroring. However, time had helped the healing process and when Michael eventually sat in our car for the first time, he was in good shape.

Michael had a complete aura around him that, even if you are used to dealing with film stars or sports stars, was unique. He was like a modern-day motor racing prince with a presence that befitted royalty, even if his fashion sense was more nightclub than royal palace. There was a calmness about him and a focus that I would say is typical of the highest level of sportsmen and women. When Michael turned to look at you, his eyes seemed almost to pierce your skull and you had that curious sense that he knew what was going on inside your head.

The first time he came to Brackley was to sign his contract. This had been negotiated by Caroline McGrory with Michael's lawyer, Brian Clarke, who had formerly been Caroline's boss at IMG, so it had all gone pretty smoothly. The difficult part, for Ross and I, was working out what to offer him. We couldn't decide.

We didn't want to insult Michael but we didn't want to upset Mercedes either by giving away the shop. I remember sitting with Ross and having quite a jovial discussion about 'where the hell do we pitch this?' On the one hand he was a multiple world champion who, in his pomp, would have commanded the highest salary on the grid; on the other hand, he had been out of the sport for three years and this was really his swansong. So trying to find a point at which both sides were comfortable was not easy. In the end we settled on at a figure that was around two-thirds of the £30 million top-end benchmark that Fernando Alonso was reputed to be earning.

Driving Michael in the snow to Oxford airport, where his plane was waiting after that visit, proved one of the most terrifying experiences of my life. Knowing that it might not be the easiest assignment, Ross had cheekily said at the end of the meeting: 'Nick, why don't you drive Michael back to the airport?' So there was I, at the wheel of my Mercedes road car, with the most successful driver in Formula One history sitting next to me. This would be nerve-wracking in any conditions but in the snow it was horrible.

I drove incredibly carefully and I couldn't help feeling that Michael was scrutinizing everything I did. Every gear shift seemed to catch his super-critical eye and I kept anticipating a short intake of breath and a judgemental remark. When it finally came, it was delivered in the form of a question: 'Has this car got snow tyres fitted, Nick?'

'Oh no, he wants me to go faster,' I thought as I laughed gamely at his stab at humour.

He didn't actually say it but if it hadn't been me – the person whose responsibility it was to negotiate his new contract – he would have said: 'I'll tell you what, mate, you get out and I'll drive…'

Afterwards I got myself back to the office, relieved that it was over. Ross met me at the door with a big grin on his face. 'How was that then?' he said with a chuckle, knowing full well what would have happened.

The thing that came over straight away with Michael was how hard-working he was. The level of detail that he would go into at engineering briefings and debriefings, when all aspects of a car's performance were being analysed with the engineers, was extraordinary – it was hours and hours and hours of discussion. Where most drivers would get bored after two hours, Michael would still be going after four hours and he wouldn't let go, which was completely extraordinary in someone who had been doing this for so many years. That commitment to the sport and to his career was reflected in absolutely everything.

On the commercial side, where I dealt with him, he had contracts with everybody and the difficulty was finding anything that you could do with him as a team that Michael hadn't already covered off through a personal endorsement.

One of my first meetings with him became quite heated and tense because Michael became exasperated by what amounted to conflicts of interest. For example, we wanted to do a deal with the Swiss watchmaker IWC Schaffhausen but Michael was already tied up with Omega. He also had a contract with Smirnoff, but our agreement with our title sponsor Petronas prevented any association with alcohol.

'I didn't want it to be like this… This isn't going as I hoped,' he summarized tersely.

Michael wanted it to work but I don't think he quite realized how difficult it might be to realign himself with a new team after so many years at Ferrari.

The other extraordinary thing about Michael was the relative normality of his family life, despite his immense wealth and fame. I remember at the British Grand Prix at Silverstone in 2010, his wife Corinna and my wife Kate and Michael's two kids and my son were upstairs in the team transporter all playing quite happily. Michael and I arrived and we just sat on the sides of the sofas, chatting like any other families.

There were strict rules for the children at races. Mick, Michael's son – then aged ten but now a Formula 2 driver who has tested with Ferrari – was not allowed in the garage; he would stand behind the hoardings at the back and peek around occasionally or look on the diagonal towards his dad's car, but the kids were not allowed on the forecourt.

Michael was always positive, regardless of how dire our team's fortunes were – and they were at times pretty awful – but he would always take the positives out of a situation and look for ways to build and improve. There was never any 'blame' emanating from him; if anything, he was the first to blame himself. And unusually perhaps for a superstar, he always thought of others and would invariably remember birthdays and react to family situations. When our son was unwell, the first person outside the family to send a 'get well soon' text was Michael, with a reminder of how important family was and that he and Corinna would hold the fort if I was away.

Michael had that knack of making people feel good about themselves by doing simple things that most sporting superstars do not do. He knew everyone's name in the team – all the mechanics, the catering staff, the truck drivers – and he would make a habit of socializing with them and taking them out for a beer. How good does it make you feel when one of the most famous people on the planet cares about you? In this respect he was the polar opposite to someone like Jacques Villeneuve and his helmet-on-visor-shut approach to his teammates.

I think Michael genuinely liked people and if he found them interesting then he would give them lots of time. For one relatively small sponsor we organized a lunch at The Square restaurant in London's Mayfair. We booked a private room for the sponsors, their senior people and guests. Michael was contracted to attend and we expected him to do what most sportspeople would do: the minimum required and then nip off as soon as he reasonably could without causing offence. In this instance, the sponsor was Autonomy, a British IT company, which was not necessarily the most intriguing of businesses for a top sportsman. But Michael stayed all afternoon. He was genuinely engaged. Of course, the company's senior staff thought the world of him after that and would have done anything for him and us.

Michael passed his people skills on to Nico, who did not have the same empathy and ability to engage with the warmth that Michael could exude. Michael spent time with his young German rival and teammate, counselling him on how to get his people onside – something Michael had excelled at during his years at Maranello. Nico is a bright guy and quickly saw the benefit of what he was being shown and started engaging with his engineers to a much greater extent after that. In fact, I would say that his championship win in 2016, ahead of Lewis, was a direct result of the tips he had picked up from Michael.

At the start of that season Nico got his engineers together and gave them a pep talk. He told them he was not as naturally quick as Lewis but that he believed they could beat Hamilton through guile, superior engineering and superior racecraft. They did. I believe Sebastian Vettel also modelled his behaviour on Michael and to great effect. I think it could be said that Jackie Stewart was the first to take driving in Formula One to a professional level, but Michael Schumacher made the next quantum leap.

There was no doubt that Michael was still quick during those final three seasons at Mercedes, even in his early forties. The unfortunate thing was that we were never able to give him a car that was competitive at the front end of the grid – the earlier cutbacks at Brackley saw to that – and consequently both he and Nico had to try harder than they possibly would have sensibly done. So we ended up with quite a few incidents and accidents and reliability issues, and so on.

One of the things I regret in all my motor racing career is that we never won with Michael. That would have been the icing on the cake. The statistics show that he drove fifty-eight Grand Prix for us in three years and managed only one podium, when finishing third at the European Grand Prix on the street circuit at Valencia in 2012.

Michael may have come back hoping to add to his incredible tally of race wins and pole positions, but it was not to be. For the first time in his career, he was outdriven in 2010 and 2011 by his teammate in almost every category that he and Nico could be compared. Michael mainly lost out to Nico when it came to low-speed corner technique, not on the high-speed sectors where commitment in the cockpit has to be exemplary, which was a feature of his driving that he never lost – you could never say he had become old and scared like some who stuck around too long.

There is no doubt that Michael made more mistakes than he would have done early on, principally because – even for a man of his pedigree – the situation was high pressure and he did not have a car capable of winning. We had come back as a Mercedes works team for the first time since the 1950s; in Michael Schumacher we had brought back a legend of the sport to rank alongside Ayrton Senna, Jackie Stewart or Jim Clark, and we had won the world championship the year before. We wanted to win so desperately and Michael had been used to winning with Ross, so there was an expectation that the combination of Ross Brawn, Michael and Mercedes would dominate, but we didn't.

Possibly we benefitted from those three seasons more than Michael did, especially early on. Although we never finished higher than fourth in the constructors' ranking and both our drivers were stuck in the lower reaches of the top ten, the impact of having the world championship-winning team together with a former world championship-winning driver was a PR and commercial dream come true. Michael clearly wanted to do it because he still wanted to drive, but I do think that it was more strategically beneficial to the team than to him and his hopes of finishing off his career in style.

The slightly counter-intuitive aspect to Michael's performance at Mercedes was that he saved his best until last: the 2012 season when he was forty-three years old. For the first time in that battle with Nico, he equalled him in qualifying over the season, with each being ahead of the other in ten races, and Schumacher achieving a slightly faster average lap time in qualifying and fractionally higher average grid positions as a result. Although his race performance in 2012 was disappointing and was badly affected by seven retirements, the stats show that Michael was still quick right to the end and that he could take Nico on and beat him. Of course, Nico then turned out to be as quick as Lewis on occasion, even if Lewis was clearly ahead overall in the four seasons that they raced together. But I believe to this day that Michael would have been more than a match for Lewis if they had been around at the same time and in the same car.

Just over a year after he called it quits for a second time and we replaced him with Lewis, Michael suffered his terrible brain injury while skiing with his son near his chalet at Meribel in the French Alps. Since then Corinna and the family have kept a very tight control on information about his condition and his treatment which, I think, is a pity. There are millions of people out there who have a genuine affection for Michael, and that's not just his fans in Germany or fans of Mercedes Benz. Because of what he achieved, people would like to know about his condition; they are inquisitive and they genuinely feel for him. I do think that reporting on how he is, regardless of whether it is good news or bad news – and possibly it is bad news – is important because people can empathize with him, because they want to show that he is not alone, and because he is someone who has sustained an injury while skiing, which unfortunately happens to ordinary people every year. It is not as unusual as being injured in Formula One, for example, and I think that families of those in recovery generally react better if they know other people are in the same boat.

From what I understand, Michael's family has been able to give him the best treatment that money can buy in a specially constructed facility at the family home in Switzerland, where he is looked after by a dedicated team around the clock. I am sure that techniques and therapies have been developed and tried there over the last few years that may well help others. This could be treatment or approaches that work as well as ideas that don't. It would be helpful for his family to share how they have dealt with this challenge because there are lots of people in a similar situation who would probably find it beneficial to have that first-hand experience.

The last time I spoke to Michael – and it is really ironic – he was providing me with a bit of advice based on his experience on what I should and should not do when buying a place on the slopes. He told me the most important thing was not to buy – as he had done – a chalet that was too low on the mountain where the snow was not reliable for skiing all through the season.

# CHAPTER EIGHTEEN

# THE LONG ROAD TO HIRING LEWIS HAMILTON

Lewis Hamilton is an exceptional driver who stands comparison with the greats of motorsport and of Formula One, and whose stellar career is vindicating all the early optimism about his prospects that I and many others felt when he made his debut in 2007.

He first zipped up a Mercedes Grand Prix driving suit in the build-up to the 2013 season and since then he has added four world championships to his maiden title with McLaren in 2008. But how he got into a silver arrow is a story that goes back to 2006, long before the wider world had ever heard of Lewis Hamilton, the famous F1 driver, and the year *before* he was given his first race drive in Formula One by what was then McLaren Mercedes.

At the age of twenty-one, Lewis was well on his way to winning the GP2 championship via some thrilling battles with the young German driver Timo Glock and Nelson Piquet Jnr. Lewis was fast, aggressive, fluent under pressure and he knew how to win. Everyone could see that he was a tremendous talent who was capable of stunning skill behind the wheel, but it wasn't clear at that stage whether McLaren was going to give him the drive or not.

Anthony Hamilton had managed his son's career all the way through karting and then through the lower formulae, and he was convinced that Lewis was good enough to earn a drive so he was touting around for potential alternatives to McLaren should the Woking-based outfit fail to deliver. Anthony was a familiar face in the paddock and had a reputation as a sharp deal-maker for his son. His discreet (and not so discreet) enquiries for Lewis may have been an attempt to apply some leverage on McLaren while they weighed whether he should get a race drive or the much lesser role of reserve or test driver in 2007.

Ron Dennis, the McLaren team principal, was worried about rushing ahead. He was concerned that Lewis might still be too young and unexposed to cope with the unique pressures of Formula One. And Ron knew better than anybody that there is an enormous gulf between the relative backwater of GP2 racing – which was staged on the undercard at F1 weekends – and the cauldron-like test of the highest formula in the sport.

Indeed, there were questions marks over Lewis in those days. Everyone could see he was exceptionally gifted, but throughout his karting and early open-wheel career he'd always had the best equipment. How good would he be in a car that wasn't the best? And was he good enough to be a great Formula One driver? In all sports, greatness is an unstoppable force that always finds a way to shine through. In motorsport, think of Ayrton Senna driving a Toleman: a virtuoso driver in a dreadful car who could nevertheless produce the goods, as he did when clawing his way through the field in the wet at Monaco at only his sixth Formula One race in 1984. Would Lewis be able to do that?

Of course, Lewis would also have to cope with the extra pressure of being the first black driver in F1 history, and there was some concern at McLaren about how he would handle the media attention that this would bring.

While Ron was still mulling it over, I was clear in my own mind. What I had seen of Lewis on the track, and my impression of him as a self-possessed young man out of the car, was enough to remove the doubts: if McLaren was going to pass, we had to be ready to pounce.

I first met Lewis and Anthony at Gil de Ferran's place in Oxford during the 2006 mid-season Formula One summer break. Gil was the sporting director of Honda F1 and an amiable ex-driver who was well connected in motor racing and had been helpful in hiring and contacting other drivers. A former Indianapolis 500 winner, Gil knew how drivers thought and what the world looked like from behind the visor, and he was respected and trusted by the youngsters coming through.

That night it was just Anthony, Lewis, me and Gil – and Gil cooked pasta for us. I remember a young-looking and polite Lewis saying little, referring to me as 'Mr Fry' and leaving Anthony to do the talking as I set out our interest. I made it clear that if McLaren did not offer Lewis a drive for 2007 then we would like to have a chance. Anthony told me that if McLaren hesitated and Lewis was left on the sidelines then they were contractually free to go elsewhere. Whether that was true or not, or whether it was all just wishful thinking, I still have no idea.

A few weeks later Gil and I met Anthony at a hotel during a Formula One race weekend and presented him with a 'what if?' proposal. This was the bare bones of a contract, set out on a single sheet of paper, that we would offer Lewis to drive for our team the following year. It was a three-year deal with relatively small numbers on it by F1 standards, offering him a basic salary of around £1 million a season. This was in line with contracts for good young drivers at the time and it included bonuses for championship points scored, or races won, or a combination of the two.

In those situations you always play to the sense of invincibility that all up-and-coming drivers seem to have and you say: 'OK, it's a million basic, but if you win a race it will be a million more, and if you win a championship we will give you several million on top of that.' Nearly all drivers at that level – and Lewis was no different – think they are the best, so if you give them a fairly sizeable upside, they believe that they can achieve it, whether that's true or not.

There was, of course, a competitive element in trying to prise Lewis away from McLaren. It would have been good to put one over on the opposition and it would have been one in the eye for Ron Dennis. I saw the opportunity to weaken McLaren by acquiring what we realized was one of their key resources, even if they seemed to be struggling to see it that way themselves.

In retrospect, I have often wondered why Ron Dennis was prevaricating. Undoubtedly he enjoyed the attention he was getting in being seen to be making up his mind amid growing press speculation that Lewis would be making his debut in 2007. But there is another element to it. McLaren, along with Ferrari, were the royalty of the Formula One paddock and, in their position, they would not normally give a race seat to a rookie because it is a big step and a big risk. When you have sponsors like Marlboro or Vodafone, they expect results, which is why teams continue with old and often unspectacular number-two drivers for years – men like Kimi after his championship-winning year, or Felipe – because they can be assured of pretty decent results from them.

After the meeting at Gil's house, the first proper contact with Lewis's camp was some years later, in 2011, when Simon Fuller was Lewis's manager. By then Lewis was a force to be reckoned with. As everyone knows, McLaren *did* give him the race seat, and his 2007 rookie season had been dazzling – with nine consecutive podium finishes and four race wins – before he went on to secure his first title in 2008. Since then, however, he had had to settle for fourth and fifth places as McLaren struggled to match the dominance of Red Bull and as Sebastian Vettel went on a run of four consecutive championship titles.

Simon and I had already worked together with Honda in 2007 and 2008, and he and I got on well. In the early summer of 2011 we were both in New York and we met up at the Plaza Hotel for a family lunch. There was Simon and me, his wife Natalie Swanston and their daughter and nanny and my wife and son. We had a couple of Bloody Marys and then after lunch retired to Simon's apartment overlooking Central Park. It was there that he raised the subject of Lewis's future. I indicated my continuing interest in a driver who had more than fulfilled his early promise and was already getting frustrated at not having machinery at McLaren to contend for another world championship.

The next encounter was a bit like something from a spy movie. Simon and I met in central London in the summer of 2012 and walked around Green Park in the sunshine while his wife and children were playing nearby. We sat in a couple of rented deckchairs to talk about what might be. While all around us office workers were enjoying their sandwiches, we quietly discussed bringing Lewis Hamilton to Mercedes, one of the biggest moves in international sport. At that stage the conversation was not about Lewis the racing driver or his salary, but much more about the opportunities Simon wanted to see to further augment Lewis's fame around the world once he was working for Mercedes.

It was clear that relationships were very poor at McLaren, not just between Lewis and the team but also between Simon and the team. Formula One looked down on Simon and regarded him suspiciously, and that was true of both Bernie and Ron Dennis. Here was a showbiz impresario who had made his name promoting the Spice Girls and who was putting his size-nines into an elite sporting environment that was run by someone else. In Bernie's eyes, Simon was variously a threat or an irritant or both. Ron took a similar view, being used to driver-managers who were brought up in car racing with a background and perspective that was closely aligned with the teams' objectives. Someone from pop music was a real curveball. To a Formula One purist like Ron, dealing with Simon on the subject of Lewis's future was not what he would have expected or considered appropriate.

But despite the tensions with McLaren, Simon was incredibly professional throughout. His job as a manager, he said, was to lay out for Lewis the alternatives; he would negotiate the best deals that he could and then it would be up to Lewis to decide what he wanted. Anthony wasn't a factor at that stage, having handed over all the strategic decision-making about his son's career to Lewis and his advisers.

Initially I couldn't get Mercedes on board with hiring Lewis. More than once we were sent back to come up with other ideas. For whatever reason, we were told to look at people like Nick Heidfeld again, who was super-keen to get the seat, and repeatedly texted me with photos of himself, his family and his dog in a futile bid to pique my interest.

We looked at Paul di Resta then driving for Force India. I also received an impassioned call from Jacques Villeneuve, of all people, who bent my ear about how wonderful he would be and how he could still drive fast after three years out of Formula One in NASCAR. Jacques did not impress me either in the car or out of it when driving for BAR Honda and, given our past history, I struggled to keep a straight face on the other end of the line. Once bitten, there was no way we were going to consider Jacques.

So we kept coming back to Lewis. Yet we never got a particularly positive reaction whenever we sent our recommendation to Dieter Zetsche, although we would not hear it directly from him. Our go-between was Norbert, who never seemed to want to discuss Lewis. I think he was afraid to go to his bosses and ask for the amount of money we would need for Hamilton, which we all knew was going to be around the £30 million-a-year mark. Perhaps there was stuff that had happened in the past that we didn't know about but, whatever it was, Norbert seemed reluctant to make a strong proposal for Lewis.

It was extremely frustrating, given the amount of time and effort I had put into cultivating first Lewis and Anthony and then Simon. On top of that, the alternatives were so poor by comparison that I could not bring myself to take any other candidate seriously. Comparing Nick Heidfeld to Lewis was like comparing someone down the local gym to Mohammad Ali.

The breakthrough came after about six months of stasis when Niki Lauda was appointed non-executive chairman of the Mercedes team. This was long after we had concluded that Michael Schumacher would not be in either of our cars for the 2013 season. On his first day in the job at the end of September 2012, Niki came to see me in my office at Brackley. I told him where we had got to with Lewis and Simon and about the logjam with Mercedes. Niki, a no-nonsense Austrian who always spoke his mind and who was all-or-nothing about everything he did in life, simply said: 'Nick, go and do it and I will ask Mercedes for forgiveness later.'

I thought: 'That's brilliant. Thank God for Niki,' and immediately set to work to try and make it happen.

Simon had made it clear to me that he was very keen for Lewis to join us. But he had to appear disinterested and not allow his poor relationship with Ron to influence Lewis one way or another.

Even at this stage, it was not an easy decision for Lewis. He had been associated with McLaren since 1998, when he had been selected to join its young driver programme, and Ron had been almost a father figure to him as he went about learning his trade at Woking. In the end it would have to be his own decision to leave. That said, Simon's relations with Ron were so poor that I suspect that, if Lewis had stayed at McLaren, Simon and his company would have been forced to resign from their management contract with him.

The straw that broke the camel's back and finally prompted a decision from Lewis came when Ron caught wind of what was going on and tried, in a very ham-fisted way, to stop him from leaving. According to a report by Jonathan McEvoy in the *Daily Mail*, Dennis flew in his private jet to Stuttgart to see Dieter Zetsche at Mercedes in the autumn of 2012, by which time Zetsche had come on board with the decision to hire Lewis.

According to McEvoy, Dennis made various claims about Lewis's behaviour and suggested to the Daimler chief executive that hiring him would lead to a PR and media backlash against Mercedes. In the course of their discussions, Dennis referred to a story in *The Sun* newspaper a year earlier about how Hamilton had partied into the early hours with ten women. After clubbing with the American rapper J Cole, he had then taken the girls and some male friends to London's Mayfair Hotel. There seemed to be a whiff of scandal about this, but Hamilton's camp brushed the episode off, with sources close to him saying at the time that 'nothing untoward' had occurred.

Ron's initiative backfired spectacularly. Far from being deterred, Dieter rang Ross and explained what he had been told. Ross then came hotfoot to my office and told me. And I rang Simon and told him. I also briefed Lewis's lawyer, Sue Thackeray, knowing that that would be enough to light the blue touchpaper. By the Singapore Grand Prix in 2012, we had pretty much finalized the contract and it was signed a few weeks later.

Yet the deal was tinged with uncertainty right to the end because Mercedes was unhappy with the amount of money involved. All the teams were benchmarking themselves against the remuneration of Fernando Alonso, who was reputedly getting £30 million a season at Ferrari. If that was the going rate, we knew we would have to pay Lewis that. But the Mercedes senior management balked at paying so much. The company stumped up around 90 per cent of the total, leaving us short by £3–4 million. Mercedes was adamant; it was not going to go any further. It fell to me to persuade Petronas to cough up the difference and I met their executives at the Singapore Grand Prix to discuss it.

Simon was in Los Angeles, I was in Singapore and my Mercedes counterparts were in Stuttgart. I spent a long time on the phone. We agreed to give Petronas some more advertising stickers on the car in return for the cash. But Petronas also wanted to be able to use Lewis and Nico's images to promote its fuels and oils. That presented no problem with Nico, whose image rights we owned, so we could pretty much tell him what to do. I had to negotiate Lewis's image rights with Simon, and thankfully I was able to persuade him that it would be good for Lewis and that we should give this to Petronas.

There was one final twist in this tale, just before the deal was finally sewn up. As is often the case in big companies when an exciting deal is nearing completion, everyone tries to get involved and take some credit. In this instance it was Niki, who intervened for the second time in this affair – this time to not such good effect.

For reasons only he knows, maybe through a misunder-standing or a misguided effort to move the deal along, Niki took it upon himself to call Simon in Los Angeles some days before all the loose ends were tied off, and told him the deal was done, assuring him that Mercedes had delivered the money. The problem was that Simon knew full well that the money had still not been confirmed and the internal Mercedes negotiation was still ongoing, because he was talk-ing to me on a daily basis.

Simon was furious. I had never experienced him losing his temper but that night he rang me in Singapore and he was screaming down the phone.

'Tell Lauda it's off. And you can tell them all to fuck off – the deal is off!' he thundered.

Simon was apoplectic because he thought Niki had misled him. It also didn't help that Niki had pulled him out of an important dinner party to do it.

While tempers were cooling, I managed to finally nail down all the financial arrangements when waiting to board my plane back to London from Singapore. I had left before the Grand Prix started, which was not unusual, but I was far more interested in getting this piece of business done than in what happened on the track. We had a good chance of getting Lewis Hamilton in a Mercedes for at least three years starting in 2013. It was a seriously exciting prospect.

Ross arranged to see Lewis at what was supposed to be a low-key meeting in London to underline the importance of driving for a team that produced its own engines. Ross found it hilarious when Lewis turned up at a central London hotel at the wheel of a garishly coloured supercar with an exhaust system loud enough to wake up half of the West End.

Lewis fully understood that having a works engine – one designed and produced by the team itself – and driving for Mercedes Benz was going to be the future, especially with the complex energy recovery systems involved in the cars at that time to recycle exhaust gasses and create extra power and acceleration. It underlines that Lewis's stellar career in Formula One has not been just about being super-quick on the track but also about picking the right strategic options out of the car. This is something that surely cannot be said of Fernando Alonso, who was never able to get himself in the right car at the right time after his last world championship-winning season in 2006.

Lewis's career at Mercedes has been nothing short of breath-taking. After finishing fourth in 2013, he has since been on a dazzling run of success, winning the world championship in 2014 and 2015, finishing second behind Nico in 2016, and then winning again in 2017 and 2018.

It has been a classic case of the right driver in the right car at the right time. Good for him.

# LOOKING BACK ON A SPORTING FAIRY TALE

My time as chief executive of the Mercedes Formula One team came to an end in March 2013 when I handed over responsibilities for the commercial side of the operation to Toto Wolff, who had taken over from Norbert Haug as director of the team's motorsports activity a few weeks earlier. It was an entirely amicable split and I stayed on as a consultant to Mercedes for another eighteen months. But it brought to an end my career in Formula One that had started eleven years earlier when I was appointed managing director of BAR Honda.

We were second in the constructors' championship in 2004 and since then I had seen Honda take over as a constructor, we had achieved our first race win with Jenson in 2006, and then completed the remarkable journey in 2009 as Brawn GP came into being and achieved victories in both the drivers' and constructors' championships. During my final couple of seasons I had seen the Mercedes team grow and develop as it battled to get to the front of the grid in a period when Red Bull, led by designer Adrian Newey and driver Sebastian Vettel, were untouchable with four successive championships.

We needed to adapt to meet the Red Bull challenge – and getting Lewis into one of our cars was my last major project, which came to fruition six months before I left.

Ross stayed on after my departure, but the changing of the guard continued as he too decided to leave at the end of the 2013 season when Mercedes finished second in the constructors' championship, with Lewis fourth and Nico sixth. Also leaving at the same time was Jock Clear who went to Ferrari in what may eventually prove to be a thorn in Mercedes's side.

Since then the team – still based in our old factory at Brackley – has surpassed even Red Bull's earlier dominance, winning the drivers' and constructors' every year from 2014 to 2018 and turning Lewis into a legend of the sport.

People sometimes compare what we achieved in 2009 to Leicester City's remarkable victory in the English Premier League in 2015–16. That is widely regarded as the biggest shock in British sporting history. There are some parallels – we were both rank outsiders at the start of the campaign (Leicester were 5,000-1; we were 150-1), we had both endured woeful seasons the previous year, and both achievements had an almost other-worldly feel about them. In both teams people felt that something unbelievable was happening that seemed to have an energy and logic all of its own.

Yet, in one respect, you could argue that what we achieved was even more unlikely than what Leicester's squad under Claudio Ranieri managed. Remember, we weren't just competing in a Formula One season in 2009; we were also fighting for our lives as a business, trying to find new owners and new sponsors, having to cut our workforce dramatically to survive, and even having to change the design of our car at the last minute to accommodate a new engine. The rulebook says you can only win at this level if you are focused 100 per cent on winning; however, we managed to pull it off while fighting fires on a whole series of other fronts at the same time.

There is always an element of myth about these types of sporting sagas that tend to develop and become embellished as the years go by. Looking back on how we did it, I would argue that, by the end of 2008, we had got to a point where we had almost all the building blocks in place to reach the top and so not even the abrupt decision by Honda to pull out could stop the forces we unleashed. We had superb facilities in the wind tunnel and machine shop built with Honda money, we had excellent people in key roles in both engineering and design, and – most important of all – in Ross we had a conductor of the orchestra who knew how to get us all playing the right music in the same key.

Bringing in someone like Ross and installing him almost as your boss might be emotionally difficult for some people, but I saw it in black-and-white terms: either we did it or we would continue along a path of mediocrity. To win, you have to be able to take difficult decisions, whether it be about drivers, designers or managers. We did it. I'm not sure the Toyota Formula One operation ever faced up to this.

On top of all that, *luckily* we failed in our attempt to persuade Honda to continue supplying us with their race engines for 2009 and instead we ended up with one of the most potent power plants in Formula One made by Mercedes Benz. That was an incredible stroke of good fortune. In fact, if there was a low point in that season for me, it was when we realized that we would not be using Honda power. At that stage, we knew we were going to have to redesign the back of our car to fit a 'foreign' power plant, and the balance and aerodynamic detailing would have to be reworked in a matter of weeks to get to the start of the first race in Australia. I was always up for a challenge, but I thought 'this is getting out of hand'. How wrong I was – and gloriously so.

If that was a nadir, the opening race in Australia was the opposite. This was when we acquired momentum that would take us through to what became an almost unassailable lead for Jenson after seven races. We turned up in Melbourne short of testing time, with only a partial understanding of the performance of our car and with very little experience to go on in terms of its reliability. We were quite prepared for the possibility that both Rubens and Jenson would not make the full distance. But that day in Albert Park went like a dream and it gave us that precious commodity: belief. Finishing one and two gave us confidence to push on through all the challenges we faced, which included operating with almost no spare cash, trying to find sponsors on a race-by-race basis, finding a new owner and fighting in the uncertain Formula One legal system for our right to use a rear diffuser that was a class above the rest.

Within the team there was definitely a coming-together and a sense of purpose that I had not seen before. The redundancies undoubtedly focused minds; Ross's inspiring leadership got people working with renewed vigour and, once we went racing, the sheer excitement – not to say preposterousness – of what we were achieving drove us all on. We were all in it together, a principle underlined by Ross's decision to share out podium appearances among team members.

At the director level, everyone played a blinder all season long – we took our opportunities and worked our luck to the point where it is hard to look back and see even one example of where we missed the boat. There was no time for egos either, and that went for Ross and me too. In a paddock notorious for its egomaniacs, I think it is fair to say we ranked pretty low on that score.

The confidence element was remarkable in itself because, once we felt its positive influence, we started to play way above our normal range of performance. The best evidence for this is a letter I found during my research for this book. Ross and I had written to Dieter Zetsche, the top man at Mercedes Benz, at a time when the company was prevaricating over whether or not to buy us. The letter comes over now as presumptuous and arrogant in the extreme. As the managers of a small Formula One team that had been hanging on by its fingertips, we had penned a note to a very important person saying in effect: 'make up your mind or we'll go elsewhere.'

Actually, I'm not sure it was arrogance; it was just what needed to be done and I think we looked at these things in a very objective way. If it was a part of the car that wasn't working, we would change it. If a deal was taking time, we hurried it along or played up the alternatives. I think once we started hitting sixes, to use a cricketing analogy, we got into the mindset of approaching everything in the same way. 'There's a problem; what are we going to do? Get on with it. Whack...'

It's all about impetus and momentum. As soon as you start to win, you start to get on a roll. What other explanation is there for how we managed, in the course of nine or ten months, to go from looking over the edge of the precipice to winning eight races and coming first and second in four of them, winning both world championships, signing – after Marlboro – probably the biggest sponsorship deal in Formula One, getting one of the biggest and best-known companies in racing to invest in us and finally to employ – whichever way you look at Michael – one of the icons of F1 history?

On the sporting side, the big challenge was always going to be how the team coped when our performance level dropped and the opposition started to catch us up. When this duly happened, from the British Grand Prix onwards, there were certainly moments of doubt and feelings that we were slipping and needed to find a way to stop it, but in general we kept our heads down and kept chipping away.

I think our years of being in the Formula One doghouse prepared us well and hardened us. We knew what it felt like to be at the back of the grid and we had no plans to start heading in that direction. Jenson may have dropped off in a big way, but he never stopped scoring points and only failed to finish once. Rubens kept him honest with his own impressive performances on the other side of the garage, and in the design race we kept our heads above water, despite having far smaller resources to spend on the car than our main rivals.

I have mentioned Ross's inspirational leadership already but another quality in him was key. He is famous for being calm in a crisis – you only have to look at television coverage of the Grand Prix at Interlagos to see that. While everyone else was on the edge of their seats and could barely watch, Ross was his usual composed, logical self. This was just the type of sporting leadership we needed when the pressure came on us in the design race and on the track as the season unfolded.

But ultimately, I would argue, the reason why we won was because the overall level of teamwork was sensational. If there was a secret ingredient it was the rather unglamorous one that every single person did their own job well and helped their colleagues to do their jobs well too.

From a business perspective, I guess our experience of fire-fighting and winning at the same time underlines a simple lesson: if you've got twenty problems facing you simultaneously, don't let them overwhelm you, take them on one at a time. That is a skill that works in any setting. In our situation it was a case of 'let's just be pragmatic, understand where we are and what needs to be done, and then start methodically working through all the issues in a fairly unemotional fashion, get them behind us and move on to the next one.' Sounds simple. It can be if you keep your head.

My favourite memory of that charmed season will always be the race in Monaco. Not the race itself, which passed me by in a blur, but what happened afterwards. Being clapped into the Sporting Club alongside Prince Albert and then, later that night, watching Jenson, wide-eyed as the fireworks lit up the sky over the opened roof above our dinner table. We were only a third of the way through the season at that point, but the feeling we all had that night was: 'Wow. We have done this. We have arrived – we are at the top of our game in one of the world's most difficult sports. Bring it on.'

And what of Formula One?

Since 2009, the world championship has been dominated by Mercedes and Lewis Hamilton. In the last five years every race has been won by Mercedes, Ferrari or Red Bull. These three teams enjoy the lion's share of the profits of Formula One and also have huge budgets provided by owners and sponsors. Mercedes F1 now employs nearly a thousand people in the design and build of their race cars and at least half as many again in the design and manufacture of their engines. The limits on team expenditure proposed by Max Mosley in 2009 have so far failed to materialize. His successor as FIA president, Jean Todt, has been unwilling to use the autocratic powers deployed by Max and Bernie for the sport's benefit. As a result the top teams remain focused with laser-like intensity on winning, and the future of the sport is low on their list of priorities.

Those who argue that Formula One has always been dominated for lengthy periods by a single team or driver, resulting in processional races (as many were in 2009), fail to acknowledge that most other sports – including football, rugby and especially cricket – have moved on and now provide a much more entertaining offering than they used to.

Worse still, while Formula One has failed to improve and evolve, the external threats to it have grown ever more potent. The rapid move towards electric and autonomous road vehicles is threatening to leave F1 on the wrong side of history and to undermine its role as a showcase for the major car manufacturers.

Rightly, in my view, Bernie was always somewhat dismissive of the voice of the car manufacturers, understanding that their participation in the sport would end the day it did not meet their needs. That time is drawing closer and Formula One may soon have to continue without the same level of support from huge multinationals that have underpinned it for years.

The choices are stark: move with the times towards electric power or switch to an entertainment-based formula that will appeal to new audiences and especially younger people. Either way, Formula One looks likely to again be dominated by independent teams of the size and scale of Brawn GP.

# CAST OF CHARACTERS

*Listed in order of appearance and with job titles or roles in 2009 as featured in the text*

Jenson Button, racing driver, Brawn GP

Ross Brawn, team principal, Brawn GP

Rubens Barrichello, racing driver, Brawn GP

Sebastian Vettel, racing driver, Red Bull Racing

Robert Kubica, racing driver, BMW Sauber F1 Team

Nico Rosberg, racing driver, AT&T Williams

Felipe Massa, racing driver, Scuderia Ferrari Marlboro

Kimi Raikkonen, racing driver, Scuderia Ferrari Marlboro

Mark Webber, racing driver, Red Bull Racing

Nick Heidfeld, racing driver, BMW Sauber F1 Team

Heikki Kovalainen, racing driver, Vodafone McLaren Mercedes

Richard Branson, founder, Virgin Group

Lewis Hamilton, racing driver, Vodafone McLaren Mercedes

Kate Fry, wife of Nick Fry

Adrian Newey, chief designer, Red Bull Racing

Hiroshi Oshima, chief operating officer, Honda Motor Company

Nigel Kerr, financial director, Brawn GP

Caroline McGrory, legal director, Brawn GP

John Marsden, human resources director, Brawn GP

Fernando Alonso, racing driver, ING Renault F1 Team

Jean Brawn, wife of Ross Brawn

Ron Meadows, sporting director, Brawn GP

Joerg Xander, head of chassis engineering, Brawn GP

Graham Miller, operations manager, Brawn GP

Luca di Montezemolo, chairman of Ferrari

Michael Schumacher, racing driver, Mercedes GP Petronas
    F1 Team

John Howlett, team principal, Panasonic Toyota Racing

Ron Dennis, team principal/chairman, Vodafone McLaren
    Mercedes

Martin Whitmarsh, chief operating officer, Vodafone
    McLaren Mercedes

Richard Goddard, Jenson's manager

Andrew Shovlin, Jenson's race engineer

Loïc Bigois, head of aerodynamics, Brawn GP

James Vowles, chief race strategist, Brawn GP

Simon Cole, chief race engineer, Brawn GP

Richard Burns, former World Rally Champion

Jock Clear, Rubens's race engineer

Vijay Mallya, team principal, Force India F1 Team

Bernie Ecclestone, commercial rights holder, Formula One

Achilleas Kallakis, Britain's biggest-ever mortgage fraudster

Carlos Slim, Mexican telecommunications billionaire

Sir Jackie Stewart, three-time Formula One world champion

Marcus Evans, owner of Ipswich Town football club

Alex Tai, director of special projects, Virgin Group

Tom Bower, author of biographies of Richard Branson

Gordon Blair, corporate restructuring expert

Eddie Jordan, former eponymous team owner

Jean Todt, team principal, Scuderia Ferrari Marlboro

Dieter Zetsche, chief executive of Daimler

Shuhei Nakamoto, senior technical director, Honda Racing
F1 Team

Geoff Willis, technical director, Honda Racing F1 Team

Takeo Fukui, chief executive and president of Honda
Motor Company

Bob Bell, technical director, AT&T Williams

Pat Symonds, chief technical officer, ING Renault F1 Team

Charlie Whiting, race director, Formula One

Graham Miller, head of operations, Honda Racing F1 Team

Ralf Schumacher, racing driver, Panasonic Toyota Racing

Atsushi Ogawa, aerodynamicist, Brawn GP

Lucien Bigois, social media executive, Brawn GP

Timo Glock, racing driver, Panasonic Toyota Racing

Flavio Briatore, team principal, ING Renault F1 Team

Max Mosley, president, FIA

Richard Woods, spin doctor to Max Mosley

Richard Berry, sponsorship manager, Brawn GP

Richard Sanders, sponsorship manager, Brawn GP

Jessica Michibata, Jenson's girlfriend

Gary Holland, mechanic and fuel-nozzle hand

Simon Arron, motorsports journalist

Frank Williams, team principal, AT&T Williams

John Button, Jenson's father

Paul Harris QC, silk representing Brawn GP

Nigel Tozzi, QC, silk representing Scuderia Ferrari
Marlboro

Kazuki Nakajima, racing driver, AT&T Williams

Christian Horner, team principal, Red Bull Racing

Adrian Sutil, racing driver, Force India F1 Team

Sébastien Buemi, racing driver, Scuderia Toro Rosso

Sébastien Bourdais, racing driver, Scuderia Toro Rosso

Jo Bauer, technical delegate, FIA

Nicola Armstrong, communications manager, Brawn GP

Alex Wurz, test driver, Brawn GP

Prince Albert and Charlene Wittstock, first couple,
    principality of Monaco

Gareth Griffith, software developer and supplier, Brawn GP

Donald Mackenzie, managing director and co-founder,
    CVC Capital Partners Group

Norbert Haug, vice-president, Mercedes Benz Motorsport

Ed Woodward, head of commercial and media operations,
    Manchester United

Tony Fernandes, founder and owner, Air Asia

Anita Aziz, marketing director, Petronas

Mike Collier, Jenson's trainer

Jules Kulpinski, Jenson's personal assistant

Chris Buncombe, Jenson's friend

Jacques Villeneuve, racing driver, BAR Honda

Takuma Sato, racing driver, BAR Honda

Romain Grosjean, racing driver, ING Renault F1 Team

Giancarlo Fisichella, racing driver, Force India F1 Team and
    Scuderia Ferrari Marlboro

Nelson Piquet Jnr, racing driver, ING Renault F1 Team

Nelson Piquet Snr, three-time Formula One world
    champion

Jonathan McEvoy, Formula One correspondent, *Daily Mail*

Craig Wilson, chief race engineer, Honda Racing F1 Team/
    head of vehicle dynamics, Brawn GP

Kamui Kobayashi, racing driver, Panasonic Toyota Racing

Ian Clatworthy, IT specialist, Brawn GP

Charlie March, owner of Goodwood House

Julian Jakobi, manager of Richard Burns

David Richards, team principal, BAR Honda

John Byfield, Jenson Button's former manager

Matt Bishop, chief communications officer, McLaren Technology Group

Brian Clarke, Michael Schumacher's lawyer

Corinna Schumacher, Michael's wife

Mick Schumacher, Michael's son

Anthony Hamilton, Lewis's father

Gil de Ferran, sporting director, Honda Racing F1 Team

Simon Fuller, manager of Lewis Hamilton

Paul di Resta, racing driver, Force India F1 Team

Niki Lauda, non-executive chairman, Mercedes GP Petronas F1 Team

Sue Thackeray, Lewis Hamilton's lawyer

Toto Wolff, executive director, Mercedes GP Petronas F1 Team

# 2009 FIA FORMULA ONE WORLD CHAMPIONSHIP RESULTS

## ROUND 1

## Australian Grand Prix, Albert Park, 29 March

Pole position: Jenson Button, 1m26.202
Fastest lap: Nico Rosberg, 1m27.706

### Points scoring positions:

| Pos. | Driver | Points |
|---|---|---|
| 1 | Jenson Button, Brawn GP | 10 |
| 2 | Rubens Barrichello, Brawn GP | 8 |
| 3 | Jarno Trulli, Panasonic Toyota Racing | 6 |
| 4 | Timo Glock, Panasonic Toyota Racing | 5 |
| 5 | Fernando Alonso, ING Renault F1 Team | 4 |
| 6 | Nico Rosberg, AT&T Williams | 3 |
| 7 | Sébastien Buemi, Scuderia Torro Rosso | 2 |
| 8 | Sébastien Bourdais, Scuderia Torro Rosso | 1 |

### Driver standings (top 8):

| | | |
|---|---|---|
| 1 | Jenson Button, Brawn GP | 10 |
| 2 | Rubens Barrichello, Brawn GP | 8 |
| 3 | Jarno Trulli, Panasonic Toyota Racing | 6 |
| 4 | Timo Glock, Panasonic Toyota Racing | 5 |
| 5 | Fernando Alonso, ING Renault F1 Team | 4 |
| 6 | Nico Rosberg, AT&T Williams | 3 |
| 7 | Sébastien Buemi, Scuderia Torro Rosso | 2 |
| 8 | Sébastien Bourdais, Scuderia Torro Rosso | 1 |

**ROUND 2**

# Malaysian Grand Prix, Sepang, 5 April

Pole position: Jenson Button, 1m35.181
Fastest lap: Jenson Button, 1m36.641

## Points scoring positions:

| Pos. | Driver | Points* |
|------|--------|---------|
| 1 | Jenson Button, Brawn GP | 5 |
| 2 | Nick Heidfeld, BMW Sauber F1 Team | 4 |
| 3 | Timo Glock, Panasonic Toyota Racing | 3 |
| 4 | Jarno Trulli, Panasonic Toyota Racing | 2.5 |
| 5 | Rubens Barrichello, Brawn GP | 2 |
| 6 | Mark Webber, Red Bull Racing | 1.5 |
| 7 | Lewis Hamilton, Vodafone McLaren Mercedes | 1 |
| 8 | Nico Rosberg, AT&T Williams | 0.5 |

\* Half points awarded due to 75% race distance not being completed.

## Driver standings (top 8):

| | | |
|------|--------|---------|
| 1 | Jenson Button, Brawn GP | 15 |
| 2 | Rubens Barrichello, Brawn GP | 10 |
| 3 | Jarno Trulli, Panasonic Toyota Racing | 8.5 |
| 4 | Timo Glock, Panasonic Toyota Racing | 8 |
| 5 | Nick Heidfeld, BMW Sauber F1 Team | 4 |
| 6 | Fernando Alonso, ING Renault F1 Team | 4 |
| 7 | Nico Rosberg, AT&T Williams | 3.5 |
| 8 | Sébastien Buemi, Scuderia Torro Rosso | 2 |

**ROUND 3**

# Chinese Grand Prix, Shanghai, 19 April

Pole position: Sebastian Vettel, 1m36.184
Fastest lap: Rubens Barrichello, 1m52.592

## Points scoring positions:

| Pos. | Driver | Points |
|------|--------|--------|
| 1 | Sebastian Vettel, Red Bull Racing | 10 |
| 2 | Mark Webber, Red Bull Racing | 8 |
| 3 | Jenson Button, Brawn GP | 6 |
| 4 | Rubens Barrichello, Brawn GP | 5 |
| 5 | Heikki Kovalainen, Vodafone McLaren Mercedes | 4 |
| 6 | Lewis Hamilton, Vodafone McLaren Mercedes | 3 |
| 7 | Timo Glock, Panasonic Toyota Racing | 2 |
| 8 | Sébastien Buemi, Scuderia Toro Rosso | 1 |

## Driver standings (top 8):

| | | |
|------|--------|--------|
| 1 | Jenson Button, Brawn GP | 21 |
| 2 | Rubens Barrichello, Brawn GP | 15 |
| 3 | Sebastian Vettel, Red Bull Racing | 10 |
| 4 | Timo Glock, Panasonic Toyota Racing | 10 |
| 5 | Mark Webber, Red Bull Racing | 9.5 |
| 6 | Jarno Trulli, Panasonic Toyota Racing | 8.5 |
| 7 | Nick Heidfeld, BMW Sauber F1 Team | 4 |
| 8 | Fernando Alonso, ING Renault F1 Team | 4 |

**ROUND 4**

# Bahrain Grand Prix, Sakhir, 26 April

Pole position: Jarno Trulli, 1m33.431
Fastest lap: Jarno Trulli, 1m34.556

## Points scoring positions:

| Pos. | Driver | Points |
|------|--------|--------|
| 1 | Jenson Button, Brawn GP | 10 |
| 2 | Sebastian Vettel, Red Bull Racing | 8 |
| 3 | Jarno Trulli, Panasonic Toyota Racing | 6 |
| 4 | Lewis Hamilton, Vodafone McLaren Mercedes | 5 |
| 5 | Rubens Barrichello, Brawn GP | 4 |
| 6 | Kimi Raikkonen, Scuderia Ferrari Marlboro | 3 |
| 7 | Timo Glock, Panasonic Toyota Racing | 2 |
| 8 | Fernando Alonso, ING Renault F1 Team | 1 |

## Driver standings (top 8):

| | | |
|------|--------|--------|
| 1 | Jenson Button, Brawn GP | 31 |
| 2 | Rubens Barrichello, Brawn GP | 19 |
| 3 | Sebastian Vettel, Red Bull Racing | 18 |
| 4 | Jarno Trulli, Panasonic Toyota Racing | 14.5 |
| 5 | Timo Glock, Panasonic Toyota Racing | 12 |
| 6 | Mark Webber, Red Bull Racing | 9.5 |
| 7 | Lewis Hamilton, Vodafone McLaren Mercedes | 8 |
| 8 | Fernando Alonso, ING Renault F1 Team | 5 |

**ROUND 5**

# Spanish Grand Prix, Catalunya, 10 May

Pole position: Jenson Button, 1m20.527
Fastest lap: Rubens Barrichello, 1m22.762

## Points scoring positions:

| Pos. | Driver | Points |
|------|--------|--------|
| 1 | Jenson Button, Brawn GP | 10 |
| 2 | Rubens Barrichello, Brawn GP | 8 |
| 3 | Mark Webber, Red Bull Racing | 6 |
| 4 | Sebastian Vettel, Red Bull Racing | 5 |
| 5 | Fernando Alonso, ING Renault F1 Team | 4 |
| 6 | Felipe Massa, Scuderia Ferrari Marlboro | 3 |
| 7 | Nick Heidfeld, BMW Sauber F1 Team | 2 |
| 8 | Nico Rosberg, AT&T Williams | 1 |

## Driver standings (top 8):

| | | |
|------|--------|--------|
| 1 | Jenson Button, Brawn GP | 41 |
| 2 | Rubens Barrichello, Brawn GP | 27 |
| 3 | Sebastian Vettel, Red Bull Racing | 23 |
| 4 | Mark Webber, Red Bull Racing | 15.5 |
| 5 | Jarno Trulli, Panasonic Toyota Racing | 14.5 |
| 6 | Timo Glock, Panasonic Toyota Racing | 12 |
| 7 | Fernando Alonso, ING Renault F1 Team | 9 |
| 8 | Lewis Hamilton, Vodafone McLaren Mercedes | 9 |

**ROUND 6**

# Monaco Grand Prix, Monte Carlo, 24 May

Pole position: Jenson Button, 1m14.902
Fastest lap: Felipe Massa, 1m15.154

## Points scoring positions:

| Pos. | Driver | Points |
|------|--------|--------|
| 1 | Jenson Button, Brawn GP | 10 |
| 2 | Rubens Barrichello, Brawn GP Formula One Team | 8 |
| 3 | Kimi Raikkonen, Scuderia Ferrari Marlboro | 6 |
| 4 | Felipe Massa, Scuderia Ferrari Marlboro | 5 |
| 5 | Mark Webber, Red Bull Racing | 4 |
| 6 | Nico Rosberg, AT&T Williams | 3 |
| 7 | Fernando Alonso, ING Renault F1 Team | 2 |
| 8 | Sébastien Bourdais, Scuderia Toro Rosso | 1 |

## Driver standings (top 8):

| 1 | Jenson Button, Brawn GP | 51 |
|---|-------------------------|-----|
| 2 | Rubens Barrichello, Brawn GP | 35 |
| 3 | Sebastian Vettel, Red Bull Racing | 23 |
| 4 | Mark Webber, Red Bull Racing | 19.5 |
| 5 | Jarno Trulli, Panasonic Toyota Racing | 14.5 |
| 6 | Timo Glock, Panasonic Toyota Racing | 12 |
| 7 | Fernando Alonso, ING Renault F1 Team | 11 |
| 8 | Lewis Hamilton, Vodafone McLaren Mercedes | 9 |

**ROUND 7**

# Turkish Grand Prix, Istanbul Park, 7 June

Pole position: Sebastian Vettel, 1m28.316
Fastest lap: Jenson Button, 1m27.579

## Points scoring positions:

| Pos. | Driver | Points |
|------|--------|--------|
| 1 | Jenson Button, Brawn GP | 10 |
| 2 | Mark Webber, Red Bull Racing | 8 |
| 3 | Sebastian Vettel, Red Bull Racing | 6 |
| 4 | Jarno Trulli, Panasonic Toyota Racing | 5 |
| 5 | Nico Rosberg, AT&T Williams | 4 |
| 6 | Felipe Massa, Scuderia Ferrari Marlboro | 3 |
| 7 | Robert Kubica, BMW Sauber F1 Team | 2 |
| 8 | Timo Glock, Panasonic Toyota Racing | 1 |

## Driver standings (top 8):

| | | |
|------|--------|--------|
| 1 | Jenson Button, Brawn GP | 61 |
| 2 | Rubens Barrichello, Brawn GP | 35 |
| 3 | Sebastian Vettel, Red Bull Racing | 29 |
| 4 | Mark Webber, Red Bull Racing | 27.5 |
| 5 | Jarno Trulli, Panasonic Toyota Racing | 19.5 |
| 6 | Timo Glock, Panasonic Toyota Racing | 13 |
| 7 | Fernando Alonso, ING Renault F1 Team | 11 |
| 8 | Felipe Massa, Scuderia Ferrari Marlboro | 11 |

**ROUND 8**

# British Grand Prix, Silverstone, 21 June

Pole position: Sebastian Vettel, 1m19.509
Fastest lap: Sebastian Vettel, 1m20.735

## Points scoring positions:

| Pos. | Driver | Points |
|------|--------|--------|
| 1 | Sebastian Vettel, Red Bull Racing | 10 |
| 2 | Mark Webber, Red Bull Racing | 8 |
| 3 | Rubens Barrichello, Brawn GP | 6 |
| 4 | Felipe Massa, Scuderia Ferrari Marlboro | 5 |
| 5 | Nico Rosberg, AT&T Williams | 4 |
| 6 | Jenson Button, Brawn GP | 3 |
| 7 | Jarno Trulli, Panasonic Toyota Racing | 2 |
| 8 | Kimi Raikkonen, Scuderia Ferrari Marlboro | 1 |

## Driver standings (top 8):

| | | |
|------|--------|--------|
| 1 | Jenson Button, Brawn GP | 64 |
| 2 | Rubens Barrichello, Brawn GP | 41 |
| 3 | Sebastian Vettel, Red Bull Racing | 39 |
| 4 | Mark Webber, Red Bull Racing | 35.5 |
| 5 | Jarno Trulli, Panasonic Toyota Racing | 21.5 |
| 6 | Felipe Massa, Scuderia Ferrari Marlboro | 16 |
| 7 | Timo Glock, Panasonic Toyota Racing | 13 |
| 8 | Nico Rosberg, AT&T Williams | 11.5 |

**ROUND 9**

# German Grand Prix, Nürburgring, 12 July

Pole position: Mark Webber, 1m32.230
Fastest lap: Fernando Alonso, 1m33.365

## Points scoring positions:

| Pos. | Driver | Points |
|------|--------|--------|
| 1 | Mark Webber, Red Bull Racing | 10 |
| 2 | Sebastian Vettel, Red Bull Racing | 8 |
| 3 | Felipe Massa, Scuderia Ferrari Marlboro | 6 |
| 4 | Nico Rosberg, AT&T Williams | 5 |
| 5 | Jenson Button, Brawn GP | 4 |
| 6 | Rubens Barrichello, Brawn GP | 3 |
| 7 | Fernando Alonso, ING Renault F1 Team | 2 |
| 8 | Heikki Kovalainen, Vodafone McLaren Mercedes | 1 |

## Driver standings (top 8):

| | | |
|------|--------|--------|
| 1 | Jenson Button, Brawn GP | 68 |
| 2 | Sebastian Vettel, Red Bull Racing | 47 |
| 3 | Mark Webber, Red Bull Racing | 45.5 |
| 4 | Rubens Barrichello, Brawn GP | 44 |
| 5 | Felipe Massa, Scuderia Ferrari Marlboro | 22 |
| 6 | Jarno Trulli, Panasonic Toyota Racing | 21.5 |
| 7 | Nico Rosberg, AT&T Williams | 16.5 |
| 8 | Timo Glock, Panasonic Toyota Racing | 13 |

## ROUND 10

# Hungarian Grand Prix, Hungaroring, 26 July

Pole position: Fernando Alonso, 1m21.569
Fastest lap: Mark Webber, 1m21.931

### Points scoring positions:

| Pos. | Driver | Points |
|------|--------|--------|
| 1 | Lewis Hamilton, Vodafone McLaren Mercedes | 10 |
| 2 | Kimi Raikkonen, Scuderia Ferrari Marlboro | 8 |
| 3 | Mark Webber, Red Bull Racing | 6 |
| 4 | Nico Rosberg, AT&T Williams | 5 |
| 5 | Heikki Kovalainen, Vodafone McLaren Mercedes | 4 |
| 6 | Timo Glock, Panasonic Toyota Racing | 3 |
| 7 | Jenson Button, Brawn GP | 2 |
| 8 | Jarno Trulli, Panasonic Toyota Racing | 1 |

### Driver standings (top 8):

| | | |
|------|--------|--------|
| 1 | Jenson Button, Brawn GP | 70 |
| 2 | Mark Webber, Red Bull Racing | 51.5 |
| 3 | Sebastian Vettel, Red Bull Racing | 47 |
| 4 | Rubens Barrichello, Brawn GP | 44 |
| 5 | Jarno Trulli, Panasonic Toyota Racing | 22.5 |
| 6 | Felipe Massa, Scuderia Ferrari Marlboro | 22 |
| 7 | Nico Rosberg, AT&T Williams | 21.5 |
| 8 | Kimi Raikkonen, Scuderia Ferrari Marlboro | 18 |

**ROUND 11**

# European Grand Prix, Valencia Street Circuit, 23 August

Pole position: Lewis Hamilton, 1m39.498
Fastest lap: Timo Glock, 1m38.683

## Points scoring positions:

| Pos. | Driver | Points |
|------|--------|--------|
| 1 | Rubens Barrichello, Brawn GP | 10 |
| 2 | Lewis Hamilton, Vodafone McLaren Mercedes | 8 |
| 3 | Kimi Raikkonen, Scuderia Ferrari Marlboro | 6 |
| 4 | Heikki Kovalainen, Vodafone McLaren Mercedes | 5 |
| 5 | Nico Rosberg, AT&T Williams | 4 |
| 6 | Fernando Alonso, ING Renault F1 Team | 3 |
| 7 | Jenson Button, Brawn GP | 2 |
| 8 | Robert Kubica, BMW Sauber F1 Team | 1 |

## Driver standings (top 8):

| | | |
|------|--------|--------|
| 1 | Jenson Button, Brawn GP | 72 |
| 2 | Rubens Barrichello, Brawn GP | 54 |
| 3 | Mark Webber, Red Bull Racing | 51.5 |
| 4 | Sebastian Vettel, Red Bull Racing | 47 |
| 5 | Lewis Hamilton, Vodafone McLaren Mercedes | 27 |
| 6 | Nico Rosberg, AT&T Williams | 25.5 |
| 7 | Kimi Raikkonen, Scuderia Ferrari Marlboro | 24 |
| 8 | Jarno Trulli, Panasonic Toyota Racing | 22.5 |

**ROUND 12**

# Belgian Grand Prix, Spa-Francorchamps, 30 August

Pole position: Giancarlo Fisichella, 1m46.308
Fastest lap: Sebastian Vettel, 1m47.263

## Points scoring positions:

| Pos. | Driver | Points |
|------|--------|--------|
| 1 | Kimi Raikkonen, Scuderia Ferrari Marlboro | 10 |
| 2 | Giancarlo Fisichella, Force India Formula One Team | 8 |
| 3 | Sebastian Vettel, Red Bull Racing | 6 |
| 4 | Robert Kubica, BMW Sauber F1 Team | 5 |
| 5 | Nick Heidfeld, BMW Sauber F1 Team | 4 |
| 6 | Heikki Kovalainen, Vodafone McLaren Mercedes | 3 |
| 7 | Rubens Barrichello, Brawn GP | 2 |
| 8 | Nico Rosberg, AT&T Williams | 1 |

## Driver standings (top 8):

| | | |
|------|--------|--------|
| 1 | Jenson Button, Brawn GP | 72 |
| 2 | Rubens Barrichello, Brawn GP | 56 |
| 3 | Sebastian Vettel, Red Bull Racing | 53 |
| 4 | Mark Webber, Red Bull Racing | 51.5 |
| 5 | Kimi Raikkonen, Scuderia Ferrari Marlboro | 34 |
| 6 | Lewis Hamilton, Vodafone McLaren Mercedes | 27 |
| 7 | Nico Rosberg, AT&T Williams | 26.5 |
| 8 | Jarno Trulli, Panasonic Toyota Racing | 22.5 |

**ROUND 13**

# Italian Grand Prix, Monza, 13 September

Pole position: Lewis Hamilton, 1m24.066
Fastest lap: Adrian Sutil, 1m24.739

## Points scoring positions:

| Pos. | Driver | Points |
|------|--------|--------|
| 1 | Rubens Barrichello, Brawn GP | 10 |
| 2 | Jenson Button, Brawn GP | 8 |
| 3 | Kimi Raikkonen, Scuderia Ferrari Marlboro | 6 |
| 4 | Adrian Sutil, Force India Formula One Team | 5 |
| 5 | Fernando Alonso, ING Renault F1 Team | 4 |
| 6 | Heikki Kovalainen, Vodafone McLaren Mercedes | 3 |
| 7 | Nick Heidfeld, BMW Sauber F1 Team | 2 |
| 8 | Sebastian Vettel, Red Bull Racing | 1 |

## Driver standings (top 8):

| | | |
|------|--------|--------|
| 1 | Jenson Button, Brawn GP | 80 |
| 2 | Rubens Barrichello, Brawn GP | 66 |
| 3 | Sebastian Vettel, Red Bull Racing | 54 |
| 4 | Mark Webber, Red Bull Racing | 51.5 |
| 5 | Kimi Raikkonen, Scuderia Ferrari Marlboro | 40 |
| 6 | Lewis Hamilton, Vodafone McLaren Mercedes | 27 |
| 7 | Nico Rosberg, AT&T Williams | 26.5 |
| 8 | Jarno Trulli, Panasonic Toyota Racing | 22.5 |

**ROUND 14**

# Singapore Grand Prix, Marina Bay, 27 September

Pole position: Lewis Hamilton, 1m47.891
Fastest lap: Fernando Alonso, 1m48.240

## Points scoring positions:

| Pos. | Driver | Points |
|---|---|---|
| 1 | Lewis Hamilton, Vodafone McLaren Mercedes | 10 |
| 2 | Timo Glock, Panasonic Toyota Racing | 8 |
| 3 | Fernando Alonso, ING Renault F1 Team | 6 |
| 4 | Sebastian Vettel, Red Bull Racing | 5 |
| 5 | Jenson Button, Brawn GP | 4 |
| 6 | Rubens Barrichello, Brawn GP | 3 |
| 7 | Heikki Kovalainen, Vodafone McLaren Mercedes | 2 |
| 8 | Robert Kubica, BMW Sauber F1 Team | 1 |

## Driver standings (top 8):

| | | |
|---|---|---|
| 1 | Jenson Button, Brawn GP | 84 |
| 2 | Rubens Barrichello, Brawn GP | 69 |
| 3 | Sebastian Vettel, Red Bull Racing | 59 |
| 4 | Mark Webber, Red Bull Racing | 51.5 |
| 5 | Kimi Raikkonen, Scuderia Ferrari Marlboro | 40 |
| 6 | Lewis Hamilton, Vodafone McLaren Mercedes | 37 |
| 7 | Nico Rosberg, AT&T Williams | 26.5 |
| 8 | Fernando Alonso, ING Renault F1 Team | 26 |

**ROUND 15**

# Japanese Grand Prix, Suzuka, 4 October

Pole position: Sebastian Vettel, 1m32.160
Fastest lap: Mark Webber, 1m32.569

## Points scoring positions:

| Pos. | Driver | Points |
|------|--------|--------|
| 1 | Sebastian Vettel, Red Bull Racing | 10 |
| 2 | Jarno Trulli, Panasonic Toyota Racing | 8 |
| 3 | Lewis Hamilton, Vodafone McLaren Mercedes | 6 |
| 4 | Kimi Raikkonen, Scuderia Ferrari Marlboro | 5 |
| 5 | Nico Rosberg, AT&T Williams | 4 |
| 6 | Nick Heidfeld, BMW Sauber F1 Team | 3 |
| 7 | Rubens Barrichello, Brawn GP | 2 |
| 8 | Jenson Button, Brawn GP | 1 |

## Driver standings (top 8):

| | | |
|------|--------|--------|
| 1 | Jenson Button, Brawn GP | 85 |
| 2 | Rubens Barrichello, Brawn GP | 71 |
| 3 | Sebastian Vettel, Red Bull Racing | 69 |
| 4 | Mark Webber, Red Bull Racing | 51.5 |
| 5 | Kimi Raikkonen, Scuderia Ferrari Marlboro | 45 |
| 6 | Lewis Hamilton, Vodafone McLaren Mercedes | 43 |
| 7 | Nico Rosberg, AT&T Williams | 34.5 |
| 8 | Jarno Trulli, Panasonic Toyota Racing | 30.5 |

**ROUND 16**

# Brazilian Grand Prix, Interlagos, 18 October

Pole position: Rubens Barrichello, 1m19.576
Fastest lap: Mark Webber, 1m13.733

## Points scoring positions:

| Pos. | Driver | Points |
|---|---|---|
| 1 | Mark Webber, Red Bull Racing | 10 |
| 2 | Robert Kubica, BMW Sauber F1 Team | 8 |
| 3 | Lewis Hamilton, Vodafone McLaren Mercedes | 6 |
| 4 | Sebastian Vettel, Red Bull Racing | 5 |
| 5 | Jenson Button, Brawn GP | 4 |
| 6 | Kimi Raikkonen, Scuderia Ferrari Marlboro | 3 |
| 7 | Sébastien Buemi, Scuderia Toro Rosso | 2 |
| 8 | Rubens Barrichello, Brawn GP | 1 |

## Driver standings (top 8):

| | | |
|---|---|---|
| 1 | Jenson Button, Brawn GP | 89 |
| 2 | Sebastian Vettel, Red Bull Racing | 74 |
| 3 | Rubens Barrichello, Brawn GP | 72 |
| 4 | Mark Webber, Red Bull Racing | 61.5 |
| 5 | Lewis Hamilton, Vodafone McLaren Mercedes | 49 |
| 6 | Kimi Raikkonen, Scuderia Ferrari Marlboro | 48 |
| 7 | Nico Rosberg, AT&T Williams | 34.5 |
| 8 | Jarno Trulli, Panasonic Toyota Racing | 30.5 |

**ROUND 17**

# Abu Dhabi Grand Prix, Yas Marina, 1 November

Pole position: Lewis Hamilton, 1m40.948
Fastest lap: Sebastian Vettel, 1m40.279

## Points scoring positions:

| Pos. | Driver | Points |
|---|---|---|
| 1 | Sebastian Vettel, Red Bull Racing | 10 |
| 2 | Mark Webber, Red Bull Racing | 8 |
| 3 | Jenson Button, Brawn GP | 6 |
| 4 | Rubens Barrichello, Brawn GP | 5 |
| 5 | Nick Heidfeld, BMW Sauber F1 Team | 4 |
| 6 | Kamui Kobayashi, Panasonic Toyota Racing | 3 |
| 7 | Jarno Trulli, Panasonic Toyota Racing | 2 |
| 8 | Sébastien Buemi, Scuderia Toro Rosso | 1 |

## Driver standings (top 8):

| | | |
|---|---|---|
| 1 | Jenson Button, Brawn GP | 95 |
| 2 | Sebastian Vettel, Red Bull Racing | 84 |
| 4 | Rubens Barrichello, Brawn GP | 77 |
| 4 | Mark Webber, Red Bull Racing | 69.5 |
| 5 | Lewis Hamilton, Vodafone McLaren Mercedes | 49 |
| 6 | Kimi Raikkonen, Scuderia Ferrari Marlboro | 48 |
| 7 | Nico Rosberg, AT&T Williams | 34.5 |
| 8 | Jarno Trulli, Panasonic Toyota Racing | 32.5 |

## Final driver standings

| Pos. | Driver | Points |
|---|---|---|
| 1 | Jenson Button, Brawn GP | 95 |
| 2 | Sebastian Vettel, Red Bull Racing | 84 |
| 3 | Rubens Barrichello, Brawn GP | 77 |
| 4 | Mark Webber, Red Bull Racing | 69.5 |
| 5 | Lewis Hamilton, Vodafone McLaren Mercedes | 49 |
| 6 | Kimi Raikkonen, Scuderia Ferrari Marlboro | 48 |
| 7 | Nico Rosberg, AT&T Williams | 34.5 |
| 8 | Jarno Trulli, Panasonic Toyota Racing | 32.5 |
| 9 | Fernando Alonso, ING Renault F1 Team | 26 |
| 10 | Timo Glock, Panasonic Toyota Racing | 24 |
| 11 | Felipe Massa, Scuderia Ferrari Marlboro | 22 |
| 12 | Heikki Kovalainen, Vodafone McLaren Mercedes | 22 |
| 13 | Nick Heidfeld, BMW Sauber F1 Team | 19 |
| 14 | Robert Kubica, BMW Sauber F1 Team | 17 |
| 15 | Giancarlo Fisichella, Scuderia Ferrari Marlboro/Force India Formula One Team[1] | 8 |
| 16 | Sébastien Buemi, Scuderia Toro Rosso | 6 |
| 17 | Adrian Sutil, Force India Formula One Team | 5 |
| 18 | Kamui Kobayashi, Panasonic Toyota Racing[2] | 3 |
| 19 | Sébastien Bourdais, Scuderia Toro Rosso | 2 |
| 20 | Kazuki Nakajima, AT&T Williams | 0 |
| 21 | Nelson Piquet Jr, ING Renault F1 Team | 0 |
| 22 | Vitantonio Liuzzi, Force India Formula One Team[3] | 0 |
| 23 | Romain Grosjean, ING Renault F1 Team[4] | 0 |
| 24 | Jaime Alguersuari, Scuderia Toro Rosso[5] | 0 |
| 25 | Luca Badoer, Scuderia Ferrari Marlboro[6] | 0 |

---

1 Stood in for an injured Felipe Massa after the Belgium Grand Prix.

2 Stood in for an injured Timo Glock after the Japanese Grand Prix.

3 Replaced Giancarlo Fisichella after the Italian Grand Prix.

4 Replaced Nelson Piquet Jr after the Hungarian Grand Prix.

5 Replaced Sébastien Bourdais after the German Grand Prix.

6 Stood in for an injured Felipe Massa at the European and Belgium Grands Prix.

## Final constructor standings

| Pos. | Team | Points |
|------|------|--------|
| 1 | Brawn GP | 172 |
| 2 | Red Bull Racing | 153.5 |
| 3 | Vodafone McLaren Mercedes | 71 |
| 4 | Scuderia Ferrari Marlboro | 70 |
| 5 | Panasonic Toyota Racing | 59.5 |
| 6 | BMW-Sauber | 36 |
| 7 | AT&T Williams | 34.5 |
| 8 | ING Renault F1 Team | 26 |
| 9 | Force India Formula One Team | 13 |
| 10 | Scuderia Toro Rosso | 8 |

# ILLUSTRATION CREDITS

## Section one

Jenson Button and Rubens Barrichello finish 1-2 at the Australian Grand Prix (*Courtesy of Nick Fry*)

The team celebrating with Richard Branson after our win in Melbourne (*dpa picture alliance archive/Alamy Stock Photo*)

Celebrating the win at the Hungarian Grand Prix, 2006 (*Courtesy of Nick Fry*)

The Beckhams at the British Grand Prix, 2007 (*Courtesy of Nick Fry*)

Pit practice (*Courtesy of Nick Fry*)

Ross Brawn with Saneyuki Minagawa (*Courtesy of Nick Fry*)

Nick with Shuhei Nakamoto at a Japanese shrine (*Courtesy of Nick Fry*)

Achilleas Kallakis (*Shutterstock*)

Vijay Mallya (*dpa picture alliance archive/Alamy Stock Photo*)

Tony Fernandes with Nico Rosberg, 2008 (*Roland Weihrauch/EPA/Shutterstock*)

Richard Goddard (*Courtesy of Ed Gorman*)

The 2008 team principals gather at Monza (*Ercole Colombo/LAT Images/Motorsport Images*)

Bernie Ecclestone with Ed Gorman (*Courtesy of Ed Gorman*)

Brawn GP transporter at the Barcelona test (*Courtesy of Ed Gorman*)

Brawn GP number plate (*Courtesy of Ed Gorman*)

BGP001 front wing (*Courtesy of Ed Gorman*)

Jenson Button waiting in the pitlane at the Barcelona test (*Courtesy of Ed Gorman*)

Jenson Button in the BGP001 at the Barcelona test (*Courtesy of Ed Gorman*)

BGP001 double diffuser (*Victor Fraile/Corbis via Getty Images*)

The team factory, Brackley, Northamptonshire (*Courtesy of Nick Fry*)

Michael Schumacher and John Owen in the wind tunnel at Brackley (*Courtesy of Nick Fry*)

## Section two

Jenson Button wins in Malaysia (*Paul Gilham/Getty Images*)

Jenson hugs Nick after winning in Monte Carlo (*Fred Dufour/ AFP/Getty Images*)

Jenson and Nick on the podium at Monaco (*dpa picture alliance archive/Alamy Stock Photo*)

Nick celebrating Jenson's fifth win with Jessica Michibata and John Button (*Dave M. Benett/Getty Images*)

The start of the Turkish Grand Prix (*Photo by Paul Gilham/ Getty Images*)

Rubens Barrichello with Jock Clear and Andrew Shovlin at the German Grand Prix (*James Moy/Sutton Images/ Motorsport Images*)

Jenson and Lewis Hamilton at the Belgium Grand Prix (*Denis Charlet/AFP/Getty Images*)

Sebastian Vettel and Fernando Alonso on the grid at Singapore (*Vladimir Rys/Bongarts/Getty Images*)

Nick with Jenson at Interlagos (*Courtesy of Nick Fry*)

Jenson finishes fifth in Brazil to clinch the driver's title (*Vanderlei Almeida/AFP/Getty Images*)

Jenson and Ross Brawn celebrate winning the title (*Clive Mason/ Getty Images*)

Nick and Kate at the FIA end-of-season gala dinner (*Courtesy of Nick Fry*)

The Brawn GP shareholders with Jenson and Rubens at Abu Dhabi (*Courtesy of Nick Fry*)

The launch of the new Mercedes team, 2010 (*Courtesy of Nick Fry*)

The team with Petronas staff in Kuala Lumpur (*Courtesy of Nick Fry*)

Niki Lauda with Paddy Lowe (*Courtesy of Nick Fry*)

Lewis Hamilton with Rafferty (*Courtesy of Nick Fry*)

# ACKNOWLEDGEMENTS

The authors would like to thank Jock Clear, Bernie Ecclestone, Nigel Kerr, Ron Meadows, Andrew Shovlin and Shoichi Tanaka for sharing their recollections of 2009 with us. We are grateful to Matthew Gwyther and Jonathan McEvoy for their advice and to Maurice Hamilton for reading a draft. We would also like to thank Charlotte Atyeo for her work on preparing the manuscript for printing, our editor at Atlantic Books, James Nightingale, and all the team at Atlantic. We are grateful to Toby Mundy of Toby Mundy Associates and Mark Smith, then the CEO of Bonnier Zaffre publishing, who were instrumental in getting this project off the ground, and to Mark Lucas of The Soho Agency for his wise counsel. Finally we would like to thank our wives, Kate Buckingham-Fry and Jeanna Gorman, for their love and support.

# A NOTE ABOUT THE AUTHORS

Nick Fry was brought up in south London, the eldest of three boys, where he attended his local primary school and then Hollyfield mixed secondary school.

From an early age, and encouraged by his father who worked in Fleet Street, Nick became fascinated by motorsport and remembers watching James Hunt at Crystal Palace in October 1970 in the Formula 3 *Daily Express* Trophy Race. (Hunt collided with another car near the finish line and got into a fight – something you can still enjoy on YouTube.) Other early heroes included the Formula One drivers Chris Amon, François Cevert and Jackie Stewart with whom Nick would work alongside later in life.

After attending Swansea University, where he read Economics and Economic Geography, Nick joined the Ford Motor Company in 1977 as a graduate trainee and became an analyst for truck sales. He remained with the company for twenty-four years, helping to develop a number of successful high-performance cars including the Ford Escort Cosworth.

He was variously production manager for Ford Manufacturing Operations UK, European service director, and ultimately product planning and business director based in Cologne in Germany. Along the way Nick also enjoyed a productive spell as managing director at Aston Martin Lagonda – a partly owned Ford subsidiary – where he oversaw the development of the iconic Aston Martin DB7, the most successful Aston Martin ever built in terms of numbers of cars produced.

In 2001 Nick moved to Prodrive, the world-leading experts

in high-performance car engineering and motorsport, as managing director. During his stint at the company's base at Banbury, he oversaw the global expansion of the business and doubled its turnover in three years. On becoming group managing director, he took over responsibility for Prodrive's racing and rallying activity. Under Nick's leadership, Prodrive won two World Rally Championships with Subaru and drivers Richard Burns and Petter Solberg, and achieved victories for Ferrari at Le Mans and in the European GT Championship. He also had responsibility for the Ford V8 Racing Team in Australia and the Subaru North American Rally Team.

Nick moved into Formula One in 2002 when he added the managing director portfolio at BAR Honda to his responsibilities at Prodrive (from which he departed a year later). His first job was to restructure the previously unsuccessful team owned by British American Tobacco. Under Nick's leadership the team secured second place in the F1 constructors' world championship with drivers Jenson Button and Takuma Sato in 2004, and then secured the team's first Grand Prix win with Button at the 2006 Hungarian Grand Prix.

Having grown the team, now under Honda's exclusive ownership, Nick secured a £50 million investment in a state-of-the-art wind tunnel at the team's base at Brackley in Northamptonshire. Then, in late 2007, he negotiated the hire of the multiple world championship-winner Ross Brawn to be team principal alongside Nick as CEO. Brawn came on board to run the design and engineering while Nick took care of the commercial aspects.

When Honda abruptly pulled out of Formula One in late 2008 in the face of the world financial crisis, Nick and Ross led a management buyout and went on to win the drivers' and constructors' world championships in 2009 in the colours of Brawn GP. Throughout 2009 Nick led the search for a new owner and eventually agreed a sale of a majority stake to Mercedes Benz. As CEO of the new Mercedes AMG Petronas F1 team, and having secured the services of drivers Nico Rosberg and Michael Schumacher, Nick also secured multiple new sponsorship contracts as the team achieved its first Grand Prix victory for a Mercedes works team since 1955.

After leaving Formula One in 2013, Nick helped set up Stonehaven Partners, which provides commercial and marketing support to leading sports teams, and was appointed a UK business ambassador by prime minister David Cameron. He has since been involved in a number of start-ups and investments in other established businesses and is currently chairman of the professional e-sports team Fnatic.

When not working, Nick enjoys family life with his wife Kate at home in Oxfordshire, mountain-biking, competitive sailing and skiing. He has been an active fundraiser for his local children's hospice, is a patron of cancer-treatment charity Hope for Tomorrow and supports AT the Bus, a charity providing mental health care for young people. Any profit Nick makes from this book will go to charity.

***

Ed Gorman was brought up in rural Warwickshire and attended Marlborough College and Cambridge University.

After starting out as a freelance journalist covering the Soviet war in Afghanistan in the 1980s, he joined *The Times* and worked for the paper for twenty-five years. He was a foreign news correspondent, covering wars in Afghanistan, the Balkans and Sri Lanka, then Ireland correspondent for four years during the Troubles and then the paper's sailing and Formula One writer. His final roles were as deputy foreign editor and deputy head of news.

In recent years he has been editorial director of the sports management company OC Sport and has published a memoir about his time in Afghanistan entitled *Death of a Translator*.

Ed is now a freelance writer and works from home in West Sussex where he lives with his wife Jeanna.

# INDEX

Aabar Investments, 54
Abu Dhabi, 54, 188,
    194–6, 214
aerodynamics, 27,
    58–9, 73–4, 144–6
Air Asia, 154–5, 157,
    159
Albert Park,
    Melbourne, 5,
    7–9, 11, 100–107
Albert, Prince of
    Monaco, 134–6,
    243
Alonso, Fernando, 20,
    84, 118, 176, 186,
    190, 201, 216,
    233, 235
Armstrong, Nicola,
    129, 133
Arron, Simon, 103
Ascari, Alberto, 140
Autonomy (IT
    company), 219
*Autosport* magazine,
    61, 123
Aziz, Anita, 157

Bale, Christian, 122
Banco do Brasil, 110
BAR (British
    American
    Racing), 57
BAR Honda Formula
    One Team, 14,
    57, 237
Barcelona, Spain,
    82–5, 121–2
Barrichello, Rubens,
    62, 76–7, 83,
    86–7, 173, 178,
    193, 203

Abu Dhabi Grand
    Prix (2009), 196
Australian Grand
    Prix (2009), 6, 10
Belgian Grand Prix
    (2009), 175–6
Brazilian Grand
    Prix (2008), 16
Brazilian Grand
    Prix (2009),
    185–92
European Grand
    Prix (2009),
    171–3
German Grand
    Prix (2009),
    164–6
Italian Grand Prix
    (2009), 181–3
Malaysian Grand
    Prix (2009), 114
Monaco Grand
    Prix (2009),
    128–9, 133
Singapore Grand
    Prix (2009), 183
Spanish Grand
    Prix (2009), 121,
    123–4
Turkish Grand Prix
    (2009), 139
Bauer, Jo, 128
Bell, Bob, 62
Benetton, 63, 69, 136
Berry, Richard, 99
BGP001 (car), 59–60,
    73–8, 81–5
Bigois, Loïc, 27, 74–5
Bigois, Lucien, 75
Bishop, Matt, 210

Blair, Gordon, 46, 49,
    156
BMW Sauber, 16, 105,
    119, 122, 156–7
Bourdais, Sébastien,
    123
Boutique nightclub,
    Melbourne, 12
Bower, Tom, 42
Brabham, David, 131
Brackley Operations
    Centre, 17–19,
    23–4, 25–9, 31,
    47, 55, 156, 197,
    238
    and Honda, 57–62,
    64–6
    and Ross Brawn,
    62–9, 71–2
    wind tunnel, 58–9
Branson, Richard, 8,
    41–3, 99–103
Brawn GP, 237–43
    and Bernie
    Ecclestone,
    89–90, 95–6
    budget, 110–12
    cars, 9–10, 59–60,
    72–8, 81–5,
    104–5, 144–6,
    167, 211
    establishment of,
    7–8, 82
    and Lewis
    Hamilton, 225–36
    management
    buyout (MBO),
    45–55, 72–3
    and Mercedes
    Benz, 149–59,
    197–8, 230–35

and Michael
Schumacher, 208,
211–23
pitstops, 104–5
sponsorship,
99–103, 109–10,
122, 132–3,
149–59
*see also* Brackley
Operations
Centre
Brawn, Jean, 20, 50
Brawn, Ross, 5, 10–11,
32, 34–7, 40–42,
113–14, 117,
123–4, 136, 154
and Bernie
Ecclestone, 51–2
and Brackley
Operations
Centre, 62–9,
71–2
and Brawn GP
MBO, 7, 13,
18–24, 45–6, 49,
53, 55, 238–42
Briatore, Flavio, 84,
92, 119–20, 132,
136, 176–7
British American
Tobacco (BAT),
57–8, 207
Buemi, Sébastien,
123, 191
Buncombe, Chris,
162
Burns, Richard, 28,
204–6, 208
Button, Jenson, 62,
82–3, 85–6, 102,
173–5, 178–9,
199–202, 204–10
Abu Dhabi Grand
Prix (2009),
194–6

Australian Grand
Prix (2009), 5–12,
99–107
Bahrain Grand
Prix (2009),
120–21
becomes world
champion, 191–3
Belgian Grand Prix
(2009), 173–5
Brazilian Grand
Prix (2006), 186
Brazilian Grand
Prix (2008), 16
Brazilian Grand
Prix (2009),
185–92
British Grand Prix
(2009), 161–4
Chinese Grand
Prix (2009),
119–20
European Grand
Prix (2009),
171–2
German Grand
Prix (2009),
164–6
Hungarian Grand
Prix (2009),
166–7
Italian Grand Prix
(2009), 180–82
Japanese Grand
Prix (2009), 183
Malaysian Grand
Prix (2009),
112–16
Monaco Grand
Prix (2009),
127–9, 133–7
and Ross Brawn, 71
Singapore Grand
Prix (2009), 183

Spanish Grand Prix
(2009), 121–5
Turkish Grand Prix
(2009), 139–40
Button, John, 115–16,
187, 191, 200
Byfield, John, 207
Byrne, Rory, 83

Cameron, David, 47
*Campaign* magazine,
122
Canon, 110
Charlene, Princess of
Monaco, 134–5
Clark, Jim, 140, 221
Clarke, Brian, 216
Clatworthy, Ian, 194
Clear, Jock, 28, 83,
172, 238
Cole, Simon, 28, 195
Collier, Mike, 162,
192
computational fluid
dynamics, 59–60
Coulthard, David, 162
Court of Arbitration
for Sport,
Lausanne, 117
'crashgate' scandal,
176–7
CVC Capital Partners,
96, 140

*Daily Mail*, 180, 232
Dennis, Ron, 22, 52,
78–9, 91, 114,
130, 142–6, 159,
180, 209–10,
226–8, 230, 232–3
Donington Park, 162
Doohan, Mick, 14
'double-diffuser', 9,
73–5, 84, 105–7,
116–18
Ducasse, Alain, 132

Ecclestone, Bernie,
    31, 49, 51–2,
    89–97, 103,
    116–17, 140, 152,
    244
Emirates airline, 195,
    197
Energy Recovery
    System (KERS),
    72, 121, 129
Ettington Park, 164–5
Evans, Marcus, 41

Fangio, Juan Manuel,
    11, 140
Fédération
    Internationale
    de l'Automobile
    (FIA), 9, 90,
    105–6, 116–17,
    180
Ferguson, Sir Alex,
    63, 154
Fernandes, Tony,
    154–5, 157, 159
de Ferran, Gil, 227,
    229
Ferrari, 21, 63, 69, 77,
    141, 157, 212–13,
    243
Fisichella, Giancarlo,
    176
Force India, 30–31,
    176
Ford Motor
    Company, 52, 91,
    151, 198
Formula One
    Management
    (FOM), 49–50
Formula One Teams
    Association
    (FOTA), 21, 78

Fry, Kate, 11–12, 20,
    50–51, 62, 102,
    135, 164–5, 196
Fukui, Takeo, 53,
    61–2, 66
Full Tilt, 132–3
Fuller, Simon,
    229–32, 234–5

Gené, Marc, 131
Glazer family, 153–5,
    158
Glock, Timo, 84, 114,
    225
Goddard, Richard,
    22, 82, 102, 162,
    200–201, 203, 205
Graham
    (watchmakers),
    110
Grands Prix
    Abu Dhabi (2009),
        194–6
    Australian (2009),
        5–12, 99–107, 240
    Bahrain (2009),
        120–21
    Belgian (2009),
        173–6
    Brazilian (2006),
        186
    Brazilian (2008),
        16
    Brazilian (2009),
        185–92
    British (2009),
        161–4
    Chinese (2009),
        118–20
    European (2009),
        171–2
    German (2009),
        164–6
    Hungarian (2006),
        86

    Hungarian (2009),
        166–7
    Italian (2009),
        180–82
    Japanese (2009),
        183
    Malaysian (2009),
        112–16
    Monaco (2009),
        127–33, 243
    Singapore (2009),
        183
    Spanish (2009),
        121–5
    Turkish (2009),
        139–40
Griffith, Gareth, 135
Grosjean, Romain,
    175, 190

Hamilton, Anthony,
    226–7, 230
Hamilton, Lewis, 8–9,
    84, 120–21, 191,
    196, 202, 142,
    162, 168, 172,
    175, 183–4, 243
    and Mercedes
    Benz, 225–36
Harris, Paul, 117
Haug, Norbert,
    149–51, 153, 155,
    157–8, 210, 231,
    237
Heidfeld, Nick, 6,
    114, 213, 231
Henri Lloyd (clothing
    brand), 110, 122
Herbert, Johnny, 162
Hill, Damon, 162, 212
Hockenheim,
    Germany, 93–4
Holland, Gary, 104–5

Honda Motor Company, 7, 13–21, 24, 26, 38–9, 42–3, 57, 125–6, 239
and Brackley, 58–62, 64–9
and Brawn GP MBO, 47–50, 52–6, 72–3
engine power, 76
Honda, Soichiro, 14
Horner, Christian, 121, 124, 141
Howlett, John, 22
Hungaroring, Hungary, 11, 166–8
Hunt, James, 162

Interlagos, Brazil, 16, 185, 242
Ipswich Town FC, 41
Itaipava beer company, 194
IWC Schaffhausen, 217

Jakobi, Julian, 205
Jordan, Eddie, 31, 52, 92, 146
JP Morgan Bank, 153–4

Kallakis, Achilleas, 34–40, 43–4, 101
Kerr, Nigel, 15, 19, 21, 28, 32–3, 37, 45–6, 111, 149–52
KERS (Kinetic Energy Recovery System), 72–3, 121, 129
Kling, Karl, 11
Kobayashi, Kamui, 190
Kovalainen, Heikki, 6, 142, 172, 190

Kroll (corporate detective agency), 37, 39–40
Kubica, Robert, 6, 10
Kulpinski, Jules, 162

Lauda, Niki, 231–2, 234–5
Le Mans, 130–31
Legard, Jonathan, 11
Leicester City FC, 238
Liberty Media, 97
*Life to the Limit* (Button), 102, 185

Mackenzie, Donald, 140
Mallya, Vijay, 30–34, 131–2
Manchester United FC, 63, 153–4, 158
Mansell, Nigel, 162
Maranello, Italy, 21, 64, 65, 87, 209, 219
March, Charlie, 203
Marsden, John, 19, 21, 28
Massa, Felipe, 6, 9, 166–7, 178–9, 186, 191, 214
McEvoy, Jonathan, 180, 232–3
McGrory, Caroline, 19, 21, 28, 37, 99, 196, 207, 216
McLaren, 22, 78, 141–2, 145–7, 150–51, 159, 208–10, 226–30, 232
Meadows, Ron, 21, 27, 74, 83, 111, 166, 211

Melbourne, Australia, 5–12, 99–101, 106–7, 240
Mercedes Benz, 54, 60, 77–8, 133, 145, 149–59, 197–8, 237–8
Mercedes F1, 243
Michibata, Jessica, 102, 135
MIG Bank, 110, 122
Miller, Graham, 21, 65
Minagawa, Saneyuki, 74
di Montezemolo, Luca, 21–2, 180
Mosley, Max, 89–90, 116–17, 152, 180–81, 243

Nakajima, Kazuki, 119, 190
Nakamoto, Shuhei, 60–62
Nevland, Erik, 121
Newey, Adrian, 12, 62–3, 237
*News of the World*, 180

Omega, 217
Omura, Mr, 19, 38, 48, 52
Oshima, Hiroshi, 13–19, 61

Petronas, 157, 197, 217, 233–4
Piquet Jnr, Nelson, 176–8, 225
Piquet Snr, Nelson, 178
Pista Magica, Monza, 180–81
Prodrive, 28, 46, 204–5

Raikkonen, Kimi, 6,
    10, 128–9, 133,
    176, 190
Ranieri, Claudio, 238
Red Bull, 12, 119,
    121, 124, 141,
    182, 187, 237–8,
    243
Renault, 20, 24, 86,
    105, 176, 199
di Resta, Paul, 231
Richards, David, 207
Rosberg, Keke, 204
Rosberg, Nico, 6,
    113–14, 84,
    203–4, 211,
    219–22, 234, 236
Rutan, Burt, 42, 100

Sanders, Richard, 99
Sato, Takuma, 173
Schumacher,
    Corinna, 218, 222
Schumacher,
    Michael, 21, 63,
    140, 193, 202,
    208, 211–23
Schumacher, Mick,
    218
Schumacher, Ralf, 67
Senna, Ayrton, 15,
    193, 221, 226
Shovlin, Andrew,
    27–8, 81, 175,
    187, 191, 199
'silver arrow' (car),
    211–12, 225
Silverstone,
    Northampton-
    shire, 81, 161–4
Slim, Carlos, 36
Smirnoff, 217

Sony Pictures, 110,
    122
Spa, Belgian, 173–5
Spencer, Freddie, 14
Spyker, 41
Stewart, Jackie, 38–9,
    195, 221
Stowe Castle,
    Buckinghamshire,
    32
Subaru, 151, 204–5,
    273
Sun, The, 233
Sutil, Adrian, 123,
    139, 190
Swanston, Natalie,
    229
Symonds, Pat, 62–3,
    176–7

Tai, Alex, 41
Terminator Salvation
    (film), 122
Thackeray, Sue, 233
Times, The, 24, 174
Todt, Jean, 52, 63, 65,
    67, 91, 209, 244
Toro Rosso, 119
Toyota, 22, 24, 48–9,
    63, 67, 75, 105,
    113, 141, 239
Tozzi, Nigel, 117
Trulli, Jarno, 67,
    113–14, 123, 190

Valencia, Spain,
    171–2
Vettel, Sebastian, 220,
    229, 237
    Grands Prix 2009,
    6, 10, 84, 118–21,
    128, 139–41,

163–4, 166,
    168, 172, 182–3,
    185–9, 196
Villeneuve, Jacques,
    85, 173, 219, 231
Virgin Group, 8,
    41–3, 99–103,
    110, 196
Volkswagen, 177
Vowles, James, 27–8

Walkinshaw, Tom, 52
Watson, John, 162
Webber, Mark, 6, 118,
    139, 162, 165–6,
    168, 172, 182,
    191, 196
Whiting, Charlie,
    62–3, 77, 107, 117
Whitmarsh, Martin,
    22, 78, 142,
    209–10
Williams, 24, 62, 75,
    105, 113, 141,
    157, 204, 207
Williams, Alex, 35
Williams, Frank, 114,
    180, 207
Willis, Geoff, 60–61
Wilson, Craig, 187
Wolff, Toto, 237
Woods, Richard, 90
Woodward, Ed,
    153–4, 158
Wurz, Alex, 130–31

Xander, Joerg, 21

Yamanashi, Tadashi,
    22

Zetsche, Dieter, 54,
    153, 231–3, 241